Cooking For Crowds For Dummies®

T0065768

Food Quantity Tables

Use the following tables to determine how much food you need to prepare for your big gatherings. You'll find much more information on this topic in Chapter 3.

Appetizers

Type of Appetizer	Number of Different Appetizer Types	Per Person	Crowd of 25	Crowd of 50
Appetizers preceding a full meal	At least 4	6 to 8 pieces	150 to 200 total appetizers	300 to 400 total appetizers
Appetizers without a meal	At least 6	12 to 15 pieces	300 to 375 total appetizers	600 to 750 total appetizers

Drinks

Type of Drink	Per Person
Soft drinks	1 to 2 eight-ounce servings per hour
Punch	1 to 2 four-ounce servings per hour
Tea	1 to 2 eight-ounce servings per hour
Coffee	1 to 2 four-ounce servings per hour

Soups and Stews

Soup or Stew	Per Person	Crowd of 25	Crowd of 50
Served as a first course	1 cup	5 quarts	2½ gallons
Served as an entree	1½ to 2 cups	2 to 2½ gallons	4 gallons

Main Courses

Entree	Per Person	Crowd of 25	Crowd of 50
Baby-back ribs, pork spareribs, beef short ribs	1 pound	25 pounds	50 pounds
Casserole	N/A	2 to 3 13-x-9-inch casseroles	4 to 5 13-x-9-inch casseroles
Chicken, turkey, or duck (boneless)	½ pound	13 pounds	25 pounds
Chicken or turkey (with bones)	¾ to 1 pound	19 pounds	38 pounds
Chili, stew, stroganoff, and other chopped meats	5 to 6 ounces	8 pounds	15 pounds
Ground beef	½ pound	13 pounds	25 pounds
Maine lobster (about 2 pounds each)	1	25	50
Oysters, clams, and mussels (medium to large)	6 to 10 pieces	100 to 160 pieces	200 to 260 pieces

For Dummies: Bestselling Book Series for Beginners

Cooking For Crowds For Dummies®

Cheat Sheet

Main Courses *(continued)*

Entree	Per Person	Crowd of 25	Crowd of 50
Pasta	4 to 5 ounces	7 pounds	16 pounds
Pork	14 ounces	22 pounds	44 pounds
Roast (with bone)	14 to 16 ounces	22 to 25 pounds	47 to 50 pounds
Roast cuts (boneless)	½ pound	13 pounds	25 pounds
Shrimp (large — 16 to 20 per pound)	5 to 7 shrimp	7 pounds	14 pounds
Steak cuts (T-bone, porterhouse, rib-eye)	16 to 24 ounces	16 to 24 ounces per person	16 to 24 ounces per person
Turkey (whole)	1 pound	25 pounds	50 pounds

Side Dishes

Side Dish	Per Person	Crowd of 25	Crowd of 50
Asparagus, carrots, cauliflower, broccoli, green beans, corn kernels, peas, black-eyed peas, and so on	3 to 4 ounces	4 pounds	8 pounds
Corn on the cob (broken in halves when serving buffet-style)	1 ear	20 ears	45 ears
Pasta (cooked)	2 to 3 ounces	3½ pounds	7 pounds
Potatoes and yams	1 (medium)	6 pounds	12 pounds
Rice and grains (cooked)	1½ ounces	2½ pounds	5 pounds

Desserts

Dessert	Per Person	Crowd of 25	Crowd of 50
Brownies or bars	1 to 2 per person	2½ to 3 dozen	5½ to 6 dozen
Cheesecake	2-inch wedge	2 9-inch cheesecakes	4 9-inch cheesecakes
Cobbler	1 cup	2 9-x-9-x-2-inch pans	4 9-x-9-x-2-inch pans
Cookies	2 to 3	3 to 4 dozen	6 to 8 dozen
Ice cream or sorbet	8 ounces	1 gallon	2 gallons
Layered cake or angel food cake	1 slice	2 8-inch cakes	4 8-inch cakes
Pie	3-inch wedge	2 to 3 9-inch pies	4 to 5 9-inch pies
Pudding, trifles, and the like	1 cup	1 gallon	2 gallons
Sheet cake	2-x-2-inch piece	¼ sheet cake	½ sheet cake

For Dummies: Bestselling Book Series for Beginners

Cooking
For Crowds
FOR
DUMMIES®

Cooking For Crowds

FOR

DUMMIES®

by **Dawn Simmons, Curt Simmons**

WILEY

Wiley Publishing, Inc.

Cooking For Crowds For Dummies®

Published by
Wiley Publishing, Inc.
111 River St.
Hoboken, NJ 07030-5774
www.wiley.com

For general information on our other products and services, please contact our Customer Care Department within the U.S. at 800-762-2974, outside the U.S. at 317-572-3993, or fax 317-572-4002.

For technical support, please visit www.wiley.com/techsupport.

Wiley also publishes its books in a variety of electronic formats. Some content that appears in print may not be available in electronic books.

Library of Congress Control Number: 2005923790

ISBN-13: 978-0-7645-8469-5

10 9 8 7 6 5 4 3 2 1

1O/RY/QV/QV/IN

About the Authors

Dawn Simmons is a freelance writer, online course instructor, and caterer. She loves cooking for crowds and is always on the look-out for new recipes. You can reach Dawn at dawnfsimmons@hotmail.com

Curt Simmons is a freelance writer and trainer. The author of more than fifty general technology books, Curt enjoys technology, gardening, and eating Dawn's cooking. You can reach Curt at curt_simmons@hotmail.com

Dedication

This book is for our children, Hannah Christine and Mattie Alleen.

Dawn would also like to dedicate this book to her aunts, Martha Branch and Julia Aycock, who first gave her a love of cooking.

Authors' Acknowledgments

We would like to thank our friends and family who have offered support and encouraging words during this project. Thanks to everyone at Wiley, especially Mikal Belicove for the green light, Tim Gallan and Kristin DeMint for keeping things moving in the right direction, Mike Tully for testing our recipes, and Patty Santelli for doing the nutritional analysis. We would like to especially thank our agent, Margot Hutchison, for her support.

Publisher's Acknowledgments

We're proud of this book; please send us your comments through our Dummies online registration form located at www.dummies.com/register/.

Some of the people who helped bring this book to market include the following:

Acquisitions, Editorial, and Media Development

Senior Project Editor: Tim Gallan

Acquisitions Editor: Mikal Belicove

Copy Editor: Kristin DeMint

Editorial Program Assistant: Courtney Allen

Technical Editor and Recipe Tester: Mike Tully

Nutritional Analyst: Patricia Santelli

Editorial Manager: Christine Meloy Beck

Editorial Assistants: Melissa S. Bennett, Hanna Scott

Cover Photos: © Penina/FoodPix

Cartoons: Rich Tennant (www.the5thwave.com)

Composition Services

Project Coordinator: Adrienne Martinez

Layout and Graphics: Lauren Goddard, Stephanie D. Jumper, Lynsey Osborn, Julie Trippetti

Illustrator: Liz Kurtzman

Proofreaders: Leeann Harney, Dwight Ramsey, TECHBOOKS Production Services

Indexer: TECHBOOKS Production Services

Publishing and Editorial for Consumer Dummies

Diane Graves Steele, Vice President and Publisher, Consumer Dummies

Joyce Pepple, Acquisitions Director, Consumer Dummies

Kristin A. Cocks, Product Development Director, Consumer Dummies

Michael Spring, Vice President and Publisher, Travel

Kelly Regan, Editorial Director, Travel

Publishing for Technology Dummies

Andy Cummings, Vice President and Publisher, Dummies Technology/General User

Composition Services

Gerry Fahey, Vice President of Production Services

Debbie Stailey, Director of Composition Services

Contents at a Glance

Table of Contents

Recipes at a Glance

Salads and Side Dishes

Soups and Stews

Punches and Drinks

Desserts

Summer Dishes

Holiday Dishes

Wedding Dishes

Beef Dishes

Chicken Dishes

Pork Dishes

Seafood Dishes

Introduction

*L*et's face it: Everyone loves to eat (sure you do; just admit it), and your authors especially love to eat with friends and family nearby. Nothing is more nostalgic than family get-togethers, holiday crowds, and all the fun and food that go along with a group of people. But what if you're the one who has to cook for that crowd? In that case, nostalgia and romantic notions of crowd gatherings can quickly go out the window. In fact, cooking for a crowd can be rather intimidating and stressful.

That's why we're here. We wrote *Cooking For Crowds For Dummies* just for you. After all, if you're reading this book, you probably have a crowd event looming on the horizon and know you need some extra help.

We love crowd events and we love to cook for them, and in this book, we want to help you plan, organize, cook, and manage your own event so that everyone in your crowd can't wait to come back. We bet you're hoping the same, which is why you're reading this book.

How to Use This Book

This book is designed to help you cook for a crowd. Maybe you don't even know how to start, or maybe you need extra help determining your menu and planning food quantities. Maybe you need some great recipes that are specific to crowd gatherings, and maybe you need help pulling everything together. Don't worry — we cover the gamut here.

We wrote this book so you can find the information you need quickly and easily. We don't ramble on about things that don't matter, and you don't have to read the entire book if you don't want to. In fact, you can read the book from cover to cover or simply jump around to the topics you're interested in at the moment.

One more point to note: The sidebars throughout the book contain extra information. You don't have to read them, but they often explain some technique or issue in more detail. Some sidebars provide additional information about cooking tools, the history of certain food items, and other tidbits of information that you may find fun, helpful, and amusing.

Foolish Assumptions

As we wrote this book, we made a few assumptions about you:

- We assume you know a thing or two about cooking, but we don't assume you're a professional chef or caterer. In the pages that follow, you'll find real-life tips, suggestions, and recipes you can use right away, but we don't dwell on the basics of cooking.

- We assume you can get your hands on common, everyday items and ingredients. If you want to cook a recipe in this book, you'll be able to find the ingredients at your local supermarket; you won't need to buy ingredients from exotic places.

- We assume you want to cook for a crowd in a practical, down-to-earth way and want to do your best. We think that's great, and we've written this book for you from that perspective.

- We assume you need help with the crowd factor. You may cook Aunt Linda's meatloaf better than anyone else in your family, but cooking it for 40 people is a bit overwhelming. Don't worry; you've come to the right place.

- We assume you care. You care about the food you cook and about the people who will enjoy your food.

- We assume you're an intelligent person. After all, you bought this book!

Conventions Used in This Book

Before you use the recipes in this book, here are a few guidelines that will help ensure your success:

- Before you start cooking, make sure you read through the entire recipe. Doing so will help you confirm that you have all the ingredients and cooking tools before you begin.

- Pepper means ground black pepper unless otherwise specified.

- If a recipe calls for mayonnaise, don't substitute salad dressing.

- All butter is unsalted.

- If a recipe calls for butter, don't substitute margarine or another butter replacement product.

- All eggs are large.

- All milk is whole.

- Flour is all-purpose unless otherwise specified.

- ✔ All onions are yellow unless otherwise specified.

- ✔ All temperatures are Fahrenheit. (See the Metric Conversion Guide in Appendix A at the end of the book for information about converting temperatures to Celsius.)

- ⟳ A tomato symbol like the one shown here tells you that a recipe is vegetarian. (We don't include this symbol for drinks and desserts, though; those recipes are naturally okay for vegetarians.)

How This Book Is Organized

Cooking For Crowds For Dummies is divided into five parts, which we describe in brief here. Each part contains appropriate chapters that cover everything you need to know about cooking for a crowd. With this design, you can find the information you need quickly and easily.

Part 1: So, You Need to Cook for a Crowd . . .

In this part, you find some basic information about cooking for a crowd. If a crowd event has just landed in your lap and you feel a bit panicked and bewildered, this is the place to start. In Chapter 1, you find an overview of the many topics this book covers. You see how to get your thoughts organized, how to plan for your crowd, and how to enjoy the process along the way. In Chapter 2, you find out how to plan your menu. You consider your budget and the purpose of the event, and then you see how to plan for appetizers, main courses, side dishes, soups and stews, desserts, and drinks. In Chapter 3, you find out how to estimate food quantities so you know how much food you need for your particular crowd. We also discuss serving dishes, preparation issues, and how to determine what tools you need.

Part II: Tried-and-True Recipes for Crowds

Cooking for a crowd isn't the same as cooking a nice dinner for your family. You have a lot more people to feed, and what you decide to serve has a big impact on your event. In this part, we give you 81 recipes that are designed specifically for crowd events. In Chapter 4, we show you 12 perfect appetizers. In Chapter 5, you find 21 recipes for main dishes. In Chapter 6, you find 12 recipes for delicious side dishes. In Chapter 7, you review 10 recipes for soups and stews. In Chapter 8, you explore 12 recipes for delightful punches and drinks. Finally, in Chapter 9, we give you 15 decadent dessert recipes.

Part III: Special Events and Holidays

Crowd events often occur during summertime get-togethers, holiday events, and weddings. Because these events are special, we've assembled a collection of 40 festive recipes. In Chapter 10, we provide 15 recipes that are perfect for summertime get-togethers. In Chapter 11, you get 15 recipes that are perfect for holidays. Finally, in Chapter 12, you find 10 recipes that work especially well for wedding crowds.

Part IV: Bringing It All Together

After you've planned your event and have gathered the recipes you want to use, what do you do next? You need to bring everything together and prepare your crowd meal. In this part, we show you just how to do that in an orderly fashion, which will ensure a successful event and keep your stress to a minimum. In Chapter 13, you see how to schedule and prepare food so that you can be sure you're ready on time. In Chapter 14, we take a look at the big day, showing you how to use a workflow, how to transport and manage food, and how to serve all those people.

Part V: The Part of Tens

Check out this part to find some quick and easy extra information that can help make your event a smashing success. In Chapter 15, we show you ten ways to avoid common food preparation problems. In Chapter 16, you find more than ten quick and easy decorating tips for crowds, and in Chapter 17, you read about ten practical tactics to keep you from pulling out your hair. To top it off, Chapter 18 gives you more than ten tips for keeping your food safe.

Icons Used in This Book

Throughout this book, we use icons to call your attention to certain details. The icons and the information that goes along with them are designed to help you, save you time, and steer you away from common problems, so be sure to check them out.

This icon points out information that will save you time as you cook for a crowd. Because saving time is vitally important when you crowd-cook, be sure to read these tidbits.

This icon is used to call attention to a particularly important piece of information that you shouldn't forget.

 When you see this icon, you'll find some extra information that can make your life easier or provide you with an alternate way to do something.

 If you see this icon, watch out! We use it sparingly, but when we do, take note. It provides information that can help you avoid a common problem.

Where to Go from Here

It's time to start working toward a successful crowd event. If you're just getting started, begin with Part I. If you can't wait to check out the recipes, go to Parts II and III. If you're anxious to start thinking about the rundown of the big day itself, be sure to head for Chapter 14 so you get off on a good foot. If you want to find something in particular, use the table of contents and the index for extra help and direction. No matter where you start, your crowd is coming, so get to cooking (or planning, at least)!

Part I
So, You Need to Cook for a Crowd . . .

The 5th Wave   By Rich Tennant

"You can clean up before company arrives, but use the shower, not the bath — I'm marinating the steaks."

In this part . . .

No matter whether you volunteered to cook for a crowd or found yourself suddenly owning the responsibility, this part helps you get started. After all, cooking for a crowd is very different from a family meal around the dining room table. Before you ever start cooking, you first need to tackle some fundamental planning issues. In this part, we help you do just that. You find out how to plan for a crowd, how to create a menu that will be perfect for your particular event, and how to easily estimate food quantities, plan serving dishes, manage your crowd, and much more.

Chapter 1

A Crowd by Any Other Name

In This Chapter

▶ Dealing with the initial shock when you're enlisted as crowd cook

▶ Thinking ahead for a successful day

▶ Enjoying the process

A crowd by any other name is . . . well, still a crowd! And when you cook for a crowd, you're entering a new dimension of cooking. No doubt, you've picked up this book because some kind of crowd-cooking event is looming in your future. Maybe the reception for Aunt Betty's wedding has become your responsibility. Maybe all your in-laws (and we do mean *all*) are coming to your home for Thanksgiving. Maybe you want to throw the best backyard summer party the world has ever seen, or maybe you love cooking for a crowd but want to do it better.

When you break it all down, a crowd is simply a group of people. Yet, cooking for that group of people can be bit nerve-wracking and challenging. But it should also be fun! In this chapter, you get your feet wet with crowd cooking. We give you an overview of the process, tell you some things to start thinking about, and, in upcoming chapters, explore the details of what makes a crowd-cooking event a success. Armed with this book and a strong desire to achieve greatness, you can rest assured that your crowd event will be a smashing success (and as an added bonus, you'll get to keep your sanity).

How Did I Get in This Predicament?

It usually happens slowly and gains momentum, sort of like an avalanche. A family member mentions that everyone needs to get together for Thanksgiving. You offer to help. Someone compliments you on how good a cook you are. Someone else suggests that you be in charge of the event. Still another person thinks your house is the perfect gathering place. Within moments, you find yourself agreeing to host Thanksgiving dinner for a group of 30, and in a seemingly out-of-body experience, you hear yourself saying, "Don't bring a thing. I would love to cook the whole meal for the family."

Sound familiar? This scenario happens to many people, ourselves included. It usually happens because you have some cooking talent and others perceive you as a go-getter. People trust you. People think you're talented. And for those reasons, you're suddenly in charge of the baby shower or backyard swim party. You got into this mess because you have the capacity for success and those around you know it. After all, crowds don't gather around people who can't cook and can't follow through on promises.

Give yourself a break. You're in this predicament because others trust you, and that's a good thing.

However, you may be cooking for a crowd because you volunteered. Maybe you're someone who really likes having company in your home or organizing events. Maybe you really love to cook, and seeing other people enjoying the food you make warms your heart. That's no crime. In fact, the world should have more people like you!

Regardless of how you arrived in this predicament, let us give you some encouragement: You wouldn't be here if you didn't have the capacity for success, and our purpose in writing this book is to help you make your upcoming crowd event a success. Just envision friends and loved ones enjoying your food, laughing, and having a good time. Think of the pats on the back as people leave and tell you thanks for a great day and a great meal. Imagine the thank-you notes in the mail from friends and family telling you how much fun they had and how they wish you'd do it again soon.

Understanding what it takes

Step back in time for a moment and picture this scenario: It's Christmas day, and you're 8 years old. You, your family, and all your extended family have gathered at Grandma's house for Christmas dinner, something you do every year.

When you first walk into Grandma's house, you can feel the chaos. People are running around everywhere trying to set the table. The kitchen looks like a nuclear explosion of food and dirty dishes. Grandma has resorted to chain smoking, and when everyone finally sits down for dinner, you face a smorgasbord of mismatched, random food items (not to mention three different potato casserole dishes).

Sound familiar? Even if you didn't grow up going to Grandma's house for Christmas, you've probably been to a crowd event where the air was filled with panic and the food dishes seemed disconnected and unplanned at best. In fact, this scenario may describe most of the crowd events you've attended. And there's a very good reason why.

Most people who attempt crowd cooking don't take into account the *crowd factor* — simply put, the issues that accompany cooking for a crowd. Without considering the crowd factor, you're sure to experience a number of difficulties. Although the crowd factor includes several different aspects, it generally involves issues such as

- ✔ **Planning:** Cooking for a crowd requires additional planning. You can't just cook more than what you normally would for your immediate family; you need to make some specific plans that will help you accomplish your goals. We explore the planning process in Chapters 2 and 13.

- ✔ **Organizing:** Sure, you know that organization is important, but crowd events require an extra measure of organization. Even if you're typically organized, you'll find that crowd cooking takes more organizing than you may think. We show you how to get organized in Chapters 3, 13, and 15.

- ✔ **Picking appropriate foods:** Some foods work great for an intimate dinner party, and some foods work great for a casual family affair — when you cook for a crowd, you need to be careful about what food items you choose to prepare. Don't worry, we give you our best tried-and-true crowd recipes in this book, and you'll find them in Chapters 4 through 12.

- ✔ **Finding space:** Crowds take up a lot of room. As such, an important factor is space. You need to figure out how many people will show up and where you'll put them all. We help you plan that in Chapter 13.

- ✔ **Keeping time:** One of the single greatest mistakes that cooks make is underestimating the time they need. Have you ever been to an event where dinner was an hour late? We thought so; failure to accurately plan timing is the culprit. Don't worry — we help you stay on track.

- ✔ **Following a systematic approach for success:** A crowd event is really a long list of processes that you need to complete. Throughout this book, we show you how to accomplish them effectively, efficiently, and without a migraine headache.

The truth is, crowd cooking isn't a talent you can inherit from Aunt Sue. Successful crowd cooks are as such because they're able to understand and manage the crowd factor. They know how to organize and plan, what foods to choose, what foods to avoid, and how to anticipate problems. The good news is that you can learn how to tackle these issues with poise and grace, and giving you control over the crowd factor is the main focus of this book.

Determining the purpose of your event

The purpose of your crowd event may seem apparent. Maybe you're cooking for a holiday or a specific type of event, such as a wedding shower. Regardless, you should stop and ask yourself a few questions that will help you organize your thoughts and define your goals:

- ✔ What is the overall purpose of the event? In other words, why is everyone getting together?

- ✔ What are three things you'd really like people to say about the event when it's over?

- ✔ Is there anything particularly special about this event that you need to consider?

If you stop for a moment and really think about these three questions, you'll help yourself form an overriding purpose. Again, the purpose of the event may seem apparent, but knowing what you want the event to look and feel like and what you want people to think about it when all is said and done is important. After you have this purpose firmly planted in your mind, you can bring it to fruition.

Taking a breather and mustering confidence

We, your authors, know all about that panicky feeling that wells up in your throat, making you feel like you're suffocating. It usually happens after you've agreed to cook for a crowd, when the thought, "I'm really going to do this," comes to your mind.

Before you go into panic mode, stop. Have a seat. Take a deep breath. You have no reason to panic, because you can pull off this event. We know; we've done it ourselves and have helped other people do it. We'll help you, too — after all, that's why we wrote this book.

The truth is simple: If you have some cooking skills under your belt, you can cook for a crowd. You just need some help pulling everything together and knowing what to do. In the coming pages, we help you plan, get organized, cook your food, and pay attention to the details you may forget.

So take it easy. Exchange that worried face for a smile. We're here to help you, and your event is going to be great!

Planning for a Crowd

We say it here and we say it time and again throughout this book: Planning is the key to crowd cooking. Planning is the key to conquering the crowd factor, to organizing and getting everything ready on time, and to creating a great event.

As such, we help you plan from A to Z throughout this book, but for starters, it's a good idea to think carefully about some initial planning issues so you can get off to a good start.

Exploring your needs

As you think about cooking for a crowd, step back for a moment and consider some basics. You'll most likely need things in your kitchen that you don't currently have. This includes not only some basic ingredients but also such things as cookware, serving pieces, coffee and tea makers, and much more.

Because you often need more things when you cook for a crowd than when you cook for your immediate family, it's important to think about what you're lacking from the very start. We help you plan throughout this book, pointing out needs that may not have come to mind.

One of the great needs that you should consider is your need for help. Depending on your crowd, you may not be able to do the job alone. Sure, you can be the primary cook if you want, but you may need other people to handle all the tasks that come into play, especially if your crowd is greater than 20 people. The point is simple: Far too often, crowd cooks try to handle everything on their own and end up stressed and exhausted beyond measure. Don't try to be a hero. Think about what you can physically handle, and don't hesitate to get extra help. After all, you want to enjoy the day, too. You can find out more about these planning issues in Chapters 13 and 14.

Logistically speaking

As you think about your crowd, you need to consider logistics, which means space, among other things. The size of your home and its layout will determine how many people you can handle. Naturally, if you know from the start that your home isn't large enough for your crowd event, you'll need to turn to other locations, such as community centers, churches, and other types of meeting halls.

Thinking about food

In this book, we talk a lot about planning your menu (especially in Chapter 2) and provide you with a bunch of recipes that are just right for a crowd (see Chapters 4 through 12). However, you need to remember one word as you get ready to cook for a crowd: balance. Wanting to pull out all the stops when you cook for a crowd is natural. Of course you want everyone to be happy with the food you've prepared and to "ooh" and "aah" over what you've made. But that desire often leads to the Overcomplicated Recipe Syndrome.

When this syndrome strikes, you end up choosing only recipes that are complicated and outside the norm. You want every dish to be spectacular, as if a five-star chef has camped out in your home for a month. That thought is noble, but it isn't realistic.

As such, when you cook for a crowd, you need to find a balance in what you're doing. Sure, you can serve some complicated dishes, and you probably should, but you need to balance those dishes with ones that you can prepare quickly and easily. Too much of a good thing will only lead to a bunch of problems on your end.

In this book, you only find recipes that work well for crowd events, and we tend to err on the side of making things look and taste great with minimal work. After all, you have a lot to do and can easily overcommit yourself with the food preparation. We help you avoid that situation.

Finding Joy in the Moment

We don't mean to sound like cheerleaders, and we certainly won't tell you that cooking for a crowd is a simple process (if it were, you wouldn't need a book to help you). But we do want you to enjoy your event and be able to feel as if things are under control. And you can — with a lot of planning and organization (and all the tips in this book, of course).

After all, crowd events typically involve people you know and love. You're not a professional caterer, and you don't want to be one. But you do want to cook for a large group of people that you know and love and want the meal to be outstanding. We concur. We want you to have fun and be successful.

With that said, you're not perfect, and everything may not go perfectly. You can expect some problems and pitfalls along the way. You can expect that some dishes may not be as great as you want them to be. Congratulations! You're a real human being.

As you prepare to cook for a crowd, you can find joy during this time by keeping an overall perspective on what you're doing. Deal with the details, but keep the big picture in mind. Be flexible; you may have to adapt along the way. Flexibility will help you adjust to changes easily and keep a healthy perspective.

Chapter 2

Planning Your Menu

*O*kay, we admit it. Planning is never much fun. Yet, careful planning is what makes things in life turn out well, and cooking for a crowd is no exception. As such, if you want your crowd event to go swimmingly, you need to spend some time planning your menu.

As you think about planning your menu, you may feel a sense of panic and be overwhelmed. These feelings are normal, so don't worry. In this chapter, we help you plan your menu and break the process into manageable chunks. With the information you gain here, you'll be able to plan an effective, affordable, and reasonable menu for your crowd event.

While you plan your meal, don't get frustrated. Bringing all the elements of a great crowd meal together takes time, but the efforts of planning are well worth the results. After reading this chapter, you may have some ideas about how to balance your budget with your event. You also may still be wondering what to serve. For some inspiration as you think about planning, we suggest that you turn to the recipe chapters in this book and browse through them. There you'll find many delicious recipes that work perfectly for crowd events. If you need some help figuring out how much food you need for your crowd, be sure to check out Chapter 3.

Dollars and Sense

Naturally, cooking for a crowd will cost you a bit of money, so it's important that you start out with a firm look at your budget — let us tell you, the expense can spiral out of control if you're not careful. As such, this section will help you get a handle on your budget.

Gaining the overall perspective

It's settled: You're the one making the meal for the crowd. You breathe and take it all in. But then comes the time to start planning. Ask yourself the following questions:

- ✔ **How much can you spend?** You have to make that decision before you can go any further. In your head you may be thinking "leg of lamb with rosemary potatoes," but your budget may be more along the lines of barbecued brisket and baked beans.

- ✔ **What are the age group and gender of the guests you'll be cooking for?** If you're the designated cook for your son's high-school graduation party, you should keep in mind that teenagers, both girls and boys, can eat, eat, and eat some more. However, if you're cooking for 20 tots for your 4-year-old's birthday party, you can bank on the fact that they aren't going to eat as much, and the menu can be simple.

- ✔ **What items can you borrow?** Borrowing items can save you a lot of money. For example, if you're hosting a semiformal wedding reception for 25 people with an upscale buffet served on china, you'll certainly save money if you can borrow the dishes rather than rent them.

- ✔ **What are you responsible for cooking?** Are you cooking the appetizers, dessert, and everything in between? Or are you cooking only the main course?

Before you start planning your budget, it's important to get a firm idea of the event in mind. Think about the kind of event you're hosting and carefully estimate how many people are likely to attend.

Planning your budget

Planning a budget doesn't have an exact formula, because a number of factors come into play. We can, however, offer you this list of issues and ideas that will help you get a firm handle on what you can spend. Remember that your budget should be a relatively firm guideline for how much money you spend — not necessarily 100 percent set in stone. The idea is to come up with a budget that helps you have a great event without maxing out your credit cards. Keep these issues in mind:

- ✔ **Before you start planning anything, think about your bottom line.** Are you trying to have a backyard get-together for $100, or are you cooking for a wedding reception, where the bride and groom have given you $800 to work with? Try to find a reasonable bottom line and work from there. Don't start with what you'd ideally prefer and then see what happens with your budget — you won't like the results. Rather, start with a reasonable budget and work backwards.

✔ **Plan the event according to your budget, not the other way around.** You need to pair the event with what you can afford. In many cases, you won't have quite as much disposable money as you'd like. For example, say you're cooking Thanksgiving dinner for a crowd of 20. You want something really elegant, but your budget won't allow you to prepare everything you want. Instead of overspending, find ways to compromise. You may spend more on the entree and try to find a few less expensive side dishes and appetizers to make up the difference. Remember, you can cook great food without breaking the bank, so think about how you can find a win-win resolution with what you want and what your budget will allow.

✔ **Borrow what you can.** You may need extra plates, tables, chairs, glasses, cooking tools, and such items. Borrow, borrow, borrow — we mention this concept time and time again throughout this book. Don't waste your budget on items that you'll rarely use and can borrow from friends and family. Nothing is wrong with getting some help and borrowing things you need instead of buying them.

✔ **Watch out for budget creep.** As you plan, think about everything you need to buy so that your needs and budget are accurate.

✔ **Be reasonable and flexible.** You may try to tackle the world with the best crowd meal ever, but be reasonable about what you can spend and what you can prepare. We spend more time on these issues throughout the book.

Starting Off on the Right Foot: Appetizers

Let the event start out right by serving a variety of tasty, appetizing foods. When you serve appetizers, you need to ask yourself a couple of questions in order to determine the amount and the types of appetizers that you'll be serving.

First, you need to decide whether the appetizers are the main event or the warm-up for a wonderful meal to come. Either way, when you select what appetizers you want to serve, make sure you have a variety of items.

Matching appetizers to the meal

As you plan your appetizers, you should always look toward the main meal. You don't want to serve appetizers that don't match the main course, because the purpose of an appetizer is to get your guests ready for the meal. As such, appetizers tend to work best with certain kinds of foods, such as the following:

✔ **Backyard:** Assorted chips, dips, and salsas; meat and cheese trays; and fruit trays all work well. Avoid appetizers that spoil easily.

✔ **Formal and semiformal:** Serve such items as chilled shrimp with dipping sauce, oysters on the half shell, miniquiches, stuffed mushrooms, finger sandwiches, tartlets, baked brie with crackers, and cocktail meatballs.

✔ **Home-Style:** Serve various chips and dips, meat and cheese trays, cracker trays, cocktail sausages, cocktail meatballs, cheese balls, chicken nuggets, and other standard appetizer items.

✔ **Italian:** Appetizers such as fried cheese, fried mushrooms, stuffed mushrooms, fried ravioli, fried zucchini, antipasto platters, bruschetta, calamari, meat and cheese trays, vegetable trays, cocktail meatballs, and marinara dipping sauce all work well.

✔ **Mexican:** Appetizers such as cheese dip *(queso),* guacamole, salsa, tortilla chips, seven-layer dip, quesadillas, nachos, stuffed jalapeños, taquitos, flautas, empanadas, meat and cheese trays, and vegetable trays all work well.

As a general rule, just use common sense and try to think of appetizers that complement the main meal. Throughout this book, you can find a bunch of appetizer recipes that work well for crowds.

A question we often hear is "Do I have to serve appetizers?" As a general rule, serving them is a good idea. Appetizers give early guests something to do and keep guests from twiddling their thumbs as they wait for the main meal. Unless the meal comprises only appetizers, always try to work in a few of them.

Serving appetizers everyone loves

As you're thinking about your budget and planning ahead, you may wonder what kinds of appetizers you should use. The answer depends on how much you want to spend and what type of event you're cooking for. However, don't fall into the trap of thinking that appetizers have to be fancy and unusual. Rather, it's best to lean toward the practical side and serve appetizers that most people will love. Salmon pâté may sound cool, but you'll do better serving a more practical dish that people will enjoy. You can make easy and delicious crowd appetizers without spending a fortune, and you'll find plenty of recipes in this book that will help you make people smile without breaking your back or budget.

Savory Sides, Breads, and Condiments

As you think about your meal, you need to think about side dishes, breads, and condiments. Many times, these items don't get the attention they deserve, but they do greatly impact the success of your crowd meal, so keep them in mind.

Selecting the side dishes

Selecting side dishes should be easy if you keep one question in mind — the same question you ask yourself concerning the appetizers: Does it go with the main course? Side dishes should be foods that your guests will enjoy and that complement the main meal.

As you plan your side dishes, go back to Granny's rule of thumb for a well-rounded meal: Have one side green (because greens have the vitamins) and one side starch (such as mashed potatoes, rice, corn, and so on). You get the picture. Try to keep the meal balanced.

 When selecting your sides, remember to pay attention to the location of the event and what serving pieces you have to use. Be realistic about your limitations. Because keeping items hot can be difficult, it's always a good idea to serve some cold side dishes, such as a green salad or fruit salad, and some hot sides, such as rice pilaf.

Something else to keep in mind when planning your sides is the overall table presentation, especially if you're serving the meal buffet-style. Think about when you go to an all-you-can-eat buffet. Half of the reason people eat so much is because of how it's presented — all the different colors and textures of the food are stimulating to the appetite. With that in mind, try to make sure that you have a variety of colors in your side dishes.

If you aren't sure what sides go with what type of meat, think about what foods are served together at your favorite restaurant. Or look in your favorite cookbook or cooking magazine, and you should be able to find some inspiration as to what sides will best complement your meal.

The following is a list of standard, easy-to-make sides that your guests will surely enjoy:

- ✔ **Green salads with assorted dressings**
- ✔ **Vegetable salads:** Potato, pea, coleslaw, and so on
- ✔ **Fruit salads:** Strawberry banana, assorted melons, or tropical fruits
- ✔ **Potatoes:** Mashed, scalloped, French fried, or in casseroles
- ✔ **Rice:** White, brown, wild, or flavored
- ✔ **Pasta:** Macaroni and cheese, fettuccine, or spaghetti
- ✔ **Vegetables:** Steamed broccoli or cauliflower, cheese covered, sautéed, stir fried, or in casseroles
- ✔ **Beans and peas:** Barbecued beans, ranch-style beans, black beans, navy beans, pinto beans, black-eyed peas, green peas, or creamed peas

Pass the rolls, please: Breads and rolls

Despite the low-carb craze, most people still love bread. A nice piece of bread is satisfying and completes a meal perfectly. You have many different kinds of breads and rolls to choose from.

As usual, pay attention to the type of meal you're serving and choose bread that complements the meal. You don't want to make a social faux pas and serve corn bread with rack of lamb. Remember, the bread should go with the food, not compete with it; the bread should be flavorful, but not the star attraction.

Another important detail to consider when planning what bread you'll serve is to know whether the bread will need to be served hot. If so, do you have the necessary equipment or serving pieces to keep the bread warm?

Regardless of whether the bread needs to be warm or room temperature, you need to make sure it stays fresh. An easy way to keep the bread fresh is to line the serving dish with a clean linen, place the bread on top, and cover the bread with another clean linen. Remember, the more bread is exposed to air, the staler it becomes.

Because you have so many different types of breads to choose from, don't forget to think about the overall event when deciding what to serve. If you're serving, for example, a home-style meal of pot roast, mashed potatoes and gravy, green beans, salad, and yeast rolls for 40 people, it's okay to make things easy on yourself and serve yeast rolls from your local bakery.

If for whatever reason you can't bear the thought of store-bought rolls, consider buying the yeast rolls from the freezer section. All you have to do is make sure you allow enough time for them to rise and bake. At least you don't have to make the dough, which will save you some time. However, if you have the time and are talented at making bread, by all means, make it.

The following is a suggestion list of what types of breads or rolls to serve with different types of food:

- **Barbecue:** White or wheat sliced bread, bake-and-serve dinner rolls, hamburger buns, or hot dog buns

- **Formal and semiformal:** Yeast rolls, dinner rolls, or croissants

- **Home-Style:** Corn bread, white or wheat sliced bread, yeast rolls, potato rolls, biscuits, or bake-and-serve dinner rolls

- **Italian:** Garlic bread made out of Italian loaf or French loaf bread; hearty, chewy rolls; or Vienna rolls

- **Mexican:** Corn tortillas, flour tortillas, corn bread, or jalapeño corn bread

- **Sandwiches:** Croissants, hamburger buns, white or wheat sliced bread, hoagie buns, submarine buns

Butter, spreads, and more

Condiments are those items that nobody really thinks about — at least until they're missing. Condiments deserve some planning, too — just pay attention to the food you're serving and let the dishes guide you in your decision making.

When planning your menu, always make sure you *write down* all the condiments you'll be serving. We know, it's easy to think you'll remember the salt and pepper shakers, but the school of hard knocks tells us to leave nothing to chance.

For the most part, we strongly encourage you to buy your condiments already made, mostly because you'll save time and, in many instances, money. However, if you have a recipe for a really great homemade salad dressing and you can budget the time to make it, go for it. Such special touches are always welcomed and wanted.

Flavored butters are another condiment that you can make from scratch if you have the time. These butters go great with just about any bread, and you can make them sweet or savory — whichever goes best with your menu.

Following is a list of standard condiments, just as a reminder:

- Assorted jellies
- Butter
- Coffee creamer
- Honey
- Ketchup
- Mayonnaise
- Mustard
- Pepper
- Salad dressing
- Salt
- Soy sauce
- Steak sauce
- Sugar
- Sugar substitute
- Syrup
- Tabasco sauce

The preceding list gives you just the basic types of condiments. The next list, however, provides ideas of some condiments that you may also need in order to complete the menu.

- Bacon bits
- Cheddar cheese, shredded
- Chives
- Croutons
- Crushed red pepper
- Guacamole
- Onions, diced or sliced
- Parmesan cheese, grated or shredded
- Salsa
- Sour cream

Soups and Stews

Soups and stews can be a hearty course or the main meal. When deciding which ones to serve, keep their function in mind: Will you serve them as an appetizer, a side dish, or the main meal? Also make sure they match up with the other items you're serving.

Soups and stews (and how you serve them) tend to be regional in nature. For example, Southern states tend to love vegetable beef soup, and clam chowder is a hit in New England. As such, let common sense and personal preference be your guide. A soup or stew can work great as an appetizer or side dish, and many of the heavier ones can serve as a main meal.

 Regardless of which category your soups and stews fall into, remember to include crackers, croutons, or a hearty bread to go along with them. Adding soup spoons to your inventory list is also a good idea.

The Meat of the Matter: Main Course

When planning your menu, everything should build up to the main course. Naturally, the entree will likely get most of your attention and consume most of your budget. As such, you should keep a few things in mind as you plan the main course.

Lining up your budget and your options

As you're thinking about the main course, you need to plan based on the event itself and what you want to do. The main course may already be planned based on the kind of event, but if not, finish reading this chapter and then spend some time looking through Chapter 5. You'll find plenty of main course dishes that are tried and true and won't break the bank.

As you plan the main course, remember to consider your budget. You may start off with an idea for a rather extravagant dish but decide that you can't invest the time or money on that particular entree. As such, plan something delicious and wonderful but make sure you can physically accomplish it with a reasonable amount of time and money.

 We highly recommend that you cook a trial run of the main course before the crowd event. Doing so will give you an opportunity to make sure you're happy with the result and feel confident about cooking it.

Balancing the main course with the rest of the meal

Cooking for a crowd is always a balance. You need to balance your money, time, and cooking skills. You may need several days of planning and cooking work to pull off the event, and you may need extra help.

As such, plan the entree that you really want to serve but make sure you carefully consider appetizers, side dishes, and desserts. Try to pair the main course with other dishes that are easier and quicker to make, or ones that you can at least make ahead of time. Overcommitting your time and budget when you cook for a crowd is very easy, so plan carefully. Again, check out the recipes in this book. We give you only tried-and-true recipes that work great for crowds, complete with the time you need to make them. Let this book be your friend; use the resources in it.

Delighting Your Guests with Desserts

Nothing completes a meal like a sweet treat. For some people, the dessert is the pinnacle of the meal. For others, it's a sweet ending to a wonderful meal. Regardless of which category you or your guests fall into, desserts are a very important part of any meal.

Desserts can be as simple as a nice platter of cookies or as complex and time-consuming as a made-from-scratch cheesecake and can fit in many places in between.

When planning your desserts, keep in mind what type of meal you're serving. Make sure the dessert portion of the meal complements the foods everyone will enjoy throughout the evening. You also need to make sure that the food goes with the event, which should be no problem if you keep that idea in mind when planning the rest of the meal. If you're having a formal wedding reception with beef Wellington and rice pilaf, you probably don't want to serve cherry cobbler for dessert.

The following is a list of suggestions for what types of desserts go well with certain types of meals:

✔ **Mexican:** *Flan,* a traditional Mexican dessert; *sophillas,* which are fried flour tortillas sprinkled with cinnamon sugar and served with butter and honey; *churros,* a fried pastry sprinkled with cinnamon sugar; or dessert *empanadas,* which are Spanish pastries.

- ✔ **Italian:** Cheesecake, tiramisu, Italian cream cake, carrot cake, fruit sorbet, or dessert ravioli

- ✔ **Home-Style:** Fruit cobbler, ice cream, cookies, brownies, assorted cakes, or assorted pies

- ✔ **Barbecue:** Fruit cobbler, ice cream, cookies, brownies, assorted cakes, assorted pies, watermelon, or cantaloupe

- ✔ **Formal and semiformal:** Cheesecake, assorted cakes, petits fours, crème brûlée, assorted pastries, or gourmet cookies

Quenching the Thirst: Drinks

As you plan your menu, also remember to think through what types of drinks go best with your meal. Consider the location: If you're having an outside crowd event and it's the middle of summer, you need to increase the amount of cold drinks that you serve. Likewise, if the event is outside in the winter, you need to plan for additional hot drink options.

The good thing about drinks is that you have so many to choose from, and they usually involve the least amount of work for your crowd event.

As you plan your selections, always pay attention to the event itself to decide what drinks to serve. If your crowd event is a baby or wedding shower or some kind of reception, a good choice is a tasty punch. However, if you're serving at a backyard barbecue, you may want to offer some thirst-quenching iced tea. You can find some great alternatives for punch and tea recipes in Chapter 8.

Refreshingly cool: Cold drinks

When you're deciding what cold drinks to serve, make sure you consider the people you'll be serving. Will a lot of young children be present? If so, keep in mind that most children (and parents) may prefer something fruity to a regular soft drink.

When serving soft drinks, it's important when planning your menu and looking at your budget to decide whether to serve them from cans or 2-liter plastic bottles. Generally speaking, the plastic 2-liters are less expensive than cans. However, some people prefer to serve canned soft drinks because they think that if they do, they don't have to provide cups and ice. We recommend the contrary: Regardless of how you serve soft drinks, always make sure you provide cups and ice.

One advantage of using bottles is that you tend to not have as much waste, because most people won't drink a whole can. What usually happens is they get a can, start drinking it, and set it down, and eventually the drink gets warm — and face it, no one wants to drink a warm soft drink. All that's left to do is get a new can.

When serving tea, lemonade, or limeade, you need to make sure you have a large enough container or enough smaller containers to hold the amount that you need for the event. Keep that fact in mind when you're making up your list of things to borrow. Many times churches, auxiliary clubs, and the like will have a large drink container.

The following is a list of standard cold drink choices:

- Coke or Pepsi
- Diet Coke or Diet Pepsi
- Dr. Pepper
- Sprite or 7-Up
- Ginger ale
- Root beer
- Orange or grape soda
- Iced tea
- Punch
- Lemonade
- Limeade
- Sparkling water

Soothing and satisfying: Hot drinks

During the winter months, hot drinks are typically a requirement for a crowd event. Make sure you use good quality coffee cups, either ceramic or disposable. If you're serving hot drinks to children, go for "warm" hot chocolate rather than "hot" chocolate, and so on. Here are a few quick suggestions to consider:

- Coffee
- Flavored coffees
- Hot apple cider
- Hot chocolate
- Hot punches

Easing Your Decision Making: Sample Menus

Wouldn't it be nice if someone just handed you a good menu so you could start from there? Okay, you've convinced us — we'll do the dirty work! In this section, you find a collection of sample menus for a variety of crowd events. The recipes for every menu item are in this book, so feel free to use our sample menus or modify them to suit your needs. We left room on the following pages for you to take notes. Or at least read through them to help you start thinking in the right direction!

Blissful beginnings: Wedding receptions

Nothing is quite like the joy and beauty of a wedding, coupled with the delicious food that follows. The following menu is the perfect combination of formal foods that are delightful yet practical.

Following is a list of great appetizers to serve alone or along with the suggested dinner for either an informal or formal wedding. In addition to these tasty, satisfying appetizers, you may want to add a basic fruit or vegetable tray.

- Ham and Asparagus Wraps — see Chapter 12
- Basil Pesto Kebabs — see Chapter 4
- Mini Sausage Quiches — see Chapter 11
- Bacon and Blue Cheese Bites — see Chapter 11
- Shrimp with Mustard Sauce — see Chapter 12
- My Big Fat Greek Drummettes — see Chapter 12

The following is a suggested menu for a buffet-style dinner reception:

- Tossed Salad with Strawberries and Walnuts — see Chapter 6
- Classic Waldorf Salad — see Chapter 6
- Tomato and Rice Florentine Soup — see Chapter 7
- Regal Beef Tenderloin — see Chapter 12
- Glazed Carrots — see Chapter 6
- Scalloped Potatoes — see Chapter 6
- Broccoli with Red Peppers — see Chapter 6
- Chocolate Chip Cookie Dough Truffles — see Chapter 12
- Society Punch — see Chapter 8

When serving a meal reception, always include some type of bread and butter. Croissants or dinner rolls would go great with the preceding menu.

Time to celebrate: Baby or wedding showers

Baby and wedding showers are always great fun, but someone has to prepare the food, and the designated cook may very well be you. In most cases, baby and wedding showers provide guests with a tempting assortment of appetizers and bite-size goodies; the following menu will work perfectly for any of these kinds of events. Sometimes, however, the spread is a little more substantial. With that thought in mind, we've included additional menu items for those occasions when you need a slightly heavier fare.

- Stuffed Cherry Tomatoes — see Chapter 4
- Artichoke and Spinach Dip — see Chapter 4
- Sunflower Crispies — see Chapter 4
- Summer Broccoli Salad — see Chapter 10
- Sage Pea Salad — see Chapter 10
- Smoked Ham and Cheese Roll-Ups — see Chapter 4
- Chunky Chicken Salad Sandwiches — see Chapter 10
- Raspberry Thumbprints — see Chapter 9
- Heavenly Turtle Brownies — see Chapter 9
- Frosty Pineapple Limeade — see Chapter 8

Warm and thankful hearts: Holiday meals

Holidays are all about food and family. Whether you're celebrating Thanksgiving, Christmas, Memorial Day, or any other holiday, this formal family meal is sure to be enjoyed by all.

- Olive Bites — see Chapter 12
- Sausage Balls — see Chapter 4
- Festive Pumpkin Pie Dip — see Chapter 11
- Candy-Coated Pecans — see Chapter 4
- Classic Waldorf Salad — see Chapter 6
- Heavenly Hash-Brown Casserole — see Chapter 11
- Creamy Green Bean and Mushroom Casserole — see Chapter 11
- Three Meat and Mushroom Stromboli — see Chapter 4
- Welcome Home Baked Ham — see Chapter 11
- Peppermint Mousse — see Chapter 11
- Chocolate Chip Cream Cheese Ball — see Chapter 11
- Chocolate Peanut Butter Tassies — see Chapter 12
- Peppermint Hot Cocoa — see Chapter 8
- Coconut Eggnog — see Chapter 11

The gang's all here: Family get-togethers

The odds are good that your first crowd meal will be a family gathering. Perhaps Uncle John turns 80, your parents celebrate their 50th wedding anniversary, or the annual family reunion comes your way — or perhaps the get-together is less formal. Regardless of the occasion, this menu works well for all kinds of family gatherings.

- ✔ Cheese and Corn Chowder — see Chapter 7
- ✔ Good Luck Black-Eyed Peas — see Chapter 6
- ✔ Country-Style Green Beans — see Chapter 10
- ✔ Easy Mac and Cheese — see Chapter 6
- ✔ Timesaver Pot Roast — see Chapter 5
- ✔ Chocolate Chip Cookie Bars — see Chapter 9
- ✔ Carrot Cake — see Chapter 9
- ✔ Peach Tea — see Chapter 8

Fun in the sun: Summer shindigs

Everyone loves a day in the sun with family and friends. Whether you're spending the day at the park or having a group over for a backyard pool party, this menu will put a sunny smile on everyone's face.

- ✔ Fruit Salsa and Cinnamon Chips — see Chapter 4
- ✔ Baked Beans — see Chapter 6
- ✔ Zesty Corn on the Cob — see Chapter 10
- ✔ Creamy Red Potato Salad — see Chapter 10
- ✔ Barbecued Brisket — see Chapter 5
- ✔ Strawberry Pretzel Delight — see Chapter 9
- ✔ Pucker-Up Lemon Ice — see Chapter 10
- ✔ Lemon Tea with Almond — see Chapter 8

An Italian feast

We love Italian food, and you probably do, too. The good news is that Italian meals work well for crowds, because this cuisine lends itself well to more servings. Here's a great Italian feast that your crowd is sure to love:

- Three Meat and Mushroom Stromboli — see Chapter 4
- Artichoke and Spinach Dip — see Chapter 4
- Basil Pesto Kebabs — see Chapter 4
- Tossed Salad with Strawberries and Walnuts — see Chapter 6
- Lasagne Soup — see Chapter 7
- Tomato and Rice Florentine Soup — see Chapter 7
- Sausage and Spinach Manicotti — see Chapter 5
- Baked Ziti — see Chapter 5
- Tempting Tiramisu — see Chapter 9
- Sweet Bruschetta — see Chapter 12

Don't forget to include the bread — no Italian meal is complete without it! Try some savory bruschetta, toasted garlic bread, or some rosemary bread with a side of olive oil dipping sauce. Also remember to include fresh grated Parmesan cheese.

Winter gatherings

The weather may be cold outside, but the food is hot and welcoming inside. This menu is perfect for any cold day and also works well as a holiday meal if you want something along the lines of home cooking.

- Broccoli Cheese Soup — see Chapter 7
- Hearty Vegetable Beef Soup — see Chapter 7
- Mom's Meatloaf — see Chapter 5
- Scalloped Potatoes — see Chapter 6
- Country-Style Green Beans — see Chapter 10
- Hot Cranberry Tea — see Chapter 8
- Buttered Maple Apple Cider — see Chapter 8
- Rocky Road Cake — see Chapter 9

Always include crackers and or some kind of hearty, crusty bread when you're serving soups and stews.

On the lighter side

This menu is great when you don't want to serve a full meal but want a little more than just appetizers:

- ✔ Fruit Salsa and Cinnamon Chips — see Chapter 4
- ✔ Stuffed Cherry Tomatoes — see Chapter 4
- ✔ Ham and Asparagus Wraps — see Chapter 12
- ✔ Summer Broccoli Salad — see Chapter 10
- ✔ Classic Waldorf Salad — see Chapter 6
- ✔ Sage Pea Salad — see Chapter 10
- ✔ Toasted Muffulettas — see Chapter 10
- ✔ Peach Tea — see Chapter 8
- ✔ Punch Bowl Layered Dessert — see Chapter 9

Sweets, and Nothing but the Sweets

We love desserts, and so does most everyone we know. Sometimes desserts are all you need for your get-together. The following menu is a good example of how to put different sweets together that not only taste great but also work well with other wonderful indulgences (all are vegetarian friendly, of course):

- Candy-Coated Pecans — see Chapter 4
- Mint Chocolate Candy Cookies — see Chapter 9
- Raspberry Thumbprints — see Chapter 9
- Vanilla Pudding Layered Dessert — see Chapter 9
- Surprise Devil's Food Cupcakes — see Chapter 9

Death by Chocolate

The previous menu sample, "Sweets, and Nothing but the Sweets," is indulgent, to say the least. However, for those die-hard chocolate fans, this section should have all your guests happy and in a sugar-induced state of mind.

- Café Mocha — see Chapter 8
- Peppermint Hot Cocoa — see Chapter 8
- Chocolate Chip Cookie Bars — see Chapter 9
- Peppermint Fudge Brownies — see Chapter 9
- Heavenly Turtle Brownies — see Chapter 9
- Rocky Road Cake — see Chapter 9
- Chocolate Chip Cream Cheese Ball — see Chapter 11
- Chocolate Peanut Butter Tassies — see Chapter 12

Chapter 3

Estimating Food Quantities, Serving Dishes, and More

*I*f you've planned your crowd menu (see Chapter 2 for help), the question that naturally follows is "How much food do I need?" That question can be difficult to ponder, and it can cause crowd cooking to seem a bit overwhelming. After all, if you have 30 guests coming for Thanksgiving, how do you figure out how much dressing you need? Or how many bite-size snacks do you need for a backyard pool party of 20?

Don't worry; we're here to help you quickly and easily solve the food quantity question once and for all. We also help you figure out what serving dishes you should use for your particular event. Armed with the knowledge you gain in this chapter, you'll be way ahead of the game.

Estimating Food Quantities

Let us warn you upfront: Nothing is worse than cooking for a crowd and not having enough food. Ideally, you want your guests to be able to reasonably eat as much they want without any particular dish running out. This idea may seem excessive, but we err on the side of having too much rather than too little. We do everything possible to steer clear of the sinking feeling in our stomachs that we get when we realize that people are still happily eating and we're running out of food.

So, as you explore the issue of estimating food quantities in this section, we give you some exact measurements and some general suggestions to follow. But cooking for a crowd isn't an exact formula, so you have to take some factors into consideration. Does your crowd really enjoy eating? Will a significant number of children be present? Are most people in your crowd highly weight conscious? All these questions and similar ones impact how much food you prepare; what's important is that you err on the side of excess.

Cooking and Mathematics 101

No, you don't have to go back to high-school algebra (thank goodness). After all, $x + 2x$ doesn't equal "cake." However, math has a lot to do with recipes, and rightly so. In many ways, cooking is an art, but when you add it all up, the combination of ingredients is really nothing more than good science.

If you want to put that science to work, you need to know the basics of cooking measurements. If you happen to know these already, just skip over this section and review it when you need it. If not, now is a good time to review these basic cooking measurements. Tables 3-1 and 3-2 present them in a handy way so you can refer to this section time and time again when you need a refresher. (If you're looking for metric measurement conversions, flip to Appendix A at the back of the book — you'll find just what you need.)

Table 3-1	Volume Measurements		
Teaspoons	*Tablespoons*	*Cups*	*Fluid Ounces*
3	1	N/A	½
6	2	⅛	1
12	4¼	2	
16	N/A	⅓	N/A
18	6	N/A	N/A
24	8	½	4
30	10	N/A	5
32	N/A	⅔	N/A
36	12	¾	6
48	16	1	8

Table 3-2	Fluid Measurements	
2 cups	1 pint	16 ounces
4 cups	1 quart	32 ounces
8 cups	½ gallon	64 ounces
16 cups	1 gallon	128 ounces
2 pints	1 quart	32 ounces
8 pints	1 gallon	128 ounces
2 quarts	½ gallon	64 ounces
4 quarts	1 gallon	128 ounces

You may notice that some recipes call for a "dash" or a "pinch" of an ingredient. Generally, a dash or pinch is less than ⅛ teaspoon.

Converting a small serving recipe to a large quantity recipe

Everyone has favorite recipes, but sometimes a recipe only makes six to eight servings. When you cook for a crowd, you may need 20 servings or more. So can you double or triple a recipe and get the same results? The answer: yes and no. It depends on the recipe.

If you need to increase a small serving recipe to a large serving recipe, you have several factors to take into account. What type of food is it? Will it be cooked? If so, will you be cooking it in a larger, deeper pan, or in the type of pan the recipe calls for?

When you try to increase the number of servings in a recipe, always multiply by a whole number. For example, if your original recipe makes 8 servings, but you need to make it for 21 people, round up and multiply the recipe by 3, which gives you 24 servings. Because of the cooking and complication factor, we generally don't recommend that you go beyond tripling a recipe.

Although it seems reasonable that you can multiply any recipe this way, it isn't so. Some recipes can easily be converted to a large quantity by doubling or tripling the ingredients, but the simple math conversion won't work for others. For example, you can't triple a cheesecake recipe and end up with a very large cheesecake. The cheesecake won't cook thoroughly. Therefore, you have to make several cheesecakes, not one big one.

Cooking time issues

As you think about cooking time, you must remember that it's impacted by what you're doing with the recipe. If you create larger portion recipes, you need to adjust the cooking time based on the size of the pan and how much you're increasing the recipe. If you cook several items in your oven at the same time, the cooking time will generally need to be extended a bit. Because you can't come up with a mathematical formula for converting cooking time (and who would want to, anyway?), just use good common sense and keep checking on what's in the oven. However, the more you open the door and check, the more cooking time you need to add. As you can see, cooking time can turn into a ridiculously complicated issue, but let your cooking sense guide you and don't get distracted with other tasks.

To double or triple a recipe, keep a few tips in mind:

✔ **You need a pan large enough to handle the larger recipe.**

✔ **If you double or triple a recipe, you must also adjust the cook time.** There's no exact way to do this, so you have to use your good cooking sense and keep your eye on the dish. Basically, if you put the ingredients in a deeper pan, you need more cook time. If you put something in a more shallow pan (which causes the food to spread out), you need less.

✔ **Overly complicated recipes tend to cause problems when you try to increase the quantity.** If the recipe seems complicated to you, you're better off creating several dishes of the same thing rather than trying to create one big one.

Making Enough to Serve Everyone

Suppose you're cooking brisket for a July 4th backyard party for 40, with creamed corn on the side. How much brisket and corn do you need? We know these questions plague you; after all, this answer isn't something you should know off the top of your head. So we've created several handy food quantity charts that you can refer to over and over again. Check out the following sections for details.

We also compressed these quantity charts onto a simple tear-out card, a Cheat Sheet if you will, that you can find at the beginning of this book. Just rip it out and keep it in your kitchen for quick reference.

Quantity planning for appetizers and drinks

Appetizers and drinks don't have to be a pain in the neck, but planning them tends to be confusing. Don't worry; this section will guide you.

Little nibbles: Appetizers

As you determine the appetizer quantity, consider what purpose the appetizers will serve. If you're serving appetizers before a main meal, you don't need as many as you do if the appetizers are the meal itself. Because appetizers are different from other food items, how much you need depends on several factors. Appetizers don't lend themselves to a quantity chart per se, but let the following list guide you:

- **For appetizers preceding a full meal,** you should have at least four different types of appetizers and six to eight pieces per person. For example, say you have 20 guests. In that case, you'd need at least 120 total appetizer pieces.

- **For appetizers without a meal,** you should have at least six different types of appetizers. You should also have 12 to 15 pieces per person. For example, if you have 20 guests, you need at least 240 total appetizer pieces. This estimate is for a three-hour party. Longer parties require more appetizers.

- **The more variety you have, the smaller portion size each type of appetizer will need to have.** Therefore, you don't need to make as much of any one particular appetizer.

- **When you serve appetizers to a crowd, always include bulk-type appetizers.** Bulk-type foods are items that aren't individually made, such as dips or spreads. If you forgo the dips and spreads, you'll end up making hundreds of individual appetizer items, which may push you over the edge. To calculate bulk items, assume 1 ounce equals 1 piece.

- **Always try to have extra items, such as black and green olives and nuts, for extra filler.**

When appetizers precede the meal, you should serve dinner within an hour. If more than an hour will pass before the meal, then you need to increase the number of appetizers. Once again, always err on the side of having too much rather than too little.

Thirst quenchers

Concerning drinks, let the following list guide you:

- **Soft drinks:** One to two 8-ounce servings per person per hour.
- **Punch:** One to two 4-ounce servings per person per hour.
- **Tea:** One to two 8-ounce servings per person per hour.
- **Coffee:** One to two 4-ounce servings per person per hour.
- **Water:** Always provide it. Two standard serving pitchers are usually enough.

Again, err on the side of having too much. If people are eating a lot and having fun, they tend to consume more liquid.

Quantity planning for soups, sides, main courses, and desserts

The following tables can help you determine how much food you need for some typical soups, sides, main courses, and desserts. If the item you're serving isn't listed here, you can probably find an item in the same food group to guide you.

Note: In Tables 3-3 through 3-8, you may notice a bit of a discrepancy between the serving per person and the crowd servings. We include the per-person serving based on a plated affair. However, buffet-style affairs typically figure at a lower serving per person, because buffets typically feature more side dish items than a plated meal does. Don't use the quantity tables as an exact science; use them to guide you and help you make decisions for your particular crowd. If you're serving a dish that you know everyone loves, make more than the table suggests. If you have a dish that isn't as popular, you can get by with less.

Table 3-3	Soups and Stews		
Soup or Stew	**Per Person**	**Crowd of 25**	**Crowd of 50**
Served as a first course	1 cup	5 quarts	2½ gallons
Served as an entree	1½ to 2 cups	2 to 2½ gallons	4 gallons

Table 3-4		Main Courses	
Entree	*Per Person*	*Crowd of 25*	*Crowd of 50*
Baby-back ribs, pork spareribs, beef short ribs	1 pound	25 pounds	50 pounds
Casserole	N/A	2 to 3 13-x-9-inch casseroles	4 to 5 13-x-9-inch casseroles
Chicken, turkey, or duck (boneless)	½ pound	13 pounds	25 pounds
Chicken or turkey (with bones)	¾ to 1 pound	19 pounds	38 pounds
Chili, stew, stroganoff, and other chopped meats	5 to 6 ounces	8 pounds	15 pounds
Ground beef	½ pound	13 pounds	25 pounds
Maine lobster (about 2 pounds each)	1	25	50
Oysters, clams, and mussels (medium to large)	6 to 10 pieces	100 to 160 pieces	200 to 260 pieces
Pasta	4 to 5 ounces	7 pounds	16 pounds
Pork	14 ounces	22 pounds	44 pounds
Roast (with bone)	14 to 16 ounces	22 to 25 pounds	47 to 50 pounds
Roast cuts (boneless)	½ pound	13 pounds	25 pounds
Shrimp (large — 16 to 20 per pound)	5 to 7 shrimp	7 pounds	14 pounds
Steak cuts (T-bone, porterhouse, rib-eye)	16 to 24 ounces	16 to 24 ounces per person	16 to 24 ounces per person
Turkey (whole)	1 pound	25 pounds	50 pounds

Table 3-5	Side Dishes		
Side Dish	*Per Person*	*Crowd of 25*	*Crowd of 50*
Asparagus, carrots, cauliflower, broccoli, green beans, corn kernels, peas, black-eyed peas, and so on	3 to 4 ounces	4 pounds	8 pounds
Corn on the cob (broken in halves when serving buffet-style)	1 ear	20 ears	45 ears
Pasta (cooked)	2 to 3 ounces	3½ pounds	7 pounds
Potatoes and yams	1 (medium)	6 pounds	12 pounds
Rice and grains (cooked)	1½ ounces	2½ pounds	5 pounds

Table 3-6	Side Salads		
Ingredient	*Per Person*	*Crowd of 25*	*Crowd of 50*
Croutons (medium size)	N/A	2 cups	4 cups
Dressing (served on the side)	N/A	4 cups	8 cups
Fruit salad	N/A	3 quarts	6 quarts
Lettuce (iceberg or romaine)	N/A	4 heads	8 heads
Lettuce (butter or red leaf)	N/A	6 heads	12 heads
Potato or macaroni salad	N/A	8 pounds	16 pounds
Shredded cabbage for coleslaw	N/A	6 to 8 cups (about 1 large head of cabbage)	12 to 16 cups (about 2 large heads of cabbage)
Vegetables (such as tomato and cucumber)	N/A	3 cups	6 cups

Table 3-7		Breads	
Bread	**Per Person**	**Crowd of 25**	**Crowd of 50**
Croissants or muffins	1½ per person	3½ dozen	7 dozen
Dinner rolls	1½ per person	3½ dozen	7 dozen
French or Italian bread	N/A	2 18-inch loaves	4 18-inch loaves

Table 3-8		Desserts	
Dessert	**Per Person**	**Crowd of 25**	**Crowd of 50**
Brownies or bars	1 to 2 per person	2½ to 3 dozen	5½ to 6 dozen
Cheesecake	2-inch wedge	2 9-inch cheesecakes	4 9-inch cheesecakes
Cobbler	1 cup	2 9-x-9-x-2-inch pans	4 9-x-9-x-2-inch pans
Cookies	2 to 3	3 to 4 dozen	6 to 8 dozen
Ice cream or sorbet	8 ounces	1 gallon	2 gallons
Layered cake or angel food cake	1 slice	2 8-inch cakes	4 8-inch cakes
Pie	3-inch wedge	2 to 3 9-inch pies	4 to 5 9-inch pies
Pudding, trifles, and the like	1 cup	1 gallon	2 gallons
Sheet cake	2-x-2-inch piece	¼ sheet cake	½ sheet cake

Preparation Dishes: Pots, Pans, and Everything but the Kitchen Sink

An important but often overlooked aspect of cooking for a crowd is preparation dishes. Many times, crowd cooks get so fixated on the food they're going to serve that they forget about everything they need to prepare it. Consider the following sections your crash course to understanding what you need to prepare your very own crowd meal.

The basic stuff you need

What you need in order to successfully pull off cooking for a crowd depends on what you're serving. Hopefully you've already read Chapter 2 and know what menu items you'll serve. You should also know exactly how much of each food you'll be serving.

Now with those pesky details established, take a look at some of the items you'll need. First, grab your menu and a piece of paper. You need to work step by step through each dish that you're going to prepare and serve so you have a realistic account of the actual items needed.

The key point to remember is that you'll need more items than you'd normally use. You'll also need more of certain items that you may actually have on hand. The following list tells you the standard preparation dishes you'll probably need in order to prepare everything for your crowd:

- Cake pans
- Casserole dishes
- Cheesecake pans
- Cookie sheets
- Food storage containers
- Ice chests
- Measuring cups (two sets)
- Measuring spoons (two sets)
- Mixing bowls
- Pie pans
- Slow cookers
- Stockpots

You'll likely need to get your hands on additional preparation dishes and tools. The point is to carefully create a list and think about all the extra items you'll need to prepare your food before you get to work. After all, unless you live in a school cafeteria, your kitchen probably isn't outfitted to cook for a crowd.

Beg, borrow, and steal

At this point, you may be wondering, "How do I get everything I need without blowing a large part of my budget on dishes and such?" The answer: Borrow, borrow, and borrow some more.

Your friends and family will usually be more than willing to let you borrow supplies. Just make sure that when you borrow items, you let the person know how long you need to borrow them. If you're rounding up everything ahead of time, which we highly recommend, you may be borrowing things for a couple of weeks.

Because you'll probably need to borrow preparation items, make sure you create a list of what you need. Then, when you borrow an item from someone, be sure to add his or her name to the list. Also, take your list a step further by writing detailed descriptions of what you've borrowed so you can make sure that Aunt Jenny gets her specific cookie sheet back (because believe us, Aunt Jenny will know if it's hers or not). This may seem ridiculous, but be forewarned: Pots, pans, and such will start to look alike. Let's say you borrow five cookie sheets from five different people. Two weeks from now, will you remember which cookie sheet belongs to whom?

Would You Like Paper, Plastic, or China?

When you try to decide what type of serving dishes to use, you must first decide on the overall feel or theme of the event. The following questions are a good way to decide what items will work best for you:

- ✔ What is the event? A family get-together, wedding, baby shower, or graduation (and so on)?
- ✔ Is the event formal or informal?
- ✔ Is the event inside or outside?
- ✔ Does the event have a set theme or concept?
- ✔ Has the menu been set?

After you determine the overall theme or feel of the event, let common sense help you decide what kind of serving items to use. Naturally, you wouldn't use china at a backyard barbecue, but as a general rule, err on the side of making your serving pieces a bit nicer than they need to be. After all, no one ever complains if the decor is nicer than expected.

Now that you know what type of event you're cooking for, you can start deciding what you need to use as serving dishes. It's important to keep in mind that borrowing dishes and serving pieces from friends and family is okay. Remember, most cooks won't have enough serving pieces of their own to feed a wedding party of 50.

Having fun with serving pieces

When you cook for a crowd, do your darnedest to think outside the box. China, crystal, and silver serving trays are all beautiful and practical, but you can add some interest by using the unusual for a serving dish.

When brainstorming creative serving pieces, think along the lines of objects that you usually use for another purpose other than presenting and serving food. A wide-mouth stemware piece, for example, is a great serving dish for, say, candy, nuts, or olives. When you think about stemware, you think about serving a drink — not food. But using stemware to serve food adds visual interest, which can help bring the event together because not only will the food taste great, but it'll also look great. The nice part about adding visual interest is that with a little imagination and creativity, you don't have to spend a dime. Everyone has everyday objects around the house that will do the job as creative serving pieces.

Other items you probably have lying around your house are baskets made from a variety of materials, such as wicker, willow, or plastic. Are you serving whole pieces of fruit? Try nicely arranging them in a basket. Are bread or rolls part of the meal? Line a basket with a color-coordinated linen, place the bread in the basket, and cover the bread with another linen. In so doing, you've added different textures to your presentation and are simultaneously keeping the bread from drying out.

Another tip is to let the food also take on the role of a serving piece. Have you ever seen a watermelon basket, nicely carved with a variety of melons and other assorted fruits inside? Such a presentation is beautiful and colorful and can add a lot to your table decor. And if you were planning on serving watermelon anyway, it's resourceful. Flip ahead to Chapter 16 for more ideas.

Naturally, you can exercise your creativity in many different ways. If the creative bug bites, visit www.diynet.com for all kinds of creative and fun ideas.

You'll likely use certain standard serving pieces at your crowd event: ceramic, glass, or china platters; decorative or ornate serving bowls; and other such items. Just take a close look at your recipes and decide how you want to serve those foods. The sidebar "Having fun with serving pieces" provides some ideas to get your creative juices flowing.

Don't wait until the last minute to round up your serving pieces! It's really easy to get so fixated on the food that everything else becomes secondary. Start trying to get serving pieces in your possession now so you're not frantic the week of the event!

Part II
Tried-and-True Recipes for Crowds

The 5th Wave — By Rich Tennant

"OK Cookie-your venison in lingdonberry sauce is good, as are your eggplant soufflé and the risotto with foie gras. But whoever taught you how to make a croquembouche should be shot!"

In this part . . .

Now come the big decisions: What recipes should you choose? Are certain recipes better than others? How can you create a dish that is manageable for a crowd but not boring and mundane? You've come to the right place! We love crowd cooking, and in this part, we share a bunch of our favorite recipes with you. You find crowd recipe options for appetizers, main dishes, side dishes, soups and stews, punches and drinks, and some wonderful desserts. Armed with these recipes, your event is sure to be a big success.

Chapter 4

Creating Tasty Appetizers

In This Chapter

▶ Cooling down with cold appetizers

▶ Warming up with hot appetizers

▶ Mixing up munchies

*I*f you're like us, you know that nothing beats a delicious appetizer. After all, a good appetizer whets your palate and gets you ready for the meal. When you cook for a crowd, appetizers can be a big help — they're immediately appealing and they give your guests something to do while you put the finishing touches on the main meal.

In this chapter, you find a host of appetizers that are perfect for crowd cooking. We select some of our favorites and provide only tried-and-true recipes (but if you're still hankering for more, check out *Appetizers For Dummies* by Dede Wilson and published by Wiley). You'll be glad to know that most of them are a cinch to create and are good for advance preparation, which saves you time and headaches on the big day. So warm up the oven and get ready to have some fun in the kitchen!

If you want to know how many appetizers you need to prepare, Chapter 3 will clue you in.

Cold Appetizers

Cold appetizers are appropriate for just about any kind of event. For the most part, they're easy to prepare ahead of time and easy to store. As you think about cold appetizers, make sure you choose ones that complement your main meal (flip back to Chapter 2), and be sure to try out some of our favorites.

Fruit Salsa and Cinnamon Chips

When most people think of salsa, they picture tomatoes, onions, and jalapeños. This recipe is a cool, refreshing alternative and works great as a colorful, tasty appetizer. The fruit combination is visually appetizing, and its flavors are sweet and satisfying, especially when you serve them with cinnamon chips.

This appetizer is a breeze, and you can exercise your creative flair by using different fruit combinations to suit your tastes. For an attractive look, try serving the fruit salsa in a glass bowl sitting in the middle of a platter with the cinnamon chips arranged around it.

Preparation time: *45 minutes*

Yield: *20 to 25 servings*

4 kiwis, washed, peeled, and diced	*1 pound raspberries, washed and cut in half*	*¼ cup, 2 tablespoons apricot (or your favorite flavor) fruit preserves*
4 Golden Delicious or Granny Smith apples, washed, peeled, cored, and diced	*2 pounds strawberries, washed and cut in fourths*	*Butter-flavored cooking spray*
	¼ cup sugar	*20 flour tortillas (fajita size)*
	2 tablespoons brown sugar	*4 cups cinnamon-sugar mix*

1 Preheat the oven to 350 degrees.

2 In a large bowl, mix together the fruit, sugar, brown sugar, and fruit preserves.

3 Cover the bowl tightly and refrigerate for 20 minutes.

4 Cut the tortillas into 8 triangles each.

5 Arrange the tortilla wedges in a single layer on a parchment-lined cookie sheet.

6 Spray the wedges with butter-flavored cooking spray on the side facing up.

7 Generously sprinkle with cinnamon and sugar.

8 Spray again with butter-flavored cooking spray.

9 Bake for 8 to 10 minutes.

10 Allow the chips to cool for 15 minutes before serving.

Tip: *To help speed up the chopping process, use a kitchen chopper with a sharp blade. We recommend that you hand cut the berries and the kiwi because the chopper tends to mash them.*

Vary It! *Keep in mind that you can substitute different fruits for different flavor combinations. Be creative and enjoy!*

Per serving: *Calories 364 (From Fat 41); Fat 5g (Saturated 1g); Cholesterol 0mg; Sodium 279mg; Carbohydrate 78g (Dietary Fiber 6g); Protein 6g.*

Basil Pesto Kebabs

Skewered foods are appealing in their own right. They're easy to walk around with and eat while you're socializing at a get-together. You can fashion kebabs from any assortment of foods and flavor combinations, so they're rather versatile.

When you cook for a crowd, you should make some recipes in advance, and in fact, some recipes taste better when you cook them ahead. For example, these kebabs will have a bolder, zestier taste if you allow them to marinate for 24 hours.

Preparation time: *45 minutes*

Marinating time: *4 to 24 hours*

Yield: *2 dozen*

24 large, stuffed green olives

24 large, pitted black olives

24 whole baby carrots, peeled

3 medium sweet red bell peppers

8 ounces smoked provolone, cut into ½-inch chunks

8 ounces summer sausage, sliced ¾ inch thick, then cut in half

2 tablespoons white wine vinegar

4 tablespoons refrigerated basil pesto sauce

2 cups lightly packed, fresh, washed and dried spinach leaves

24 medium-size wooden skewers

1 Put the olives, carrots, bell peppers, cheese, and sausage in a large bowl and mix.

2 In a small bowl, mix the white wine vinegar and basil pesto together.

3 Pour the vinegar/pesto mixture over the ingredients in the large bowl and mix well.

4 Cover the bowl tightly and refrigerate for 4 to 24 hours.

5 Remove the mixture from the refrigerator.

6 Place a baby carrot on the skewer, followed by a piece of spinach.

7 Add a black olive and a piece of spinach.

8 Add a piece of sausage and a piece of spinach.

9 Continue to add a different ingredient followed by a piece of spinach until you have one of each item on the skewer.

10 Repeat Steps 6 through 9 to make the additional skewers.

Tip: *You can skewer these flavorful kebabs in any order you choose. Keep in mind that the more visually appealing the presentation, the more likely people will be drawn to them.*

Vary It! *If pesto isn't your thing, substitute a zesty Italian dressing instead. You can also change the summer sausage to salami or ham. The same goes for the cheese — cheddar or mozzarella make good substitutions.*

Per serving: Calories 95 (From Fat 67); Fat 8g (Saturated 3g); Cholesterol 17mg; Sodium 362mg; Carbohydrate 3g (Dietary Fiber 1g); Protein 5g.

Presto . . . it's pesto!

Pesto sauce is a standard that you can buy at any grocery store. The name *pesto* comes from the original preparation of the sauce, which included pounding the basil with a pestle in a mortar. The good news is that pesto is easy to make, and here's how you make it. This recipe yields about 3¼ cups of pesto:

2 cups chopped fresh basil leaves

½ cup olive oil

2 garlic cloves, minced

2 tablespoons pine nuts or walnuts

1 teaspoon salt

½ cup grated Parmesan cheese

Blend the basil, oil, garlic, and nuts at high speed until puréed. Pour the mixture into a bowl and thoroughly mix in the salt and Parmesan cheese. You can either store the pesto sauce in the refrigerator for two days or you can freeze it for a month.

Stuffed Cherry Tomatoes

Stuffed cherry tomatoes are a colorful, versatile appetizer for any occasion. They're delicious and make a beautiful addition to your table. In fact, they're so versatile that they work well for a formal dinner or a casual affair.

Preparation time: *45 minutes*

Chill time: *3 hours*

Yield: *5 dozen*

60 cherry tomatoes

1 cup chopped green onions

3 pounds crisp, cooked bacon, crumbled

1½ cups mayonnaise

½ cup grated Parmesan cheese

1 Wash and thoroughly dry the tomatoes and green onions.

2 Cut a thin slice off the top of each tomato. Gently scoop out the pulp. (You can easily remove the pulp by using a small spoon; a baby-food spoon works especially well.)

3 In a large bowl, combine the remaining ingredients (including the green onions) and mix well.

4 Spoon the mixture into the tomatoes. Cover loosely with plastic wrap and refrigerate. For the best results, refrigerate at least 3 hours, preferably overnight.

Crowd Saver: To save time, you can make the filling the day before the event and stuff the tomatoes the morning of your event. This preparation will also conserve refrigerator space, because you can store the filling in a bowl instead of storing the entire platter.

Per serving: Calories 90 (From Fat 75); Fat 8g (Saturated 2g); Cholesterol 10mg; Sodium 165mg; Carbohydrate 1g (Dietary Fiber 0g); Protein 3g.

Smoked Ham and Cheese Roll-Ups

These bite-sized meat-and-cheese roll-ups are creamy and satisfying. You can substitute a number of different ingredients to create your own taste sensation.

Preparation time: *30 minutes*

Chill time: *4 to 24 hours*

Yield: *84 to 105 appetizers*

8 ounces cream cheese, softened	¾ cup coarsely chopped black olives	1 cup shredded cheddar cheese
8 ounces sour cream	1 pound deli smoked ham, shaved	12 to 15 flour tortillas (8-inch diameter)
1 package dry ranch seasoning mix		

1 In a large bowl, mix all the ingredients together, except the flour tortillas.

2 Place 4 or 5 tortillas between two paper towels and microwave for 15 to 30 seconds, until the tortillas are warm and soft.

3 Spread the mixture over each warm tortilla. Keep in mind that you'll be rolling up the tortillas, so make sure that you don't overstuff them.

4 Roll up the tortillas and place them seam side down on a plate.

5 Repeat Steps 2 through 4 until all the tortillas are rolled up.

6 Tightly wrap the plate of tortilla roll-ups and refrigerate for 4 to 24 hours.

7 To serve, slice the tortilla roll-ups in ½-inch to 1-inch-thick slices, depending on your preference.

Tip: *These appetizers are full of flavor, but if you want to add more flavor, a side of ranch dressing as a dipping sauce is a good choice.*

Vary It! *Consider trying salami and mozzarella or turkey and Swiss.*

Per serving: Calories 51 (From Fat 26); Fat 3g (Saturated 1g); Cholesterol 8mg; Sodium 172mg; Carbohydrate 4g (Dietary Fiber 0g); Protein 2g.

Serving with style . . . or not!

Crowd events are as versatile as the food items you may serve, so as you're thinking about appetizers, be sure to keep the style of the event in mind. Is the event a formal affair, or a backyard pool party? The good news is that all the recipes in this chapter work well for both ends of the spectrum. Take, for example, the stuffed cherry tomatoes. You can put these delicious treats on a nice crystal platter or cake pedestal for a wedding, or you can use a simple plastic platter lined with leaf lettuce for a backyard get-together. Just remember to think about the style of your event, and don't forget to have fun!

Hot Appetizers

Like cold appetizers, hot appetizers are rather versatile because they work well for casual and formal crowd events. They can be a bit more troublesome than cold appetizers, but they're always well received and appreciated. In this section, we give you our favorites for crowd cooking, which include simple but tasty options.

Three Meat and Mushroom Stromboli

This hearty appetizer is a good choice whenever and wherever you're serving a crowd. As with some of the other recipes, you can adapt this one to meet your likes and needs.

Preparation time: 45 minutes

Cooking time: 30 minutes

Yield: 32 appetizers

4 pounds frozen bread dough, thawed

½ cup freshly grated Parmesan cheese

1 tablespoon garlic powder

1 tablespoon dried oregano

1 teaspoon dried parsley flakes

1 teaspoon pepper

1 teaspoon salt

½ pound deli ham, thinly sliced

½ pound pepperoni, thinly sliced

½ pound salami, thinly sliced

2 cups (8 ounces) shredded mozzarella cheese

2 cups sliced, canned mushrooms

2 egg whites

1 Preheat the oven to 375 degrees.

2 Following the package directions, allow the thawed dough to rise until doubled.

3 After the dough has doubled in size, punch it down in the middle.

4 Roll each loaf into a 15-x-12-inch rectangle.

5 In a small bowl, combine the Parmesan cheese and all the spices and mix thoroughly.

6 Place a fourth of all three meats and ½ cup of the mozzarella cheese on each of the dough rectangles.

7 Sprinkle ½ cup of the mushrooms over the meats and cheese.

8 Sprinkle a fourth of the Parmesan and spices mixture over the top of the meats, mozzarella, and mushrooms.

9 Roll up each rectangle jellyroll-style, beginning with a long side.

10 Seal the seams and each end, then place the rolls seam side down on a parchment paper–lined baking sheet.

11 In a small bowl, beat the two egg whites until well mixed.

12 Brush each loaf with the egg whites.

13 Bake the loaves for 25 to 30 minutes, or until golden brown.

14 Let the loaves stand for 5 minutes, then slice each loaf into 8 pieces and serve.

Tip: *To make this stromboli even tastier, try serving it with some marinara sauce. Put the sauce in a bowl and sprinkle a little Parmesan cheese on top for a garnish. Place the bowl in the middle of a large tray and surround it with the stromboli slices.*

Per serving: *Calories 287 (From Fat 116); Fat 13g (Saturated 5g); Cholesterol 27mg; Sodium 919mg; Carbohydrate 31g (Dietary Fiber 2g); Protein 15g.*

Sausage Balls

At some time or another, just about everyone eats a sausage ball. Sausage balls and meatballs are standard appetizers, and you find them at nearly every kind of event, from formal wedding affairs to backyard get-togethers. Why are they so popular? They taste great, they're relatively inexpensive, and you can whip them up ahead of time.

The difference between this recipe and the rest is the chill time. Do yourself a favor and allow the mixture to sit for the whole 24 hours — the taste difference is incredible. People will rave over them, so make sure you prepare plenty!

Preparation time: *35 minutes*

Chill time: *1 to 24 hours*

Cooking time: *15 minutes per dozen*

Yield: *6 dozen*

32 ounces pork sausage	*½ cup finely chopped celery*
1½ cups all-purpose baking mix	*½ cup finely chopped onion*
4 cups (16 ounces) shredded sharp cheddar cheese	*½ teaspoon garlic powder*

1 Preheat the oven to 375 degrees.

2 In a large bowl, mix all the ingredients thoroughly.

3 Cover the bowl tightly and refrigerate for 1 to 24 hours.

4 Roll the mixture into 1-inch balls and place 12 of them on an ungreased baking sheet.

5 Bake for 15 minutes or until golden brown. Serve warm.

Tip: If you like your sausage balls with an extra kick, try using hot flavored pork sausage. If you desire more fire, try adding ½ cup of finely chopped and seeded fresh jalapeño peppers.

Per serving: Calories 123 (From Fat 86); Fat 10g (Saturated 5g); Cholesterol 22mg; Sodium 246mg; Carbohydrate 4g (Dietary Fiber 0g); Protein 5g.

Brown Sugar Cocktail Sausages

These cocktail sausages are great for cooking for a crowd, and you can easily adjust the recipe to make as much as you need. The basic rule for this recipe is one package of cocktail sausages to one package of bacon and 1½ cups of brown sugar.

Preparation time: *35 minutes*

Cooking time: *1 to 1½ hours*

Yield: *7 dozen*

2 packages all-beef cocktail sausages (40 to 42 sausages per package)

3 cups brown sugar

3 pounds sliced bacon

box of wooden toothpicks

1 Preheat the oven to 375 degrees.

2 Cut the slices of bacon into thirds.

3 Wrap each sausage with a piece of bacon. Secure them with wooden toothpicks and place them in a shallow baking dish.

4 Cover the sausages with brown sugar.

5 Cover the pan with foil and bake for 30 minutes.

6 Remove the foil and cook for an additional 30 minutes, or until the bacon reaches the desired crispness. Serve warm.

Remember: *Always use wooden toothpicks to secure food that you're going to cook. Plastic toothpicks will melt!*

Per serving: Calories 305 (From Fat 146); Fat 16g (Saturated 6g); Cholesterol 30mg; Sodium 542mg; Carbohydrate 31g (Dietary Fiber 0g); Protein 9g.

⟶ *Artichoke and Spinach Dip*

The standard artichoke and spinach dip has been around for a long time. This recipe, however, gives you a thrilling combination of cream cheese, Monterey Jack, and balsamic vinegar, putting a new twist on an old favorite.

Any round loaf of bread will work. However, if you really want to bring out the flavors of the dip, serve it with Hawaiian bread. The taste of the dip along with the sweetness of the bread is a wonderful taste sensation.

Preparation time: *1 hour*

Cooking time: *10 minutes*

Yield: *20 servings*

1 round loaf bread, preferably a sweet bread, such as Hawaiian bread	*2 Roma tomatoes, seeded and chopped*
1 tablespoon olive oil	*10-ounce package frozen spinach, thawed and well drained*
1 cup chopped onion	*2 teaspoons whole milk*
6-ounce jar marinated artichoke hearts, drained	*1 tablespoon balsamic vinegar*
¼ cup shredded Monterey Jack cheese	*8 ounces cream cheese, cubed*
¼ teaspoon pepper	*1 tablespoon minced garlic*
3 tablespoons dry ranch dressing mix	*3 tablespoons butter*

1 Preheat the oven to 350 degrees.

2 Cut a 1-inch slice off the top of the loaf of bread and set the slice aside.

3 Gently remove chunks of the bread from the center of the loaf, making a bowl. Make sure to leave about a ½-inch wall on all sides to prevent the bread bowl from breaking.

4 Tear the chunks into bite-size pieces; place them on a cookie sheet and set aside.

5 In a large skillet, heat the olive oil.

6 Add the chopped onion and cook until tender, but not brown.

7 Drain the artichoke hearts and coarsely cut them if necessary.

8 Add the artichoke hearts and the rest of the ingredients, with the exception of the butter and garlic, to the skillet.

9 Cook over low heat until the cheese melts and the mixture becomes smooth.

10 Place the bread bowl on a foil-lined cookie sheet. Make sure you use enough foil to wrap the bread bowl.

11 Fill the bread bowl with the dip mixture, replace the top of the bread shell, and wrap the bowl in foil.

12 Cook the filled bread bowl for about 15 minutes, or until heated thoroughly.

13 In a small bowl, melt the butter and mix in the garlic.

14 Using a cooking brush, brush the garlic butter on the tops of the bread pieces.

15 Toast the bread pieces until they're golden brown.

16 Place the bread bowl in the center of a large serving dish. Arrange the bread pieces around the bowl and serve.

Per serving: Calories 156 (From Fat 81); Fat 9g (Saturated 5g); Cholesterol 32mg; Sodium 200mg; Carbohydrate 15g (Dietary Fiber 1g); Protein 4g.

Munchies and More

Everyone likes things that go crunch. Chips and crackers are standard appetizer fare, but try adding some unexpected munchies to the mix.

Popcorn, pretzels, and nuts are tasty additions, but mix them together and add some dried fruit or chocolate, and you'll have people coming back for more! Try these recipes and give your munchies some punch!

◌ *Not Your Momma's Snack Mix*

This snack mix is in a different world from the kind your mom made when you were a kid. The combination of dried fruits, nuts, popcorn, chocolate, and a cinnamon-sugar coating will have your guests asking for the recipe.

Preparation time: *15 minutes*

Yield: *52 ½-cup servings or 26 1-cup servings*

2 bags microwave popcorn, popped and cooled	*2 cups dried cranberries or raisins*
1 cup cinnamon-sugar mix	*2 cups semisweet chocolate chips*
4 cups banana chips	*2 cups pecan halves*
	Butter spray

1 In an extra-large bowl (such as a punch bowl), combine all the ingredients except the butter spray.

2 Mix thoroughly.

3 Spray the mix liberally with the butter spray and toss.

4 Add the cinnamon sugar and toss again until the mixture is lightly coated.

5 Serve, tossing occasionally because the heavier items may sink to the bottom of the bowl.

Warning: *Be careful when you cook microwavable popcorn because it burns quickly. Even slightly burned popcorn will ruin the whole bag and ultimately give your snack mix a char-broiled taste, which you don't want.*

Per serving: *Calories 162 (From Fat 67); Fat 7g (Saturated 2g); Cholesterol 0mg; Sodium 38mg; Carbohydrate 26g (Dietary Fiber 3g); Protein 2g.*

⟡ Sunflower Crispies

When you want to serve more than just standard crackers, serve these nutty, cheesy crisps. They're flavorful enough to be eaten alone, but they make a nice cracker to serve alongside a meat-and-cheese tray.

Preparation time: *20 minutes*

Chill time: *4 hours up to 1 week*

Cooking time: *8 to 10 minutes per batch*

Yield: *8 to 10 dozen*

4 cups (16 ounces) shredded cheddar cheese	1 teaspoon salt
1 cup grated Parmesan cheese	2 cups uncooked quick oats
1 cup sunflower oil margarine, softened	1⅓ cups roasted, salted, and shelled sunflower seeds
⅓ cup water	
2 cups flour	

1 In a large bowl, beat the cheeses, margarine, and water until blended.

2 Mix in the flour and salt.

3 Stir in the oats and sunflower seeds.

4 Shape the mixture into two 12-inch-long rolls.

5 Wrap the rolls tightly in plastic wrap and refrigerate for at least 4 hours, up to 1 week.

6 Preheat the oven to 400 degrees.

7 Lightly grease two cookie sheets.

8 Cut each roll into ⅛ to ¼-inch-thick slices.

9 Slightly flatten the slices and place them on the prepared cookie sheets.

10 Bake 8 to 10 minutes or until the edges are light golden brown.

11 Immediately remove the crisps from the pan; cool on a wire rack.

Crowd Saver: *When you cook for a crowd, time is of the essence. You can make these tasty treats ahead of time and store them unbaked in the refrigerator for up to 1 week, so take advantage of the timesaving feature.*

Per serving: *Calories 53 (From Fat 35); Fat 4g (Saturated 1g); Cholesterol 5mg; Sodium 84mg; Carbohydrate 3g (Dietary Fiber 0g); Protein 2g.*

☞ Candy-Coated Pecans

Nuts are full of flavor right out of the shell, but they take on a whole new taste when you add spices. These sugary pecans taste great served alone in a bowl or make a great topping for a number of items, such as ice cream or cheesecake.

When you serve these nuts, try putting them in a wide-mouth piece of stemware instead of a bowl for added visual appeal.

Preparation time: *15 minutes*

Cooking time: *5 to 8 minutes*

Yield: *32 ¼-cup servings*

2 egg whites	*1 teaspoon vanilla extract*
2 cups brown sugar	*8 cups pecan halves*

1 Preheat the oven to 325 degrees.

2 Beat the egg whites until very stiff (the egg whites, not you).

3 Add the brown sugar and vanilla extract.

4 Mix in the pecans and stir until coated.

5 Line a baking sheet with parchment paper or an easy-release type of foil; spread the pecans on the sheet in a single layer.

6 Bake for about 5 to 8 minutes, until brown.

7 Quickly and carefully remove the pecans from the baking sheet. Allow them to cool before stacking them on top of each other to prevent them from sticking together.

Warning: *These candy-coated pecans are easy to make, but you must beat the egg whites until they're very stiff. You also must make sure to cook the pecans long enough to prevent them from becoming chewy instead of crunchy.*

Vary It! *Are you more of a cashew person? Any nut will work with this recipe, especially almonds. If you like mixed nuts, try them instead.*

Per serving: *Calories 240 (From Fat 175); Fat 19g (Saturated 2g); Cholesterol 0mg; Sodium 9mg; Carbohydrate 17g (Dietary Fiber 3g); Protein 3g.*

◔ *Kickin' Pretzels*

These spicy pretzels are so easy to make and pack such a flavor punch that your guests won't be able to put them down. You can also make them ahead of time, as long as you store them in an airtight container. You can easily double or triple this recipe, depending on the size of your crowd.

Preparation time: *15 minutes*

Cooking time: *1 to 1½ hours*

Yield: *25 to 30 ½-cup servings*

1 cup vegetable oil	*1 teaspoon cayenne pepper*
1 package dry ranch dressing mix	*2 12-ounce packages pretzel sticks*
1 teaspoon garlic salt	

1 Preheat the oven to 200 degrees.

2 In a small bowl, mix the oil, ranch dressing mix, garlic salt, and cayenne pepper.

3 Divide the pretzels into two ungreased 15-x-10-x-1-inch baking pans.

4 Pour the oil and seasonings over the pretzels and gently toss to coat the pretzels.

5 Bake for 1 to 1½ hours or until golden brown, stirring occasionally.

6 Cool completely and store in an airtight container.

Tip: *When you make snack items, feel free to get creative. These pretzels taste great, but if your idea of spicy is something that makes flames shoot from your mouth, add an extra teaspoon of cayenne pepper.*

Per serving: *Calories 153 (From Fat 70); Fat 8g (Saturated 1g); Cholesterol 0mg; Sodium 761mg; Carbohydrate 18g (Dietary Fiber 1g); Protein 2g.*

Chapter 5

Main Dishes Everyone Will Love

In This Chapter

- Enjoying a taste of home
- Going south of the border: Mexican cuisine
- Experiencing the wild Wild West: Barbecue favorites
- Celebrating like an Italian
- Pleasing the non-meat-eaters

The main dish is the heart of every meal. After all, your appetizers, side dishes, and even dessert should always point toward the main course or follow it in a complementary way. Yet, main dishes can be one of the most frustrating parts of the crowd meal. Depending on the size of your crowd, finding something that you can cook, manage, and serve can be a bit of task.

Don't worry; in this chapter, we come to the rescue with some tried-and-true favorite main dishes. We include a variety of different items so that you can find the perfect recipe for your crowd event. Fire up the stove!

Recipes in This Chapter

- Chicken and Wild Rice Casserole
- Mom's Meatloaf
- Chicken Pot Pie
- Home-Style Pork Roast with Gravy
- Timesaver Pot Roast
- King Ranch Casserole
- Mexican Lasagne
- South of the Border Burgers
- Beef Chimichangas
- Barbecued Chicken
- Sweet and Spicy Beef Ribs
- Shredded Beef and Pork Barbecue
- Barbecued Brisket
- Chicken Tetrazzini
- Baked Ziti
- Sausage and Spinach Manicotti
- Creamy Linguine with Shrimp
- Pizza Lasagne
- ⟳ Tofu Parmigiano
- ⟳ Vegetarian Stuffed Peppers

Need a Little Home Cooking? Mom's Favorites

In many cases, crowd events tend to move to the traditional side of the table. After all, most holiday meals follow a customary set of main courses and side dishes. Of course, staying within those boundaries isn't a necessity — people usually just stick to what they know best. In this section, we show you some down-home main dishes that are fun and easy to make for a crowd. You'll be the hit of the party without a lot of fuss.

Chicken and Wild Rice Casserole

This creamy casserole is warm and satisfying. Try serving it with some green beans, salad, and crescent rolls for an easy and complete meal.

Preparation time: *40 minutes*

Cooking time: *1 hour, 5 minutes*

Yield: *24 servings*

4 6.2-ounce packages fast-cooking long grain and wild rice mix

½ cup butter or margarine

8 celery stalks, chopped

2 large onions, chopped

4 8-ounce cans (32 ounces) sliced water chestnuts, drained

10 cups chopped cooked chicken

8 cups (32 ounces) shredded cheddar cheese, divided

4 10.75-ounce cans (43 ounces) condensed cream of mushroom soup

4 8-ounce containers (32 ounces) sour cream

2 cups milk

2 teaspoons salt

2 teaspoons pepper

1 cup breadcrumbs

4.5 ounces sliced almonds, toasted

1 Preheat the oven to 350 degrees. Prepare the rice mix per the package directions.

2 In a large stockpot, melt the butter; add the celery and onions and sauté them for 15 minutes, or until tender, not browned.

3 Remove the stockpot from heat and add the water chestnuts, rice, chicken, 6 cups of the cheese, soup, sour cream, milk, salt, and pepper.

4 Lightly grease the bottom and sides of two 4-quart baking dishes. Spoon half of the mixture into each dish.

5 Top each casserole with ½ cup of the breadcrumbs; bake for 55 minutes.

6 Remove the casseroles from the oven and top them each with 1 cup of the cheese and half of the toasted almonds.

7 Return the casseroles to the oven and bake for 10 minutes, or until the cheese has melted. Allow the casseroles to set for 10 minutes before serving.

Crowd Saver: *These casseroles are great timesavers because you can prepare them in advance and keep the uncooked casseroles (minus the cheese and almond topping) in the freezer for up to 1 month. Make sure you tightly wrap the uncooked casseroles before freezing.*

Tip: *To cook previously frozen casseroles, remove them from the freezer and let them stand at room temperature for 1 hour. Bake covered at 350 degrees for 30 to 35 minutes. Then uncover and bake for 55 minutes. Remove the casseroles from the oven, top them each with 1 cup of cheese and half of the almonds, and bake them for 10 minutes, or until the cheese is melted.*

Per serving: Calories 646 (From Fat 359); Fat 39g (Saturated 19g); Cholesterol 118mg; Sodium 1,349mg; Carbohydrate 40g (Dietary Fiber 3g); Protein 35g.

Mom's Meatloaf

Meatloaf has been around for such a long time, and you can find many different versions of it. This recipe is a classic, with its sweet taste from the brown sugar and that crunchy surprise of bacon under the sauce. It's easy to make and is sure to be a hit.

Preparation time: *30 minutes*

Cooking time: *1 hour, 15 minutes*

Yield: *24 servings*

Sweet and Tangy Meatloaf Sauce (see the following recipe)

6 pounds lean ground beef

7½ cups crushed butter-flavored crackers

3 small onions, chopped

6 eggs

2¼ cups ketchup

¾ cup brown sugar

1 teaspoon salt

1 teaspoon garlic powder

12 slices bacon

1 Preheat the oven to 350 degrees.

2 In an extra-large bowl, combine all the ingredients except the bacon. Mix well.

3 Press the mixture into three 9-x-5-inch loaf pans.

4 Place 4 slices of bacon lengthwise on each loaf.

5 Bake for 1 hour or until cooked through (minimum 160 degree internal temperature). Meanwhile, prepare the sauce.

6 Divide the sauce among the three loaves and bake for an additional 15 minutes.

7 Allow the loaves to set for 10 minutes before slicing each into 8 servings.

Sweet and Tangy Meatloaf Sauce

3 cups ketchup

¼ cup white vinegar

1 teaspoon salt

¼ cup, 2 tablespoons mustard

1½ cups brown sugar

In a medium bowl, combine all the ingredients and mix well, making sure all the sugar is thoroughly incorporated into the sauce.

Per serving: Calories 438 (From Fat 126); Fat 14g (Saturated 4g); Cholesterol 121mg; Sodium 1,178mg; Carbohydrate 52g (Dietary Fiber 1g); Protein 27g.

Chicken Pot Pie

Chicken pot pie is a classic and works well for a wide variety of crowd events. This recipe is delicious and gives you 24 servings for your crowd.

Preparation time: *25 minutes*

Cooking time: *35 to 40 minutes*

Yield: *24 servings*

12 cups cubed cooked chicken	*1 teaspoon salt*
4½ cups chicken broth	*1 teaspoon pepper*
4½ cups frozen green peas	*6 cups all-purpose baking mix*
12 carrots, sliced in rounds	*3¾ cups milk*
10.75-ounce can condensed cream of potato soup	*1 tablespoon garlic powder*
2 10.75-ounce cans (21.5 ounces) condensed cream of mushroom soup	*1½ teaspoons celery salt*
	¾ teaspoon paprika

1 Preheat the oven to 350 degrees.

2 In a stockpot, combine the chicken, broth, peas, carrots, soups, salt, and pepper. Bring the mixture to a boil and stir it occasionally, then reduce the heat to the lowest setting.

3 In a large bowl, combine the baking mix, milk, garlic powder, celery salt, and paprika. The mixture will be thin.

4 Grease three 13-x-9-x-2-inch baking dishes. Pour one-third of the hot chicken mixture in each of the three dishes.

5 Spoon one-third of the baking mix mixture over the top of the chicken mixture in each pan.

6 Bake uncovered for 35 to 40 minutes, or until the topping is golden brown.

7 Remove the pot pies from the oven and allow them to set for 10 minutes before serving.

Tip: *Have leftover holiday turkey? Try using turkey in this recipe instead of chicken.*

Per serving: Calories 396 (From Fat 155); Fat 17g (Saturated 5g); Cholesterol 65mg; Sodium 1,151mg; Carbohydrate 32g (Dietary Fiber 3g); Protein 28g.

Home-Style Pork Roast with Gravy

Pork roast is always a great choice for crowd events, especially holiday meals. The good news is that you can easily prepare a delicious pork roast, and the meat will give you great flexibility with your side dish and dessert choices.

Preparation time: *40 minutes*

Cooking time: *3 hours*

Yield: *24 servings*

8 tablespoons flour, divided	*1 teaspoon dried thyme*	*4 carrots, chopped*
2 teaspoons salt	*2 4-to-5-pound bone-in pork loin roasts*	*4⅔ cups cold water, divided*
2 teaspoons pepper		*⅔ cup packed brown sugar*
2 bay leaves, finely crushed	*4 medium onions, chopped*	

1 Preheat the oven to 325 degrees.

2 In a small bowl, combine 4 tablespoons of the flour, the salt, pepper, bay leaves, and thyme; then rub the dry mixture over each of the pork roasts.

3 Place each pork roast in a shallow roasting pan, fat side up.

4 Arrange half of the onions and half of the carrots around each of the roasts.

5 Pour 2 cups of cold water into each of the roasting pans.

6 Bake uncovered for 2 hours, basting with the pan juices every 30 minutes.

7 After 2 hours of cooking, sprinkle each roast with ⅓ cup of the brown sugar.

8 Bake for 1 hour more, or until a meat thermometer reads 160 degrees.

9 After the roasts have cooked, remove them from the pan to a serving platter and allow them to set for 10 minutes before slicing.

10 While the roasts are setting, prepare the gravy. Strain the drippings from both pans, reserving the broth and discarding the vegetables.

11 Pour the broth from one of the pans into a 2-cup glass measuring cup and add enough water to the broth to measure 1⅔ cups. Return the broth and water to the pan. Repeat with the second pan.

12 In each of two small bowls, combine 2 tablespoons of flour and ⅓ cup cold water. Stir until the mixture is smooth. Or, if you want to use cornstarch, use one tablespoon of cornstarch to 3 tablespoons of cold water in each bowl.

13 Add one bowl of the mixture to each pan, bring it to a boil, and cook for 2 minutes, stirring constantly. Serve the gravy with the roast.

Tip: The key to successful gravy is making sure the flour and water mixture is completely smooth before you add it to the other liquids and that the mixture is cooked thoroughly. Otherwise, the gravy will taste like flour.

Per serving: Calories 257 (From Fat 111); Fat 12g (Saturated 5g); Cholesterol 74mg; Sodium 254mg; Carbohydrate 11g (Dietary Fiber 1g); Protein 25g.

Timesaver Pot Roast

This pot roast is one of the easiest main course entrees you can prepare, but don't think it'll be bland or boring because of how easy the recipe is. This roast slow cooks for hours, making it extra tender and flavorful.

Preparation time: *15 minutes*

Cooking time: *12 hours*

Yield: *24 servings*

2 tablespoons vegetable oil, divided

2 5-to-5½-pound pot roasts

½ cup flour

2 teaspoons salt

4 10.75-ounce cans (43 ounces) condensed cream of mushroom soup

2 1-ounce packages dry onion soup mix

3 cups beef broth, divided

1 In two large skillets, heat a tablespoon of oil.

2 Pat ¼ cup of flour and 1 teaspoon of salt on each roast.

3 Place each roast in the hot oil and sear all the sides.

4 In each of two large bowls, mix half of the cream of mushroom soup, one package of dry onion soup mix, and 1½ cups of beef broth.

5 Place each pot roast in a slow cooker and cover each roast with the soup mixture.

6 Cover the slow cookers with lids and cook for 4 hours on high and 8 to 9 hours on low.

7 Check the roasts after 5 to 6 hours of cooking; if they look too dry, add ½ cup to 1 cup of beef broth.

8 After the pot roasts have cooked, remove them from the slow cookers, allow them to set for 15 minutes, then slice each of them into 12 pieces and serve.

Tip: Want some homemade gravy to go with your pot roast? It's already in the slow cooker! Pour the gravy from the slow cooker into a saucepan and bring it to a low boil. Dissolve a teaspoon of cornstarch in a tablespoon of cold water and add it to the gravy, stirring vigorously until fully incorporated.

Per serving: Calories 478 (From Fat 299); Fat 33g (Saturated 12g); Cholesterol 124mg; Sodium 957mg; Carbohydrate 7g (Dietary Fiber 1g); Protein 37g.

Feeling Festive? Mexican Cuisine

Mexican cuisine has become very popular in the United States in the past 20 years, and rightfully so. These foods, often with an American flare, give you a number of delicious recipe options that your guests are sure to love. The recipes in this section all give you plenty of servings and lots of variety.

King Ranch Casserole

This casserole is so full of flavor and easy to make, and it's a tried-and-true favorite when it comes to cooking for a crowd. For a complete meal, serve it with salad, chips, and salsa.

Preparation time: *40 minutes*

Cooking time: *1 hour, 15 minutes*

Yield: *24 servings*

2 tablespoons butter

1½ cups chopped onion

2 teaspoons garlic salt

1 teaspoon cumin

1 teaspoon chili powder

10 cups chopped cooked chicken

4 10.75-ounce cans (43 ounces) condensed cream of chicken soup

2 10.75-ounce cans (21.5 ounces) condensed cream of mushroom soup

2 10.75-ounce cans (21.5 ounces) chicken broth

2 10-ounce cans (20 ounces) diced tomatoes with green chile peppers

12 cups (3 pounds) shredded cheddar/ Monterey Jack cheese, divided

40 corn tortillas

1 Preheat the oven to 325 degrees.

2 Melt the butter in a stockpot and add the onions and garlic salt; sauté until tender, not browned.

3 Add the cooked chicken, cumin, and chili powder to the onions and cook over low heat for 5 minutes.

4 Add the condensed soups, chicken broth, and diced tomatoes with green chile peppers and bring to a boil, then reduce the heat to simmer. Add 6 cups of the cheese and stir.

5 Grease the bottoms of two 13-x-9-x-2-inch casserole dishes. Cover the bottom of each casserole dish with a very small amount of the chicken mixture — just enough to cover the bottom of each dish — using more of the liquid than the chicken.

6 Place 10 tortillas, torn into pieces, in each casserole dish.

7 Top the tortillas with one-third of the chicken mixture.

8 Place 5 tortillas, torn into pieces, on top of each dish.

9 Sprinkle 1 cup of the cheese on each dish.

10 Top each dish with half of the remaining chicken mixture.

11 Top the chicken mixture in each dish with 5 tortillas, torn into pieces.

12 Bake for 1 hour, or until thoroughly heated.

13 Remove the casseroles from the oven and sprinkle each with 2 cups of the cheese; cook until the cheese has melted.

14 Allow the casseroles to set for 10 minutes before serving.

Per serving: Calories 558 (From Fat 298); Fat 33g (Saturated 16g); Cholesterol 115mg; Sodium 1,425mg; Carbohydrate 28g (Dietary Fiber 3g); Protein 36g.

Mexican Lasagne

This Mexican version of lasagne is layered like its Italian cousin, except instead of using pasta, you use flour tortillas. Serve it with sides of guacamole, sour cream, and sliced jalapeños for those who want a little heat with the meal.

Preparation time: *40 minutes*

Cooking time: *1 hour, 10 minutes*

Yield: *24 to 30 servings*

4 pounds ground beef

2 onions, chopped

2 tablespoons, 1 teaspoon minced garlic

2 teaspoons salt

2 teaspoons cumin

2 2-ounce cans (4 ounces) sliced black olives

2 4-ounce cans (8 ounces) diced green chile peppers

2 10-ounce cans (20 ounces) diced tomatoes with green chile peppers

2 16-ounce jars (32 ounces) taco sauce

4 16-ounce cans (48 ounces) refried beans

24 8-inch flour tortillas

8 cups (2 pounds) shredded cheddar cheese

1 Preheat the oven to 350 degrees.

2 In a large skillet(s), cook the ground beef over medium heat for 10 minutes, and then add the onions, garlic, salt, and cumin; cook until the meat is no longer pink. Drain the excess fat and return the mixture to the pan.

3 Stir in the olives, chiles, tomatoes, taco sauce, and refried beans. Mix well and simmer for 20 minutes.

4 Lightly grease two 4-quart casserole dishes. Spread a thin layer of the meat mixture in the bottom of each dish.

5 Add a layer of flour tortillas, followed by another thicker layer of meat.

6 Add a layer of shredded cheese.

7 Repeat Steps 5 and 6, making sure the final layer is the meat mixture.

8 Bake covered for 40 minutes, and then remove the dishes from the oven and top each with a layer of cheese; bake uncovered until the cheese is completely melted. Allow the casseroles to set for 15 minutes before serving.

Tip: When making the layers, gently push down on the flour tortilla layer to make the casserole more compact, which helps in serving.

Vary It! You can also make this casserole with shredded chicken by following the same steps.

Per serving: *Calories 460 (From Fat 188); Fat 21g (Saturated 10g); Cholesterol 80mg; Sodium 1,105mg; Carbohydrate 36g (Dietary Fiber 5g); Protein 28g.*

South of the Border Burgers

We realize that when you think of Mexican food, you probably think of tacos and fajitas. Burgers probably don't come to mind when you're planning a fiesta, but these burgers are so good and are packed with the spicy flavors that make Mexican food taste so great that we just had to add this recipe.

Preparation time: *40 minutes*

Cooking time: *8 to 10 minutes*

Yield: *24 servings*

For the burgers:

6 pounds lean ground beef

3 cups finely chopped onions

3 4.25-ounce cans (12.75 ounces) chopped black olives

½ cup ketchup

1 teaspoon salt

4 teaspoons chili powder

4 teaspoons beef fajita seasoning

24 1-ounce slices pepper Jack cheese

24 hamburger buns

For the zesty burger sauce:

3 cups sour cream

1⅓ cup ketchup

4 4.5-ounce cans (18 ounces) chopped green chiles

4 tablespoons minced fresh cilantro

1 Prepare the grill for medium-high heat (350 to 400 degrees).

2 Prepare the zesty burger sauce: Combine all the sauce ingredients, mix well, cover, and refrigerate for 30 minutes.

3 In an extra-large bowl, combine all the ingredients except for the cheese and the buns. Mix thoroughly.

4 Shape the mixture into 48 4-inch patties; place the patties on wax paper.

5 Fold each slice of cheese into four pieces. Then, place the four pieces toward the center of each of the 24 patties.

6 Top each burger with another burger, pressing them together to seal the edges.

7 Grill the burgers over medium-high heat for 4 to 5 minutes per side, turning only once during cook time.

8 Spread the sauce on the hamburger buns, then top them with the burgers. Serve hot.

Tip: *Want uniform-looking burgers? Try using a hamburger press. You can buy a hamburger press made of plastic, or if you're a hamburger warrior who lives, breathes, and sleeps hamburgers, you can buy a heavy-duty one. However, the plastic presses work great and are inexpensive, so you may want to pick one up at your favorite grocery or cooking store.*

Per serving: Calories 489 (From Fat 217); Fat 24g (Saturated 12g); Cholesterol 106mg; Sodium 974mg; Carbohydrate 34g (Dietary Fiber 3g); Protein 35g.

Beef Chimichangas

Chimichangas are a real Mexican favorite, and they're extremely filling, because they're deep fried. You'll love the flavor of this recipe, and your guests will ask for copies!

Preparation time: *40 minutes*

Cook time: *1 hour, 30 minutes*

Yield: *24 servings (2 chimichangas per serving)*

4 pounds ground round

4 medium onions, chopped

6 cloves garlic, crushed

1 teaspoon salt

1 teaspoon cumin

8 cups 4-cheese Mexican blend shredded cheese, divided

4 16-ounce cans (48 ounces) refried beans

4 4.5-ounce cans (18 ounces) chopped green chiles, drained

2 cups picante sauce

vegetable oil

48 8-inch flour tortillas

wooden toothpicks

Toppings:

salsa

sour cream

guacamole

shredded lettuce

1 In a stockpot, cook the ground round, onions, garlic, salt, and cumin over medium-high heat for 30 minutes, or until the beef is no longer pink.

2 Remove the stockpot from heat and drain the excess grease; return the meat and onion mixture to the pot.

3 Stir in 6 cups of the cheese, the refried beans, chiles, and picante sauce.

4 Pour the vegetable oil into a Dutch oven, about 2 inches deep, and heat to 375 degrees.

5 Meanwhile, place ¼ cup of the beef mixture just below the center of each tortilla. Fold each side of the tortillas over the filling, forming rectangles. Secure with wooden toothpicks.

6 Fry the chimichangas, a few at a time, for 1½ minutes per side, or until golden brown. Then remove them from the pot and drain the excess oil.

7 Remove the toothpicks, top each chimichanga with the remaining cheese, and serve with assorted toppings.

Crowd Saver: *We realize that frying volumes of food can be somewhat time-consuming. To help speed the process along, have two pans going at once. We do recommend having a helper take care of one pan while you take care of the other.*

Vary It! *You can also bake these chimichangas instead of frying them. To bake, place them on a baking sheet, coat them with nonstick cooking spray, and bake at 425 degrees for 8 minutes. Then turn the chimichangas and bake them for 5 more minutes. Although the baked version is good, the fried one is much better.*

Per serving: *Calories 719 (From Fat 280); Fat 31g (Saturated 13g); Cholesterol 91mg; Sodium 1,368mg; Carbohydrate 70g (Dietary Fiber 9g); Protein 37g.*

Hankering for Some Barbecue?

Barbecue is a typical crowd meal, and for good reason. It's rather easy, it tastes great, and you can do all the work beforehand without any serious traumas coming your way. Because barbecue is a common crowd meal, we give you some of our favorite recipes in this section.

Barbecued Chicken

Barbecued chicken is a common favorite for a wide variety of crowd events. From back-yard get-togethers to homecoming meals to football game parties, this recipe is sure to be a big hit.

Preparation time: *50 minutes*

Cooking time: *45 to 55 minutes*

Yield: *24 servings*

6 garlic cloves, crushed	¾ cup firmly packed brown sugar	6 dashes hot sauce
2 tablespoons butter, melted		1 teaspoon salt
3 cups ketchup	3 tablespoons celery seeds	6 2½-to-3-pound broiler-fryers, quartered
2½ cups chili sauce	3 tablespoons mustard	
	6 tablespoons Worcestershire sauce	

1 In a large saucepan, sauté the garlic in the butter until tender.

2 Stir in the ketchup, chili sauce, brown sugar, celery seeds, mustard, Worcestershire, hot sauce, and salt and bring to a boil.

3 Remove the mixture from heat and reserve 1 cup of the sauce for basting.

4 Prepare the grill for medium-high heat. Grill the chicken for 15 minutes with the lid on. After the first 15 minutes, baste the chicken with the sauce.

5 Grill the chicken for an additional 30 to 40 minutes, or until a meat thermometer inserted in the thickest part of the chicken reads 170 degrees. Baste with the sauce every 10 minutes.

6 Remove the chicken from heat and serve.

Per serving: *Calories 432 (From Fat 177); Fat 20g (Saturated 6g); Cholesterol 151mg; Sodium 1,430mg; Carbohydrate 25g (Dietary Fiber 1g); Protein 38g.*

Sweet and Spicy Beef Ribs

You'll love the combination of sugar and spice in this recipe, and your crowd will come back for seconds and thirds. Be sure to make plenty!

Preparation time: *20 minutes*

Marinating time: *8 hours or overnight*

Cooking time: *2 hours, 20 minutes*

Yield: *14 to 28 servings*

Sweet Barbecue Sauce (see the following recipe)

2¼ cups sugar

1 cup packed brown sugar

3 tablespoons salt

3 tablespoons garlic powder

3 tablespoons paprika

2 tablespoons pepper, divided

½ teaspoon cayenne pepper

14 pounds beef short ribs, trimmed

1 In a large bowl, combine the sugars, salt, garlic powder, paprika, pepper, and cayenne pepper. Rub the mixture over the ribs.

2 Place the ribs in large, heavy-duty resealable plastic bags; seal and refrigerate for 8 hours or overnight.

3 Line four 15-x-10-x-1-inch baking pans with foil and grease the foil generously with vegetable oil.

4 Preheat the oven to 325 degrees.

5 Place the ribs in the pans and bake uncovered for 2 hours, or until the meat is tender.

6 After the ribs have been cooking for 45 minutes, begin preparing the barbecue sauce.

7 Prepare the grill for medium heat.

8 Remove the ribs from the oven, place them on the grill, and coat them with sauce.

9 Grill for 20 minutes over indirect heat, basting frequently with the sauce.

Sweet Barbecue Sauce

2 small onions, finely chopped

4 teaspoons vegetable oil

2 cups ketchup

12 ounces tomato paste

3 cups water

¼ cup packed brown sugar

½ teaspoon pepper

1 In a large saucepan, sauté the onions in vegetable oil until they're tender, not browned.

2 Stir in the ketchup, tomato paste, water, brown sugar, and pepper; bring to a boil, stirring occasionally.

3 Reduce the heat, cover, and simmer for 1 hour.

Tip: Remember that when a recipe tells you to marinate your meat for a long time, make sure you do! Some people may be in a hurry, but trust us; the marinate time makes the difference between "just okay" and "wow!"

Per serving: *Calories 314 (From Fat 104); Fat 12g (Saturated 5g); Cholesterol 55mg; Sodium 997mg; Carbohydrate 34g (Dietary Fiber 1g); Protein 19g.*

Shredded Beef and Pork Barbecue

This recipe gives you a variation of the standard barbecue fare. The shredded beef and pork is sure to please and is very versatile when you're serving it with other dishes.

Preparation time: *40 minutes*

Cooking time: *10 hours, 10 minutes*

Yield: *24 servings*

3 pounds boneless beef chuck or arm roast, trimmed and cut into 2-inch pieces

3 pounds boneless pork loin or shoulder roast, trimmed and cut into 3-inch pieces

3 cups chopped onions

2 medium green bell peppers, chopped

1 cup firmly packed brown sugar

2 teaspoons salt

2 teaspoons dry mustard

2 tablespoons chili powder

½ cup vinegar

4 teaspoons Worcestershire sauce

2 6-ounce cans (12 ounces) tomato paste

24 sandwich buns

1 Divide all the ingredients, except for the buns and tomato paste, between two 4-quart slow cookers.

2 Cover the slow cookers and cook on low for 10 hours.

3 Remove the meat from the slow cookers and shred it with two forks; return it to the slow cookers and stir in the tomato paste.

4 Cover and cook on high for 10 minutes, stirring occasionally. Serve on buns.

Tip: This meal is informal, so be sure to choose informal appetizers and desserts. You may want to consider the kickin' pretzels, which you can find in Chapter 4.

Per serving: *Calories 396 (From Fat 151); Fat 16g (Saturated 6g); Cholesterol 69mg; Sodium 508mg; Carbohydrate 36g (Dietary Fiber 2g); Protein 26g.*

Barbecued Brisket

Barbecued brisket is a great choice for crowds because the meat is delicious and filling. Also, you start cooking the brisket for at least 8 hours before you serve it, so you have plenty of extra time later.

Preparation time: *30 minutes*

Cooking time: *8 to 9 hours*

Yield: *24 servings*

2 4-to-5-pound beef briskets, cut in half

4 tablespoons vegetable oil, divided

1 cup chopped onion, divided

1 cup chopped celery

4 cups beef broth, divided

2 cups tomato sauce, divided

1 cup water, divided

1 cup sugar, divided

4 tablespoons dry onion soup mix, divided

4 tablespoons vinegar, divided

2 teaspoons salt, divided

2 teaspoons pepper, divided

2 teaspoons garlic powder, divided

6 cups of your favorite barbecue sauce, heated

1 In two large skillets, heat 2 tablespoons of oil per skillet; place the briskets in the oil and sear on all sides. Transfer each brisket to a slow cooker.

2 Leave the remaining oil in each skillet and add ½ cup of the onions and ½ cup of the celery to each skillet; cook for 2 minutes.

3 To each skillet add the following: 2 cups of beef broth, 1 cup of tomato sauce, ½ cup of water, ½ cup of sugar, 2 tablespoons of the dry onion soup mix, 2 tablespoons of vinegar, and 1 teaspoon each of salt, pepper, and garlic powder.

4 Bring the mixtures to a boil, stirring constantly.

5 Pour each skillet of mixture over each brisket. If you have leftover sauce, just set it to the side.

6 Cover each slow cooker and cook on high for 1 hour; reduce the heat to low and cook for 7 to 8 hours, or until the meat is tender.

7 Remove the briskets from the slow cookers to a cutting board; allow them to set for 5 minutes before slicing.

8 Place the barbecue sauce in a microwavable bowl, cover, and heat for 2 minutes. Serve the sauce on the side.

Tip: *When you cook a large cut of meat, such as a brisket, in a slow cooker, you may sometimes find it difficult to fit all the ingredients until the meat has cooked down some. So if all the sauce doesn't fit in the slow cooker, don't worry; just wait until the meat has cooked down or has softened enough that you can push it down farther before adding the rest of the sauce.*

Per serving: *Calories 380 (From Fat 131); Fat 15g (Saturated 5g); Cholesterol 89mg; Sodium 1,492mg; Carbohydrate 29g (Dietary Fiber 1g); Protein 30g.*

Spaghetti and More: Italian Cuisine

When we're faced with a crowd, we often turn our attention to Italian cuisine. After all, Italian food is rather filling and is great for crowd cooking because you can typically make larger batches at a time. In this section, you'll find our tried-and-true Italian cuisine recipes.

Chicken Tetrazzini

This delicious dish can be dressed up for formal affairs or down for informal dinner parties. Its rich taste is sure to be a hit.

Preparation time: *30 minutes*

Cooking time: *45 minutes*

Yield: *24 servings*

32 ounces uncooked vermicelli

1 cup chicken broth

8 cups chopped cooked chicken

2 10.75-ounce cans (21.5 ounces) condensed cream of chicken soup

2 10.75- ounce cans (21.5 ounces) condensed cream of celery soup

2 8-ounce containers (16 ounces) sour cream

2 6-ounce jars (12 ounces) sliced mushrooms, drained

1 cup (4 ounces) shredded Parmesan cheese

2 teaspoons pepper

1 teaspoon salt

4 cups (16 ounces) shredded cheddar cheese

1 Preheat the oven to 350 degrees.

2 Cook the vermicelli according to the package directions; drain it and return it to the pot.

3 Toss the vermicelli with the chicken broth.

4 In a large bowl, combine the vermicelli and the remaining ingredients, except the cheddar cheese.

5 Lightly grease two 11-x-7-inch baking dishes; divide the mixture between them.

6 Top each dish with 2 cups of the cheddar cheese.

7 Cover the casseroles, and then bake them for 40 minutes.

8 Uncover the dishes and bake them for 5 more minutes, or until the cheese is melted and bubbly. Allow the casserole to set for 10 minutes before serving.

Crowd Saver: *Here's a timesaving tip: Freeze the unbaked casseroles (minus the cheese) for up to 1 month. Thaw the casseroles in the refrigerator overnight, then let them stand at room temperature for 30 minutes. Follow Steps 6 through 8 to bake them.*

Per serving: *Calories 426 (From Fat 180); Fat 20g (Saturated 9g); Cholesterol 75mg; Sodium 798mg; Carbohydrate 34g (Dietary Fiber 2g); Protein 27g.*

Baked Ziti

Ziti is macaroni pasta that has been shaped into long, thin tubes. This recipe is for a great Italian dish that will surely please your guests. You'll love the rich taste and the cheesy texture.

Preparation time: *1 hour and 15 minutes*

Cooking time: *55 minutes*

Yield: *24 servings*

24 ounces uncooked ziti

4 pounds ground beef

2 28-ounce jars (56 ounces) spaghetti sauce

2 teaspoons Italian seasoning

2 teaspoons garlic powder

4 eggs

2 15-ounce containers (30 ounces) ricotta cheese

5 cups (20 ounces) shredded mozzarella cheese, divided

1 cup Parmesan cheese

1 Preheat the oven to 350 degrees.

2 Cook the pasta according to the package directions — remember to cook it al dente. Drain the pasta and set it aside.

3 Meanwhile, in a large stockpot, cook the ground beef until it's no longer pink; drain the excess grease and return the beef to the pot.

4 Stir in the spaghetti sauce, Italian seasoning, and garlic powder; simmer on low for 10 minutes.

5 In a large bowl, combine the eggs, ricotta cheese, 3 cups of the mozzarella cheese, and the Parmesan cheese.

6 Add the pasta to the bowl and toss until the pasta is well coated with the cheese mixture.

7 Grease two 13-x-9-x-2-inch baking dishes; spoon a thin layer of the meat sauce into the bottom of each dish.

8 Follow with a layer of the pasta and cheese, then another layer of the meat sauce. Layer until the pans are close to full. The top layer should be meat sauce.

9 Cover and bake for 45 minutes.

10 Remove the casseroles from the oven, uncover, and top each dish with 1 cup of mozzarella cheese.

11 Bake for 10 minutes, or until the cheese has melted. Remove the casseroles from the oven and let them stand for 15 minutes before serving.

Vary It! *For a change of pace, use half bulk Italian sausage instead of all beef.*

Per serving: *Calories 452(From Fat 201); Fat 22g (Saturated 11g); Cholesterol 135mg; Sodium 500mg; Carbohydrate 29g (Dietary Fiber 2g); Protein 33g.*

Sausage and Spinach Manicotti

Manicotti is a large macaroni tube stuffed with different ingredients, often a variety of cheese and meat. We love this recipe because the natural serving sizes are perfect for crowd gatherings.

Preparation time: *2 hours*

Cooking time: *1 hour, 15 minutes*

Yield: *28 servings*

4 8-ounce packages (32 ounces) manicotti shells	1½ cups grated Parmesan cheese	4 eggs, beaten
½ cup butter or margarine	2 pounds bulk Italian sausage	4 cups (16 ounces) shredded mozzarella cheese, divided
½ cup flour	4 cups diced cooked chicken	4 28-ounce jars (112 ounces) spaghetti sauce
1 teaspoon garlic powder	4 10-ounce packages (40 ounces) frozen chopped spinach, thawed and squeezed dry	½ cup minced fresh parsley
5 cups milk		

1 Preheat the oven to 350 degrees.

2 Cook the manicotti according to the package directions; drain it and set it aside.

3 Meanwhile, melt the butter in a large saucepan. Stir in the flour and garlic powder until the mixture is smooth.

4 Gradually whisk in the milk. Bring the mixture to a boil; cook over low heat for 2 minutes or until thickened, whisking constantly.

5 Remove the pan from heat and stir in the Parmesan cheese until melted; set aside.

6 In a stockpot, cook the sausage over medium heat until it's no longer pink, and then drain the excess grease and return the meat to the pan.

7 Add the chicken, spinach, eggs, 2 cups of the mozzarella cheese, and 1½ cups of the white sauce that you set aside.

8 Stuff the mixture into the manicotti shells.

9 Spread ½ cup of the spaghetti sauce on the bottom of each of four 13-x-9-x-2-inch baking dishes. Place the manicotti over the sauce.

10 Pour the remaining spaghetti sauce over the manicotti, then pour the remaining white sauce over the spaghetti sauce.

11 Bake uncovered for 45 to 50 minutes. Remove the casseroles from the oven and top each dish with ½ cup of the mozzarella cheese; bake an additional 5 to 10 minutes or until the cheese has melted.

12 Remove the dishes from the oven, sprinkle each with ¼ cup of parsley, and allow them to set for 15 minutes before serving.

Per serving: Calories 422 (From Fat 169); Fat 19g (Saturated 9g); Cholesterol 92mg; Sodium 836mg; Carbohydrate 40g (Dietary Fiber 4g); Protein 24g.

Creamy Linguine with Shrimp

If you like shrimp linguine, you'll love this version because it adds an extra punch with cooked bacon. Be sure to try this one out!

Preparation time: *1 hour*

Yield: *24 servings*

4 12-ounce packages (48 ounces) linguine pasta	*4 cups half-and-half*
½ cup olive oil	*1 cup grated Parmesan cheese*
12 garlic cloves, minced	*1 cup (4 ounces) shredded Monterey Jack cheese*
½ cup chopped fresh oregano	*4 pounds medium cooked shrimp, peeled and deveined*
½ cup chopped fresh basil	
12 plum tomatoes, seeded and chopped	*2 teaspoons salt*
2 cups chopped green onions	*1 cup toasted pine nuts (optional)*
1 pound bacon, cooked crisp and crumbled	

1 Cook the linguine according to the package directions — remember to cook it al dente.

2 In a stockpot, heat the olive oil and then sauté the garlic, oregano, and basil for 2 minutes.

3 Stir in the tomatoes and green onions with the garlic mixture and sauté for 5 minutes.

4 Add the bacon, half-and-half, Parmesan cheese, and Monterey Jack cheese; cook until the cheese is melted, stirring constantly.

5 Stir in the shrimp and salt and simmer for 10 minutes, stirring occasionally. Serve the sauce over the pasta and sprinkle with pine nuts, if desired.

Vary It! *For a variation, try substituting the same amount of crabmeat or imitation crabmeat for the shrimp.*

Per serving: Calories 439 (From Fat 138); Fat 15g (Saturated 6g); Cholesterol 172mg; Sodium 512mg; Carbohydrate 47g (Dietary Fiber 2g); Protein 28g.

Pizza Lasagne

The addition of pepperoni to an otherwise standard lasagne is a welcomed change. This lasagne is hearty and satisfying. Serve it with garlic bread and salad for a complete meal.

Preparation time: *40 minutes*

Cooking time: *1 hour, 35 minutes*

Yield: *20 to 24 servings*

3 pounds ground beef

2 small onions, chopped

5 cups water

2 8-ounce cans (16 ounces) tomato sauce

2 6-ounce cans (12 ounces) tomato paste

2 teaspoons beef bouillon granules

2 tablespoons dried parsley flakes

4 teaspoons Italian seasoning

1½ teaspoons salt

2 teaspoons garlic powder

4 eggs

24 ounces small-curd cottage cheese

1 cup sour cream

16 lasagna noodles, cooked per package directions and drained

2 3.5-ounce packages (7 ounces) sliced pepperoni

6 cups (24 ounces) shredded mozzarella cheese

1 cup grated Parmesan cheese

1 Preheat the oven to 350 degrees.

2 In a stockpot, cook the beef and onions over medium heat until the meat is no longer pink; drain the excess grease.

3 Add the water, tomato sauce, tomato paste, bouillon, parsley, Italian seasoning, salt, and garlic powder; bring to a boil.

4 Reduce the heat and simmer, uncovered, for 45 minutes.

5 In a medium bowl, combine the eggs, cottage cheese, and sour cream and mix well.

6 Lightly grease two 13-x-9-x-2-inch baking dishes; pour ½ cup of the meat sauce in the bottom of each dish.

7 To each pan, add a layer of 4 lasagna noodles, spread half of the cottage cheese mixture on top of the noodles, add a layer of pepperoni, and then sprinkle on 1 cup of the mozzarella cheese.

8 Top each dish with half of the remaining noodles and half of the meat sauce.

9 Cover and bake for 35 minutes.

10 Remove the casseroles from the oven, uncover them, and sprinkle each dish with 2 cups of mozzarella cheese and ½ cup of Parmesan cheese. Return the uncovered dishes to the oven and cook for 15 minutes, or until the cheese is melted and bubbly.

11 Remove the lasagne from the oven and let it set for 15 minutes before serving.

Tip: *Make sure you let the lasagne set for the recommended 15 minutes before serving. Doing so will help you serve it in nicely cut squares instead of watching it fall apart as you try to scoop it out.*

Per serving: *Calories 375 (From Fat 197); Fat 22g (Saturated 11g); Cholesterol 120mg; Sodium 834mg; Carbohydrate 15g (Dietary Fiber 1g); Protein 29g.*

A Couple of Vegetarian Options

In any large gathering, you're bound to have a some guests who choose not to eat meat, but there's no need for these folks to be forced to eat only salads and side dishes. The following vegetarian main dishes are crowd pleasers for vegetarians and meat-eaters alike.

☙ Tofu Parmigiano

Of course you've heard of eggplant parmigiano and chicken parmigiano, but what about tofu parmigiano? If you're a vegetarian or just want to explore a delicious twist on an Italian standard, you'll want to try this one.

Preparation time: *1 hour*

Cooking time: *20 minutes*

Yield: *20 servings*

2½ cups Italian-seasoned breadcrumbs	*3 teaspoons garlic powder, divided*	*5 12-ounce packages (60 ounces) firm tofu*
1½ cups (6 ounces) grated Parmesan cheese, divided	*2 teaspoons salt, divided*	*½ cup, 2 tablespoons olive oil*
3 teaspoons Italian seasoning, divided	*1 teaspoon pepper, divided*	*6 cups (24 ounces) shredded mozzarella cheese*
	5 8-ounce cans (40 ounces) tomato sauce	

1 Preheat the oven to 400 degrees.

2 In a medium bowl, combine the breadcrumbs, 2 tablespoons of the Parmesan cheese, 1 teaspoon of the Italian seasoning, 1 teaspoon of the garlic powder, 1 teaspoon of the salt, and ½ teaspoon of the pepper. Set aside.

3 In a large saucepan, combine the tomato sauce with the remaining Parmesan cheese, Italian seasoning, garlic, salt, and pepper. Over medium heat, bring the mixture to a soft boil and then reduce the heat to simmer. Stir occasionally.

4 Meanwhile, carefully slice the tofu into ¼-inch slices.

5 Take one slice of tofu at a time and coat it with breadcrumb mixture. Make sure you gently pat the mixture on the tofu so it sticks.

6 Cover the bottom of a large skillet with the olive oil and, over medium heat, cook the coated tofu slices until they're brown on each side. Then remove the tofu to a plate covered with paper towels to help remove the excess oil.

7 Lightly coat two 13-x-9-x-2-inch pans with nonstick cooking spray.

8 Remove the sauce from heat and place a thin layer of it in the bottom of each pan.

9 Place the tofu slices in the pans — about 10 to a pan — and cover them with the remaining sauce.

10 Top each pan with 3 cups of the mozzarella cheese and bake uncovered for 20 minutes. If desired, top with some additional Parmesan cheese after the removing the pans from the oven.

Tip: If you want the sauce to be a little thicker and chunkier, try adding some sautéed mushrooms.

Per serving: Calories 384 (From Fat 215); Fat 24g (Saturated 8g); Cholesterol 31mg; Sodium 1,224mg; Carbohydrate 21g (Dietary Fiber 4g); Protein 26g.

 Vegetarian Stuffed Peppers

If you love stuffed peppers but want to avoid the meat stuffing, here's a great recipe that uses tofu instead. This recipe makes 20 servings, so it's perfect for your vegetarian crowd.

Preparation time: *1 hour*

Cooking time: *1 hour, 15 minutes*

Yield: *20 servings*

½ cup vegetable oil

4 large onions, chopped

3 garlic cloves, minced

1 cup uncooked white rice

4 cups vegetable broth

4 pounds firm tofu, crumbled

1 cup chopped fresh parsley

4 cups chopped fresh mushrooms

8 eggs

1 cup breadcrumbs

4 cups finely chopped walnuts

¼ cup Worcestershire sauce

¼ cup soy sauce

½ cup paprika

2 teaspoons salt

1 teaspoon pepper

24 green bell peppers

4 8-ounce cans (32 ounces) crushed tomatoes

1 cup cooking wine, red

½ cup tomato paste

1 Preheat the oven to 350 degrees.

2 In a medium skillet, heat the oil over medium heat. Sauté the onions and 2 cloves of minced garlic until the onions are translucent.

3 Add the rice and sauté for 2 minutes. Stir in the vegetable broth, cover the skillet, and cook until the rice is done, about 15 minutes.

4 In a large bowl, combine the tofu, parsley, mushrooms, eggs, breadcrumbs, walnuts, Worcestershire, soy sauce, paprika, salt, pepper, and cooked rice.

5 Slice the tops off of the peppers and set the tops aside. Remove the core of the peppers with a paring knife and stuff the peppers with the tofu mixture. Replace the tops.

6 In a shallow baking dish, combine the tomatoes, wine, tomato paste, and the remaining garlic. Place the stuffed peppers in the dish, cover it with foil, and bake for 1 hour.

Per serving: Calories 424 (From Fat 236); Fat 26g (Saturated 3g); Cholesterol 71mg; Sodium 670mg; Carbohydrate 31g (Dietary Fiber 7g); Protein 24g.

Chapter 6

Delicious Side Dishes

In This Chapter

▶ Making cool salads

▶ Leaving boring vegetables, rice, and pasta by the wayside

▶ Going inside a pod: Peas and beans

Side dishes are an important part of any meal, especially a crowd meal. Almost all entrees don't stand well on their own; they need a sidekick or two.

Side dishes should always complement the main meal. If you think about a meal in terms of layers, the appetizers should complement the main course, side dishes should complement the main course, and the desserts should complement the main course. In the end, the main course serves as the center for your meal. Everything else should point to that center, the side dishes in particular.

In this chapter, we point you to some of our favorite side dishes, which are flexible with a wide variety of entrees and are easy to make for your crowd event.

Scrumptious Salads

Salads complement a wide variety of entrees. In fact, we have a hard time thinking of an entree that doesn't work well with leafy greens. However, they have a tendency to be boring — not an appealing thought when you're entertaining. No problem! With the recipes in this section, you can breathe new life into the tried-and-true salad.

⏳ Tossed Salad with Strawberries and Walnuts

This salad is absolutely wonderful. The special salad dressing, along with the strawberries and walnuts, makes for a unique and delightful combination. Be sure to try this one!

Preparation time: *20 minutes*

Yield: *24 servings*

Red Wine Vinaigrette (see the following recipe)

24 cups romaine lettuce torn in pieces

12 cups Boston or Bibb lettuce torn in pieces

7½ cups sliced fresh strawberries

3 cups (12 ounces) shredded Monterey Jack cheese

1½ cups chopped walnuts, toasted

1 In an extra-large salad bowl or punch bowl, toss together the salad greens, strawberries, cheese, and walnuts.

2 Drizzle the salad with the Red Wine Vinaigrette and toss it again, making sure all the ingredients are thoroughly coated. Serve immediately.

Red Wine Vinaigrette

1½ cups vegetable oil

1 cup sugar

¾ cup red wine vinegar

3 garlic cloves, minced

1 teaspoon salt

¾ teaspoon paprika

Place all the dressing ingredients in a large jar with a tight-fitting lid and shake well.

Tip: *When you make a lettuce salad, it's extremely important to make sure the lettuce is completely dry. Doing so keeps the lettuce crisp and also helps it last longer before becoming mushy. Try using a salad spinner (see Figure 6-1) to remove the excess moisture from the lettuce.*

Per serving: *Calories 286 (From Fat 212); Fat 24g (Saturated 4g); Cholesterol 13mg; Sodium 180mg; Carbohydrate 15g (Dietary Fiber 3g); Protein 6g.*

Figure 6-1: Nobody likes soggy lettuce! Use a salad spinner to dry your lettuce after washing it.

salad spinner

Bean and Cheese Salad

Bean and cheese salad is one of those dishes that may catch you off guard because it sounds so unusual. But don't let the unexpected scare you away — this recipe is great.

Preparation time: *20 minutes*

Yield: *24 servings*

18 cups romaine lettuce torn in pieces

1½ cups sliced green onions

3 15.5-ounce cans (46.5 ounces) garbanzo beans, drained and rinsed

3 15.5-ounce cans (46.5 ounces) black beans, drained and rinsed

3 15.5-ounce cans (46.5 ounces) pinto beans, drained and rinsed

12 ounces Colby cheese, cubed

12 ounces Monterey Jack cheese, cubed

6 tomatoes, seeded and chopped

2½ cups prepared cucumber ranch salad dressing

6 eggs, hard boiled, cooled, and sliced

1 In a large bowl, combine all the ingredients except the eggs and salad dressing. Toss gently to mix.

2 Add the salad dressing. Toss the salad gently, making sure it's coated with dressing.

3 Garnish the top of the salad with the eggs.

Crowd Saver: *To save some time before your event, do Step 1, then cover and refrigerate the salad until you're ready to serve it. Remove the salad from the refrigerator and complete Steps 2 and 3 before serving.*

Per serving: *Calories 351 (From Fat 212); Fat 24g (Saturated 8g); Cholesterol 79mg; Sodium 558mg; Carbohydrate 20g (Dietary Fiber 6g); Protein 15g.*

Toasting nuts

Not quite sure how to toast nuts? No problem. First, heat the oven to 350 degrees. Place the nuts in a small baking sheet or pie pan and cook them until they're lightly browned — about 5 to 8 minutes — shaking them once or twice to prevent scorching.

Classic Waldorf Salad

Waldorf salads are always a treat. The combination of apples, celery, and walnuts is delicious. We've found that this recipe works well with many different entrees.

Preparation time: *20 minutes*

Chill time: *30 minutes*

Yield: *24 servings*

1½ cups mayonnaise	9 medium red apples, cored and diced
3 tablespoons sugar	3 cups sliced celery
3 tablespoons lemon juice	1½ cups chopped walnuts
½ teaspoon salt	

1 In a small bowl, combine the mayonnaise, sugar, lemon juice, and salt. Mix until smooth.

2 In a large bowl, combine the apples and celery.

3 Pour the mayonnaise mixture over the apples and celery and toss until coated.

4 Cover and chill for 30 minutes.

5 Just before serving, toss in the walnuts.

Per serving: *Calories 188 (From Fat 145); Fat 16g (Saturated 2g); Cholesterol 8mg; Sodium 140mg; Carbohydrate 12g (Dietary Fiber 2g); Protein 2g.*

Where's Waldorf?

Waldorf salad was created at New York's Waldorf-Astoria Hotel in 1896. However, a chef wasn't responsible, as you may think. In fact, the *maître d'hôtel,* Oscar Tschirky, invented this popular salad. The original version contained only apples, celery, and mayonnaise. Chopped walnuts later became an integral part of the dish.

Vegetables

Vegetables are given side dishes for a great variety of entrees, and naturally, your choice and method of preparation will vary based on your main dish. Like salads, vegetables can be delightful or rather boring, so we give you some recipes that taste great, are easy to make for crowds, and keep the boredom factor at bay.

☙ *Broccoli with Red Peppers*

Broccoli recipes work great with a wide variety of meals, and this recipe, which includes red peppers and almonds, will give your green some extra zip.

Preparation time: *20 minutes*

Cooking time: *25 minutes*

Yield: *24 servings*

6 bunches fresh broccoli	*2 medium onions, thinly sliced*
2 tablespoons butter	*1½ teaspoons salt*
3 large red bell peppers, cut into short, thin strips	*1 teaspoon pepper*
	¾ cup sliced almonds, toasted

1 Wash and dry the broccoli and cut off the stems, using only the florets.

2 In a stockpot, heat some water until it comes to a boil. Add the broccoli and boil, uncovered, for 7 to 10 minutes, or until bright green and tender.

3 Drain the broccoli and rinse it under cold water; set it aside.

4 In an extra-large skillet or wok, melt the butter.

5 Add the bell peppers and onions and cook them for 5 minutes, stirring occasionally.

6 Add the broccoli and sprinkle the vegetables with salt and pepper. Cook for an additional 6 to 8 minutes, and then remove them from heat.

7 Place the vegetable mixture in a serving dish, topping it with the almonds.

Per serving: Calories 76 (From Fat 27); Fat 3g (Saturated 1g); Cholesterol 3mg; Sodium 187mg; Carbohydrate 10g (Dietary Fiber 5g); Protein 5g.

☺ Glazed Carrots

Carrots are common side dishes and are delicious and exciting. Okay, maybe not . . . they have a tendency to be bland and boring after they're cooked, but you can change that sad truth with this quick and easy recipe. (Who said vegetables can't be sweet?)

Preparation time: *5 minutes*

Cooking time: *35 minutes*

Yield: *24 servings*

6 pounds baby carrots

1 cup butter

1¾ cups brown sugar

1½ teaspoons salt

1½ teaspoons pepper

parsley sprig for garnish (optional)

1 In a large stockpot or Dutch oven, place the carrots in water and bring to a boil.

2 Reduce the heat to a high simmer and cook for 20 to 30 minutes, stirring occasionally. (Make sure that you don't overcook the carrots. They should be slightly firm, not mushy.)

3 Drain the carrots, return them to the pot, and add the remaining ingredients (except the parsley). Cook on the lowest setting for 5 to 7 minutes, gently stirring, until the sugar-and-butter mixture is bubbly. Serve hot, garnishing with a parsley sprig (if desired).

Crowd Saver: If you're in a big hurry, you can substitute canned carrot rounds instead of fresh carrots. The canned carrots don't taste as good, but they save you some time.

Per serving: Calories 171 (From Fat 74); Fat 8g (Saturated 5g); Cholesterol 20mg; Sodium 192mg; Carbohydrate 25g (Dietary Fiber 2g); Protein 1g.

✎ Scalloped Potatoes

Scalloped potatoes are standard side-dish fare, and we don't reinvent the wheel here, because the traditional dish is very tasty. However, this recipe yields enough for a crowd. (In case you're wondering, *scalloped* means to bake in a casserole with milk or a sauce and often with breadcrumbs.)

Preparation time: *35 minutes*

Cooking time: *1 hour*

Yield: *24 servings*

¾ cup butter

¾ cup flour

6 cups milk

1 cup chopped green bell pepper

3 2-ounce jars (6 ounces) diced pimentos, drained

2 cups (8 ounces) shredded provolone cheese

6 green onions, chopped

2½ teaspoons salt

1 teaspoon pepper

12 medium baking potatoes, peeled and thinly sliced

1 cup breadcrumbs

1 Preheat the oven to 425 degrees. Melt the butter in a large saucepan over low heat, and whisk in the flour until smooth. Cook for 2 minutes, whisking constantly.

2 Gradually whisk in the milk; cook over medium heat until the sauce has thickened and is bubbly. Make sure that you whisk constantly to ensure a smooth sauce.

3 Stir in the green bell pepper, pimentos, provolone cheese, green onions, salt, and pepper and cook for 10 minutes, and then remove from heat.

4 Grease three 13-x-9-x-2-inch baking dishes.

5 Divide the flour mixture, the bell pepper mixture, and the remaining ingredients — except the breadcrumbs — among the three baking dishes.

6 Cover the dishes and bake them for 35 to 45 minutes, or until the potatoes are tender.

7 Uncover the dishes and top them with breadcrumbs. Bake them for another 15 to 20 minutes, or until golden brown.

Per serving: *Calories 216 (From Fat 96); Fat 11g (Saturated 7g); Cholesterol 30mg; Sodium 402mg; Carbohydrate 24g (Dietary Fiber 2g); Protein 7g.*

Rice and Pasta

Rice and pasta dishes are great sides because they're filling and work well with a number of main dishes. Of course, they can also be boring (such as the typical rice pilaf you find at restaurants). However, with the right recipe, you can put some spice and zing into rice and pasta dishes. In this section, we show you our favorites.

Festive Rice Casserole

This festive rice casserole is a perfect side dish and is packed full of flavor. Your guests will love the additional ingredients, and the taste sensation will bring them back for more.

Preparation time: *25 minutes*

Cooking time: *1 hour, 30 minutes*

Yield: *24 servings*

2 cups slivered almonds	¾ cup butter	2⅔ cups sliced fresh mushrooms
8 cups chicken broth	5 medium onions, sliced into wedges	2 teaspoons orange zest
2 cups uncooked brown rice	¼ cup brown sugar	2 teaspoons salt
2 cups uncooked wild rice	4 cups dried cranberries	2 teaspoons pepper

1 Preheat the oven to 350 degrees. Place the almonds on an ungreased baking sheet and toast them in the oven for 5 to 8 minutes.

2 In a stockpot, combine the chicken broth, brown rice, and wild rice and bring the broth to a boil. Reduce the heat to low, cover, and simmer for 50 minutes to 1 hour or until the rice is tender and the broth is absorbed.

3 In a large skillet, melt the butter. Add the onions and brown sugar and sauté them until the butter is absorbed and the onions are translucent and soft, not brown. Reduce the heat and sauté, stirring occasionally, for 25 minutes.

4 Stir the cranberries and mushrooms into the skillet with the onions. Cover the skillet and cook for 10 minutes over low heat. The cranberries should start to swell.

5 Add the almonds and orange zest to the skillet and stir until well combined.

6 Add the contents of the skillet, along with the salt and pepper, to the stockpot with the rice and stir until well combined; let it stand for 5 minutes before serving.

Per serving: *Calories 316 (From Fat 110); Fat 12g (Saturated 4g); Cholesterol 17mg; Sodium 534mg; Carbohydrate 48g (Dietary Fiber 4g); Protein 6g.*

Tips for cooking rice

For fluffier, faster-cooking rice, try soaking it in cold water for 30 to 60 minutes prior to cooking. Then rinse the rice several times until the water comes out clear. Doing so removes any starch and residue — otherwise, the rice may be sticky. Don't use salt or butter when cooking plain rice; they kill the food's natural sweet taste.

Mushroom and Walnut Orzo Pasta

Orzo is a small pasta that looks like a large grain of rice. Chefs often use it in soups and Greek cuisine. This recipe is rather filling, and mushrooms and walnuts give the dish a unique and delicious taste.

Preparation time: *30 minutes*

Cooking time: *25 minutes*

Yield: *24 servings*

1 cup chopped walnuts	*6¾ cups uncooked orzo*
¼ cup, 1 tablespoon olive oil	*2 teaspoons salt*
6 medium onions, chopped	*2 teaspoons pepper*
3 pounds fresh mushrooms, sliced	*2 teaspoons garlic powder*
12 cups chicken broth	

1 Preheat the oven to 350 degrees.

2 In a large stockpot, heat the olive oil over medium heat. Add the onions and mushrooms and sauté them until they're tender and the onions are slightly browned.

3 Pour in the broth and bring it to a boil.

4 Stir in the orzo, reduce the heat to the lowest setting, and cover the pot. Simmer for 25 minutes or until the pasta is tender and the liquid has been absorbed.

5 Meanwhile, place the walnuts on an ungreased baking sheet and bake for 8 to 10 minutes.

6 Remove the pot from heat and stir in the walnuts, salt, pepper, and garlic powder.

Per serving: Calories 300 (From Fat 101); Fat 11g (Saturated 2g); Cholesterol 3mg; Sodium 699mg; Carbohydrate 42g (Dietary Fiber 3g); Protein 10g.

🍑 Easy Mac and Cheese

Macaroni and cheese is a common side dish, and for good reason. Most people love it, and it works well with many different entrees. This easy mac-and-cheese recipe will give you a perfect crowd side dish without any fuss.

Preparation time: *50 minutes*

Yield: *24 servings*

9 cups uncooked macaroni	*½ cup butter*
2¼ pounds processed cheese, shredded	*¾ cup heavy whipping cream*
3 cups (12 ounces) shredded cheddar cheese	*2 teaspoons salt*

1 In a large stockpot, cook the macaroni according to the package directions. Make sure to cook the macaroni *al dente* — firm, not mushy.

2 Drain the pasta and return it to the pot — don't rinse it with cold water. Immediately add the remaining ingredients and stir until the cheeses are melted and creamy.

3 Allow the mac and cheese to sit for 5 minutes before serving.

Remember: *"Al dente" is a fancy term for pasta that's fully cooked, but not overly soft. The phrase is Italian for "to the tooth," which comes from testing the pasta's consistency with your teeth.*

Tip: *If you prefer an even creamier mac and cheese, substitute the cheddar cheese with additional processed cheese. You can also make it creamier by adding an additional ¼ cup of heavy whipping cream.*

Per serving: Calories 380 (From Fat 191); Fat 21g (Saturated 13g); Cholesterol 69mg; Sodium 923mg; Carbohydrate 32g (Dietary Fiber 1g); Protein 15g.

Legumes

A legume is a pod — most people commonly call them peas and beans, but regardless of what you call them, they're great side dishes. Once again, you may face the idea of a boring side dish, but you can prepare peas and beans in many different ways, so they're anything but boring. Try out these recipes and you'll see.

Good Luck Black-Eyed Peas

Whether it's New Year's Eve and you're eating black-eyed peas for good luck or the middle of August and you simply have a craving, this recipe is the one you've been searching for. It's easy to make, and you can prepare it a day ahead and reheat it, which is always a big plus when you're cooking for a crowd.

Preparation time: *15 minutes*

Cooking time: *3 hours, 30 minutes*

Yield: *24 servings*

2 pounds dry black-eyed peas, sorted, washed, and soaked	2 teaspoons pepper
1 pound bacon, cut in thirds	1 teaspoon garlic powder
3 cups chopped, cooked ham	3 medium onions, diced
2 teaspoons salt	2 14.5-ounce cans (29 ounces) diced tomatoes

1 Place the sorted, washed, and soaked black-eyed peas, along with the bacon, in a large stockpot; add enough water to fill the pot three-quarters full.

2 Bring the water to a boil. Reduce the heat to low and cover the pot; simmer for 1 hour.

3 Add the remaining ingredients and bring the water to a boil; reduce the heat, cover the pot, and simmer for 2 hours and 30 minutes or until the peas are tender.

Remember: *Anytime you're cooking dry beans or peas, be sure to sort through them and remove any small rocks and sometimes even stickers. After you've sorted them, place them in a colander and rinse them with cold water.*

Crowd Saver: *To soak beans or peas, place them in a large pot, fill it three-quarters full with water, and allow them to soak overnight or for 8 hours. Soaking them helps cut down on cook time, thus saving you preparation time.*

Per serving: *Calories 211 (From Fat 57); Fat 6g (Saturated 2g); Cholesterol 16mg; Sodium 506mg; Carbohydrate 25g (Dietary Fiber 8g); Protein 14g.*

☙ *Creamed Peas*

Creamed peas are delicious, and as a side dish they work well with a variety of entrees. Try creamed peas with almost any traditional meal, such as pot roast, steak, meatloaf, or chicken.

Preparation time: *20 minutes*

Cooking time: *15 minutes*

Yield: *24 servings*

12 cups frozen green peas, thawed	*2 cups heavy whipping cream*
4 cups water	*¾ cup flour*
2 teaspoons salt	*¼ cup, 2 tablespoons sugar*
1 cup, 2 tablespoons butter	

1 In a large stockpot, combine the peas, water, and salt. Bring to a boil.

2 Stir in the butter and reduce the heat to low.

3 In a medium bowl, whisk together the cream, flour, and sugar.

4 Stir the mixture into the peas and cook over medium-high heat for 10 to 15 minutes, until thick and bubbly. Let the peas set for 10 minutes before serving.

Per serving: *Calories 232 (From Fat 144; Fat 16g (Saturated 10g); Cholesterol 50mg; Sodium 272mg; Carbohydrate 18g (Dietary Fiber 5g); Protein 5g.*

Just why are black-eyed peas good luck?

The tradition of good luck black-eyed peas dates back to Southern families during the Civil War era. The black-eyed pea is a form of what is known as a *cowpea,* which was grown to feed livestock and slaves. As the story goes, when Union soldiers burned all the Southern crops, they left only the cowpeas, which were grown only for livestock. Southern families then had to eat the black-eyed peas for their own survival, which made black-eyed peas lucky.

Baked Beans

Baked beans are a favorite, and rightly so. They're a perfect side dish and they taste great. You'll find a lot of baked bean recipes on the Internet and in other cookbooks, but we like this one because it's full of flavor.

Baked bean recipes vary widely, depending on the region where you live. If you love baked beans, check out www.cdkitchen.com, where you can find many different baked bean recipes under "Side Dishes."

Preparation time: *25 minutes*

Cooking time: *1 hour, 10 minutes*

Yield: *24 servings*

5 28-ounce cans (140 ounces) baked beans

2½ pounds bacon, cut into small pieces

1 large onion, chopped

2½ pounds brown sugar

¼ cup mustard

2 teaspoons salt

1 Preheat the oven to 400 degrees.

2 Pour the beans into a large roasting dish or divide them between two large casserole dishes.

3 Heat a large skillet and add the bacon and chopped onions, cooking until the onions are just tender.

4 Add the brown sugar to the skillet and stir; cook for an additional 5 to 10 minutes, until bubbly.

5 Pour the bacon mixture over the beans and mix.

6 Bake uncovered for 1 hour. Allow the beans to set for 10 minutes before serving.

Per serving: Calories 447 (From Fat 93); Fat 10g (Saturated 4g); Cholesterol 25mg; Sodium 1,174mg; Carbohydrate 80g (Dietary Fiber 9g); Protein 14g.

Chapter 7

Satisfying Slurps: Soups and Stews

Soups and stews are wonderful additions to almost any meal because they're so versatile and delicious. As an added bonus, they're rather easy to make for crowds and are very filling. From casual dining affairs to formal events, we include in this chapter a collection of soups and stews that you'll use time and time again as you cook for a crowd.

If you love soup and want more great recipes, be sure to check out *Cooking Soups For Dummies* by Jenna Holst and the fine folks at Wiley.

Vegetable Soups, Fresh from Mother Nature

Vegetable soups are a mainstay of soup recipes, and for good reason: They're delicious and easy to make. In the next few pages, you find our favorite vegetable soup recipes, with helpful tips and suggestions to guide you along the way.

Cheese and Corn Chowder

This filling chowder is a wonderful addition to a fall or winter meal. It's great because most of the ingredients are things you probably have on hand at any given time.

Preparation time: *45 minutes*

Yield: *24 1-cup servings*

12 large potatoes, peeled and cubed	½ cup butter	6 cups milk
2 teaspoons salt	4 14¾-ounce cans (59 ounces) corn	8 ounces processed cheese, cubed
2 large onions, chopped	1 pound bacon, cooked crisp and crumbled	2 cups (8 ounces) shredded Colby or cheddar cheese

1 Place the potatoes in a large soup kettle; sprinkle them with salt and cover them with water. (If you don't have a large enough soup kettle, divide the potatoes equally between two pots. When you add the remaining ingredients, you'll need to divide them in half as well.)

2 Bring the water to a boil.

3 Reduce the heat, cover, and simmer until the potatoes are tender.

4 While the potatoes are cooking, sauté the onions and butter in a skillet until tender, but not brown.

5 Add the corn and precooked bacon to the onions; heat thoroughly over low heat.

6 When the potatoes are tender, drain them and then return them to the large soup kettle.

7 Add the milk to the potatoes; heat through over low heat.

8 Stir in the corn mixture and processed cheese; continue to stir gently and heat until the cheese melts.

9 Remove from heat.

10 Add the shredded cheese and stir; serve immediately.

Tip: *When you use milk in a soup, heat it slowly (over low heat) to make sure that you don't scorch it.*

Vary It! *Using processed cheese in this soup gives it a creamy, velvety texture. However, if you prefer, you can replace the processed cheese with another 2 cups (8 ounces) of the shredded Colby or cheddar.*

Go-With: *This soup would be a nice side or appetizer to serve with the meatloaf recipe in Chapter 5.*

Per serving: *Calories 295 (From Fat 132); Fat 15g (Saturated 8g); Cholesterol 39mg; Sodium 689mg; Carbohydrate 32g (Dietary Fiber 3g); Protein 11g.*

Broccoli Cheese Soup

This creamy, heartwarming soup is a popular addition to almost any meal, and we like it because it works well for all kinds of informal gatherings.

Preparation time: 1 hour

Yield: 50 1¼-cup servings

1½ gallons water

1⅓ cups chicken bouillon granules

2 tablespoons salt

1 teaspoon garlic powder

2 tablespoons coarse black pepper

7 pounds frozen broccoli florets

1 large onion, diced

3 6-ounce jars (18 ounces) chopped pimentos

1½ pounds butter

2½ cups flour

1½ gallons warmed milk

3 pounds processed cheese, shredded

1 In a large stockpot, heat the water and add the chicken bouillon granules, cooking until dissolved.

2 Add the salt, garlic, and pepper, and bring to a boil; reduce the heat to very low.

3 Add the broccoli and onion. Simmer for 10 minutes or until the vegetables are tender, but not mushy, and remove from heat.

4 Add the pimentos, remove the pot from heat, and set it aside.

5 In a large saucepan, melt the butter.

6 Slowly add the flour to the melted butter, whisking to combine.

7 Cook for 5 minutes over very low heat, stirring occasionally. This mixture creates a *roux,* or thickening agent.

8 Add the flour mixture to the broccoli mixture and whisk together until well blended.

9 Add the milk to the soup and stir together until well blended.

10 Slowly increase the heat to high and bring the soup to a boil.

11 Immediately after the mixture begins to boil, return it to very low heat and simmer for 2 minutes.

12 As the soup continues to simmer over very low heat, add the cheese slowly, stirring until well blended.

13 Serve immediately, and if you so desire, garnish the soup with a sprinkle of grated cheddar cheese.

Tip: Heat the milk slowly, over low heat, to make sure that you don't scorch it.

Per serving: Calories 322 (From Fat 191); Fat 21g (Saturated 13g); Cholesterol 60mg; Sodium 1,242mg; Carbohydrate 21g (Dietary Fiber 2g); Protein 13g.

Tomato and Rice Florentine Soup

This hearty soup is a nice addition to a formal meal, but you can serve it for casual crowd affairs as well. In any event, it's rather filling. Consider serving it with meatloaf or pot roast (see Chapter 5 for recipes) for a hearty side dish. This recipe also works well with sausage and spinach manicotti (also in Chapter 5).

Preparation time: *35 minutes*

Cooking time: *25 minutes*

Yield: *50 1¼-cup servings*

⅔ pound butter

2 medium white onions, diced

1 tablespoon minced garlic

¾ cup flour

¾ cup chicken bouillon granules

2 gallons water

4 pounds tomato paste

1 gallon warmed milk

3 pounds frozen spinach, thawed and squeezed dry

2 pounds canned, diced Italian-flavored tomatoes

16½ cups cooked wild rice

¼ cup sugar

2 tablespoons salt

1 teaspoon pepper

1 In a large frying pan, melt the butter.

2 Add the onions and garlic and sauté until tender, but not browned.

3 Slowly whisk in the flour and the chicken bouillon granules until the mixture is smooth. Continue to cook over very low heat for 5 minutes.

4 While the flour mixture is cooking, combine the water and tomato paste in a large stockpot and whisk until smooth.

5 Heat until the mixture bubbles, then reduce the heat to low.

6 Add the flour mixture to the paste mixture and stir until blended.

7 Add the milk and stir.

8 Add the remaining ingredients and stir until well blended.

9 Simmer over low heat for 25 minutes, stirring occasionally.

10 Remove from heat and let the soup set for 15 minutes before serving.

Tip: *Heat the milk slowly, over low heat, to make sure that you don't scorch it.*

Per serving: *Calories 202 (From Fat 71); Fat 8g (Saturated 5g); Cholesterol 24mg; Sodium 772mg; Carbohydrate 26g (Dietary Fiber 4g); Protein 9g.*

Belaboring bouillon

In case you're wondering, bouillon is technically a clear, thin broth made by simmering beef or chicken in water and seasonings. The term comes from an Old French word, *boulir,* which means "to boil." Because no one likes to wait around and see bouillon made, you can buy it in concentrated cubes or granules that dissolve in water — another great timesaver of the modern world.

Meat Soups and Stews: Tummy Fillers and Crowd Pleasers

Meat-based soups and stews are common reminders of cold winter days. Nothing is tastier on a blustery day than a hearty meat soup or stew.

As you're planning for your crowd, remember that meat soups and stews work well as a side dish, but they can also function as the main course. Plan accordingly, because you may not need a meat soup or stew if you're serving another meat dish. The following recipes are some of our favorites, and we even provide a few suggestions of what to serve them with.

Too skinny? Try a little roux!

Are your soups a little on the skinny side? Roux to the rescue! Roux, pronounced *roo*, is a thickening agent. All you do is create a mixture of butter and flour and cook it until it's bubbly. As you whisk the flour in the butter, the starch granules in the flour begin to break down. When you add liquid, the granules absorb it, and the sauce thickens. A *light roux* is used as a white base sauce, but you can also brown it very deeply and use it as the basis for étouffée and brown sauce.

Lasagne Soup

If you want to serve something with an Italian flare, this hearty lasagne soup will do the trick. It's a twist on the standard lasagne meal, but one your guests will love. This soup can work as a meal, but also try it with baked ziti or the sausage and spinach manicotti (see Chapter 5 for both recipes).

Preparation time: *35 minutes*

Cooking time: *25 minutes*

Yield: *50 1-cup servings*

1 pound ground beef	*3 50-ounce cans cold water*	*4 tablespoons garlic powder*
1 pound bulk Italian sausage	*1 pound, 8 ounces full-fat cottage cheese*	*4 tablespoons Italian seasoning*
14½ pounds corkscrew pasta or wide egg noodle pasta	*¼ cup (1 ounce) fresh grated Parmesan cheese*	*3 pounds canned diced tomatoes, drained*
3 50-ounce cans condensed tomato soup	*¼ cup (1 ounce) grated mozzarella cheese*	*⅔ cup fresh basil, chopped*

1 In a frying pan, brown the ground beef until no longer pink, remove it from heat, drain the excess grease, and set it aside. Do the same for the bulk Italian sausage.

2 Cook the pasta according to the package directions. Make sure to cook it *al dente,* which means a little firm, rather than mushy. Rinse the pasta with cold water and drain.

3 Cover and refrigerate the pasta while preparing the rest of the recipe.

4 In a large soup kettle, mix the tomato soup and water.

5 Add all the remaining ingredients (including the cooked beef and sausage), except the basil.

6 Simmer over low heat for 30 minutes, stirring occasionally.

7 Mix in the pasta and basil and simmer for another 5 minutes. Serve hot.

Tip: As a garnish, try topping the soup with some shredded mozzarella.

Per serving: Calories 323 (From Fat 53); Fat 6g (Saturated 2g); Cholesterol 14mg; Sodium 687mg; Carbohydrate 54g (Dietary Fiber 3g); Protein 13g.

Hearty Vegetable Beef Soup

Vegetable beef soup is probably one of the most popular types of soup. We're not trying to reinvent the wheel here, but keep this delicious recipe on hand whenever you need one of these soups, which work best as the main course.

Preparation time: 45 minutes

Cooking time: 1 hour

Yield: 24 1-cup servings

2 pounds lean ground beef

4 medium potatoes, cut into bite-size pieces

2 cups shredded cabbage

6 cups hot water

2 16-ounce cans (32 ounces) wedged tomatoes

2 10-ounce packages (20 ounces) frozen mixed vegetables

3 tablespoons beef bouillon granules

1 cup chopped onion

½ cup chopped fresh parsley

1 teaspoon pepper

1 teaspoon salt

1 Crumble the beef into a frying pan and cook it until it's no longer pink. Remove it from heat and drain the excess grease, then set it aside.

2 In a large stockpot, boil the potatoes until they're just about tender, and then drain them.

3 Return the potatoes to the pot and add all the remaining ingredients, including the beef.

4 Cook the soup over medium heat for 5 to 10 minutes.

5 Reduce the heat and simmer for 55 minutes, stirring occasionally. Serve hot.

Tip: If you want to add a little creativity to this soup, try serving it in bread bowls. You can use any small round breads and simply carve out the insides. Then fill the bread bowls with soup. Consider using the pieces of carved bread to make your own croutons!

Per serving: Calories 109 (From Fat 27); Fat 3g (Saturated 1g); Cholesterol 11mg; Sodium 986mg; Carbohydrate 13g (Dietary Fiber 2g); Protein 8g.

Creating your own croutons

Love croutons? So do we, and you can easily make your own. Try this quick and easy crouton recipe, which makes 24 servings:

1. Preheat the oven to 350 degrees.

2. Using approximately 30 slices of your favorite bread (any kind will work — even stale bread!), cut it into cubes or tear it into bite-size pieces.

3. Mix 4 teaspoons of your favorite dried herbs and spices (such as garlic or Italian seasoning) with ½ cup of olive oil or melted butter.

4. Brush the bread pieces on all sides with the olive oil or butter mixture, place them on an ungreased baking sheet, and bake them for 15 minutes, or until brown.

5. Let the croutons cool and store them in a covered container or plastic bag.

Tortilla Soup

Tortilla soup is one of our favorites. It's delicious and filling and very versatile. Plus, it provides a nice break from the traditional American soups. This recipe works great for a dinner party or a more casual crowd affair and nicely complements any of the Mexican dishes in Chapter 5.

Preparation time: *30 minutes*

Cooking time: *1 hour*

Yield: *50 1¼-cup servings*

2¼ gallons water

1¼ cups chicken bouillon granules

2 medium onions, diced

3 tablespoons minced garlic

2 teaspoons salt

4 pounds cooked chicken, diced or chopped

2¼ pounds canned, drained, and rinsed pinto beans

2¼ pounds canned, drained, and rinsed great Northern beans

2¼ pounds canned, drained, and rinsed kidney beans

2 pounds frozen corn

10 ounces canned, chopped green chiles

2½ red bell peppers, diced

3½ pounds canned, diced Mexican-flavor tomatoes

2 teaspoons cumin

1 tablespoon cilantro

2 teaspoons salt

12 cups (3 pounds) shredded cheddar cheese

2 pounds tortilla chips

1 In a large stockpot, heat the water to a low boil.

2 Add the chicken bouillon and whisk until the granules are completely dissolved.

3 Add the diced onions, garlic, and salt and bring to a boil.

4 Reduce the heat to low and simmer for 20 minutes.

5 Add the remaining ingredients, except the tortilla chips and cheese, to the pot. Bring the mixture to a boil.

6 Reduce the heat to low and simmer for 30 minutes, stirring occasionally.

7 Stir in 4 cups (1 pound) of the cheese.

8 Simmer for an additional 10 minutes, stirring to blend in the cheese.

9 Put the remainder of the cheese, along with the tortilla chips, each in a large bowl next to the soup to serve as toppings.

Tip: *If you're pressed for time, try using the precooked, diced chicken located in the freezer section of your favorite grocery store. If you choose this option, be sure to thaw the chicken in the microwave before adding it to your soup.*

Per serving: *Calories 347 (From Fat 158); Fat 18g (Saturated 8g); Cholesterol 62mg; Sodium 1,774mg; Carbohydrate 25g (Dietary Fiber 4g); Protein 23g.*

Home-Style Beef Stew

Beef stew is a standard menu item that works well with all kinds of meals or all by its lonesome. This recipe version will give you a very flavorful and hearty stew and is sure to be a crowd pleaser. Notice that the cooking time is over 4 hours. However, you can work on other recipes as the stew is cooking, so don't let the cooking time deter you. (Stews are also great because they can save stove space if you cook them in your slow cooker.)

Preparation time: *1 hour*

Cooking time: *4¼ hours*

Yield: *20 1¼-cup servings*

2 pounds small beef stew cubed meat	4 large potatoes, peeled and diced
2 teaspoons seasoned salt	6 carrots, sliced
2 teaspoons coarse black pepper	2 cups diced onion
1½ teaspoons garlic powder	2 celery stalks, sliced
8 cups water	3½ cups canned, drained corn
⅓ cup beef bouillon granules	5½ cups diced canned tomatoes
2 tablespoons Worcestershire sauce	4 10¾-ounce cans condensed cream of mushroom soup

1 In a large frying pan, brown the meat and sprinkle on the seasoned salt, pepper, and garlic powder. Set the meat aside.

2 In a large stockpot, heat the water and bouillon granules, whisking until the granules are dissolved.

3 Add the browned meat, Worcestershire sauce, potatoes, carrots, onions, and celery to the pot and bring to a boil.

4 Reduce the heat to low and cook for 3 hours.

5 Add the corn, tomatoes, and condensed soup and bring the mixture to a boil, stirring occasionally.

6 Reduce the heat to the lowest setting and cook for 1 hour.

7 Remove the stew from heat and allow it to set for 15 minutes before serving.

Tip: *When you cook a stew, keep in mind that you need allow time for it to cook slowly. The cooking time allows all the flavors to fully develop, giving you a rich, hearty stew.*

Per serving: *Calories 232 (From Fat 82); Fat 9g (Saturated 3g); Cholesterol 29mg; Sodium 1,462mg; Carbohydrate 27g (Dietary Fiber 4g); Protein 13g.*

Getting to know stockpots and Dutch ovens

If the terms *stockpot* and *Dutch oven* make you shrug your shoulders, never fear. A *stockpot* is a tall and narrow pot with straight sides, used for making stock or broth. A *Dutch oven,* on the other hand, is a shorter and wider pot, often with curved sides, that works well for making soups and stews. So if you're into making soups and stews for crowds, you want to have these items on hand. Generally, a 6-quart, heavy Dutch oven with a lid and a 10-quart stockpot with a lid will serve you well.

STOCK POT   DUTCH OVEN

For the Seafood Lovers

We love seafood, and seafood soups are always a welcome treat. Seafood soups work well with many different types of meals and are delicious year-round.

Seafood Gumbo

Seafood gumbo is probably the most popular kind of seafood soup, and rightly so. The combination of shrimp, rice, and spices makes a delicious side dish or a meal all on its own. You can find plenty of seafood gumbo recipes in cookbooks and on the Internet, but here's our favorite.

Preparation time: *55 minutes*

Cooking time: *50 minutes*

Yield: *32 1-cup servings*

½ cup vegetable oil

2 pounds Italian sausage links, sliced

2 pounds boneless, skinless chicken breasts, cubed

1½ large onions, chopped

2 medium sweet red peppers, chopped

6 celery stalks, chopped

2 teaspoons dried marjoram

2 teaspoons dried thyme

1 teaspoon garlic powder

1 teaspoon cayenne pepper

1 teaspoon salt

6 14½-ounce cans (87 ounces) chicken broth

1⅓ cups uncooked white or brown rice

2 14½-ounce cans (29 ounces) diced tomatoes, undrained

2 pounds uncooked medium shrimp, peeled and deveined

4 cups frozen sliced okra

1 In a large skillet, heat the oil and add the sausage and chicken; cook until the sausage is browned and the chicken is cooked through. Remove the meat from the pan, but keep it warm.

2 In the drippings, sauté the onions, red peppers, and celery until tender.

3 Stir in the seasonings and cook for 5 minutes over low heat.

4 In a large soup kettle, combine the broth, rice, chicken, and sausage along with the sautéed vegetables and heat the mixture until it boils.

5 Reduce the heat, cover the kettle, and simmer for 25 minutes or until the rice is tender.

6 Add the tomatoes, shrimp, and okra; cook over medium-low heat for 15 to 20 minutes or until the shrimp turn pink, stirring occasionally. Serve immediately.

Tip: If you want your gumbo to have a bit more spice, try adding a couple of dashes of hot sauce during the boiling phase. You can also use spicy sausage links in place of the Italian sausage. Still not enough heat for your taste buds? Chop up a couple of jalapeño peppers and add them to the mix.

Per serving: Calories 173 (From Fat 85); Fat 10g (Saturated 2g); Cholesterol 71mg; Sodium 634mg; Carbohydrate 7g (Dietary Fiber 1g); Protein 15g.

Clam Chowder

When you hear the word *chowder,* you probably automatically think of clam. After all, clam chowder is the most popular. This thick, chunky mixture is sure to warm you to the bone on those cold winter days. As an added bonus, chowder is very filling, so it goes a long way if you're trying to fill up a hungry crowd. Clam chowder works well as a meal itself, or you can serve it as an appetizer for other seafood meals.

Preparation time: *35 minutes*

Cooking time: *35 minutes*

Yield: *24 1-cup servings*

9 cups water	*6 6½-ounce cans (39 ounces) minced clams*	*½ cup, 1 tablespoon butter*
6 chicken bouillon cubes		*1 cup flour*
12 medium, round, red potatoes, diced	*12 slices bacon, cut into 1-inch pieces*	*12 cups milk*
	2¼ cups chopped onion	*1½ teaspoons salt*
		1 teaspoon pepper

1 In a large soup kettle, add the water and bouillon cubes and bring to a boil.

2 Add the potatoes and simmer for 10 minutes, or until they're tender. Drain them and set them aside.

3 Drain the clams, reserving the juice, and set them aside.

4 In a large skillet, cook the bacon and onions over medium-high heat, stirring constantly, until the bacon is crisp and the onions are tender.

5 Remove the bacon and onions from the pan. Reserve 2 tablespoons of the drippings from the pan and discard the rest.

6 In the soup kettle you used to cook the potatoes, add the drippings and butter and cook over low heat until the butter has melted.

7 Slowly add the flour, stirring until the mixture is smooth.

8 Cook the flour mixture over low heat for 1 minute, stirring constantly.

9 Gradually add the reserved clam juice and milk. Cook the mixture over medium heat, stirring constantly, until thickened and bubbly.

10 Remove the kettle from heat and stir in the potatoes, clams, bacon, onion, salt, and pepper.

11 Return the kettle to low heat, stirring occasionally, and cook for approximately 10 to 15 minutes, or until heated through. Serve hot.

Per serving: *Calories 252 (From Fat 91); Fat 10g (Saturated 6g); Cholesterol 39mg; Sodium 853mg; Carbohydrate 29g (Dietary Fiber 2g); Protein 11g.*

Hey chowderhead, don't you know what gumbo is?

You've probably heard the words *chowder* and *gumbo* for most of your adult life, but if someone put you on the spot and asked for a definition, could you explain the terms? Don't worry. Lots of people eat chowders and gumbos but don't exactly know what the terms mean, so here's the skinny:

✔ *Chowder* is a thick soup or stew made from milk, bacon, onions, and potatoes. Of course, what goes in a chowder varies according to recipe and taste. Clam chowder has been popular in Canada and New

England for hundreds of years, and most historians agree that English and French fishermen brought it to North America.

✔ *Gumbo* is a soup or stew that has been thickened with okra. In fact, the word *gumbo* is taken from several African terms that mean "okra." Gumbo is a Cajun soup or stew, and as you see in the seafood gumbo recipe, it normally has a variety of ingredients. Gumbos range from mild to very spicy in flavor.

Seafood Chowder

Seafood chowder takes the standard clam chowder a step further by introducing different kinds of seafood. This taste variation is sure to be a favorite.

Preparation time: *40 minutes*

Cooking time: *40 minutes*

Yield: *24 1-cup servings*

½ cup vegetable oil

5 large onions, chopped

2 large green peppers, chopped

¼ cup flour

6 14½-ounce cans (87 ounces) stewed tomatoes, undrained

2 tablespoons celery salt

2 teaspoons garlic powder

2 teaspoons hot sauce

1 teaspoon pepper

3 pounds peeled and cooked small or medium shrimp

1 pound fresh lump crabmeat

1 pound firm whitefish, cut into bite-size pieces

2 12-ounce containers (24 ounces) oysters, drained

1 In a Dutch oven, heat the oil and add the onions and green peppers. Cook over medium-high heat until tender.

2 Add the flour, stirring constantly, and cook 1 minute.

3 Stir in the tomatoes — remember, don't drain them! — and seasonings.

4 Bring the mixture to a boil, cover it, and reduce the heat and simmer for 20 minutes.

5 Add the shrimp, crabmeat, fish, and oysters; stir until well mixed.

6 Cover and simmer for 20 minutes; serve hot.

Tip: *Remember, chowders can be very thick. If this recipe is too thick for your taste, add 2 cups of water when you add the tomatoes.*

Per serving: *Calories 209 (From Fat 61); Fat 7g (Saturated 1g); Cholesterol 151mg; Sodium 854mg; Carbohydrate 12g (Dietary Fiber 3g); Protein 22g.*

Chapter 8

Stirring It Up: Punches and Drinks

In This Chapter

▷ Going the traditional route with punches

▷ Cooling off and quenching your thirst

▷ Keeping toasty on a wintry day

*T*ypically, when someone plans for a crowd event, that person forgets about the drinks to offer. One may think, "Tea, cola, coffee — that's it, plain and simple." However, with just a little work, you can easily make some creative punches, teas, lemonades, and other desirable drinks that will surely create smiles. So why not plan ahead and invest a small amount of time in drinks?

You don't have to spend a lot of time and energy worrying about what drinks to serve. After all, your event may easily dictate the choices you should make. This chapter helps you out, too. We give you our favorite drink recipes, and we include only those that work great for crowd events. If you're serving vegetarians, rest assured that they can safely enjoy any of the drinks in this chapter without a guilty conscience. Try them!

Note: Generally speaking, the serving size for punches and drinks is about 1 cup.

Socking It to 'Em: Punches

When you cook for a crowd, a good punch always works great. Punches are usually very easy to make because they're typically combinations of other products, such as juice and carbonated beverages.

An attention-getting garnish: The ice ring

If you want to make your punch extra special, take a little bit of extra time to make an ice ring. Ice rings are easy to make, keep your punch cold, and are nice to look at as well. Here's how to make one:

1. Fill a bundt pan, a ring-shaped cake pan, or a gelatin mold halfway with whatever type of soft drink (or ginger ale) or fruit juice the recipe calls for, and then allow it to partially freeze.

2. After the ring is partially frozen, add edible flowers or fruit and then fill the mold with additional soft drink or fruit juice.

3. Freeze the mold completely. Just before you're ready to serve the punch, put the ice ring in it. Your guests will think you deserve a creativity award!

Of course, you can make an ice ring without adding the flowers or fruit; simply fill up the mold from the get-go and freeze it.

Punches are best served very cold. To help keep your punches cold, you can either make flavored ice cubes or an ice ring. Flavored ice cubes are easy — just fill ice cube trays with either the punch itself or one of the fruit juices from the punch. If you want something more creative (yet still easy), see the sidebar, "An attention-getting garnish: The ice ring."

Fruity Punch

So many fruit punch recipes are on the books that you may have trouble deciding which one is the best. This fruit punch, one of our all-time standbys, has seen so many requests that we've lost track. The combination of the cranberry, lemonade, and orange flavors gives it a distinctive flavor.

Preparation time: *10 minutes*

Chill time: *3 hours*

Yield: *20 servings*

4 cups cranberry cocktail juice

½ gallon prepared lemonade

2 cups orange juice

4-ounce jar maraschino cherries, drained

2 liters ginger ale, chilled

1 In a gallon-size pitcher, combine the cranberry juice, lemonade, and orange juice.

2 Stir in the cherries, cover the pitcher, and refrigerate it for 3 hours.

3 Pour the juice and the cherries into a punch bowl.

4 Add the ginger ale, stir, and serve.

Tip: Be sure to allow this punch to cure for 3 hours. If you want to save some time, make the base (fruit juices) up to 2 days in advance. Just make sure you keep it tightly covered in the refrigerator — you don't want your punch tasting like the onion dip you also made in advance!

Per serving: Calories 120 (From Fat 1); Fat 0g (Saturated 0g); Cholesterol 0mg; Sodium 12mg; Carbohydrate 30g (Dietary Fiber 0g); Protein 0g.

Sunshine Fruit Punch

This tangy, refreshing punch is a wonderful choice for any occasion. The chunks of fruit make this punch a more filling choice.

Preparation time: 15 minutes

Chill time: 30 minutes

Yield: 25 to 30 servings

46 ounces pineapple juice

12 ounces frozen orange juice concentrate, thawed

1 cup lemonade concentrate, thawed

1 cup water, divided

3 large, ripe bananas

20-ounce package frozen, sweetened, sliced or whole strawberries, thawed

½ cup sugar

2 liters ginger ale, chilled

1 In a large punch bowl, combine the pineapple juice, orange juice concentrate, lemonade concentrate, and ½ cup of water.

2 Place the bananas, strawberries, ½ cup of water, and sugar in a blender. Blend until smooth.

3 Stir the banana and strawberry mixture into the juice mixture. Cover and refrigerate for 30 minutes.

4 Right before serving, stir in the ginger ale.

Per serving: Calories 127 (From Fat 2); Fat 0g (Saturated 0g); Cholesterol 0mg; Sodium 7mg; Carbohydrate 32g (Dietary Fiber 1g); Protein 1g.

Society Punch

This standard punch works for any event, although you typically see it at weddings and other formal crowd affairs. It's quick and easy, so put it to work when you need it.

Preparation time: *10 minutes*

Yield: *40 servings*

2 liters ginger ale, chilled	*46 ounces pineapple juice, chilled*	*64 ounces white grape juice, chilled*

Combine all the ingredients in a large punch bowl and stir; serve immediately.

Tip: *Try making an ice ring for this wonderful, sophisticated punch. You can make a plain ice ring or go all out and make a decorative one. The ring keeps the punch cold and creates a visual appeal. See the sidebar "An attention-getting garnish: The ice ring" for instructions.*

Per serving: *Calories 65 (From Fat 0); Fat 0g (Saturated 0g); Cholesterol 0mg; Sodium 8mg; Carbohydrate 16g (Dietary Fiber 0g); Protein 0g.*

Heading South: Teas, Lemonade, and Limeade

When you think about summer drinks, teas, lemonade, and limeade usually come to mind. They're all so refreshing and come in a variety of flavors. Naturally, you can serve standard tea, lemonade, and limeade without any fuss, but if you want something a bit different (and still easy to prepare), try these delicious variations.

As you serve iced tea, keep in mind that as the ice melts, the tea will become diluted. To prevent the tea from losing its great flavor, serve it over ice cubes made out of the tea.

Frosty Pineapple Limeade

This drink combines the taste of pineapple with limeade for a tart summer treat. It's simple to whip up, but keep in mind that it needs to chill for 8 hours — the wait is definitely worth it, in our opinion.

Preparation time: *10 minutes*

Chill time: *8 hours*

Yield: *30 to 35 servings*

1 gallon pineapple juice	*3 cups sugar*
3 cups fresh lime juice (about 16 limes) or lime juice concentrate	*4 liters lime-flavored sparkling water*

1 Pour the pineapple juice into an extra-large plastic pitcher.

2 In a bowl, mix the lime juice with the sugar and stir until the sugar is dissolved.

3 Add the lime-and-sugar mixture to the juice and stir.

4 Cover the pitcher and freeze for 8 hours.

5 Just before serving, remove the pitcher from the freezer and run it under hot water to loosen the frozen mixture — it doesn't have to come out in one piece.

6 Place the frozen mixture in a large punch bowl and allow it to slightly thaw.

7 Pour the sparkling water over the frozen mixture and stir it until well mixed; serve.

Tip: *The concept of this recipe is similar to sherbet punch. Allow the punch to sit out long enough for it to become slushy, but remember to stir it occasionally to keep all the flavors blended.*

Per serving: *Calories 136 (From Fat 1); Fat 0g (Saturated 0g); Cholesterol 0mg; Sodium 2mg; Carbohydrate 35g (Dietary Fiber 0g); Protein 1g.*

Lemon Tea with Almond

Iced tea comes in all different flavors these days, but one thing remains the same: A tall glass of it is sure to quench any thirst. Your guests will love this lemon tea with almond. It's a bit unique but still easy to prepare.

Preparation time: *25 minutes*

Yield: *32 servings*

½ gallon water

30 individual tea bags

1½ cups sugar

2 12-ounce cans (24 ounces) frozen lemonade concentrate

3 teaspoons almond extract

1½ gallons cold water

fresh lemon slices for garnish (optional)

1 In a large saucepan, bring the water to a boil.

2 Remove the water from heat, add the tea bags, cover the pan, and let the tea steep for 10 minutes.

3 After the tea has steeped, remove the tea bags.

4 Stir the sugar into the tea until it has dissolved.

5 Pour the tea into an extra-large drink pitcher or drink dispenser and stir in the frozen lemonade concentrate, almond extract, and cold water. Drop the fresh lemon slices into the tea (if desired) and serve the tea over ice.

Per serving: *Calories 77 (From Fat 0); Fat 0g (Saturated 0g); Cholesterol 0mg; Sodium 1mg; Carbohydrate 19g (Dietary Fiber 0g); Protein 0g.*

Peach Tea

Someone came up with the idea of mixing tea with fruit, and what an idea it was! Peach tea has become wildly popular along with some other fruit-flavored teas, such as raspberry and apricot. Peach tea is sweet, satisfying, and very easy to make.

Preparation time: *25 minutes*

Yield: *32 servings*

½ gallon water

30 individual tea bags

1 cup sugar

2 12-ounce cans (24 ounces) frozen peach juice concentrate

1½ gallons cold water

fresh peach slices for garnish (optional)

1 In a large saucepan, bring the ½ gallon of water to a boil.

2 Remove the water from heat, add the tea bags, cover the pan, and let the tea steep for 10 minutes.

3 Remove the tea bags and stir the sugar into the tea until it has dissolved.

4 Pour the tea into an extra-large drink pitcher or drink dispenser and stir in the frozen peach concentrate and cold water. Drop the fresh peach slices into the pitcher. Serve the tea over ice.

Tip: *If you can't find frozen peach juice concentrate, substitute 3 cans of peach nectar. You can find peach nectar with the other canned juices at your local grocery store.*

Per serving: *Calories 65 (From Fat 0); Fat 0g (Saturated 0g); Cholesterol 0mg; Sodium 7mg; Carbohydrate 17g (Dietary Fiber 0g); Protein 0g.*

Sparkling Raspberry Lemonade

Think about summer, and what drink comes to mind? Lemonade. Cool and refreshing with just the right amount of sweetness and tartness, lemonade is a classic drink to be enjoyed by all.

As with teas, people over the years have become creative. Again, our friend fruit got together with lemonade and spawned a whole new generation of lemonade connoisseurs.

Preparation time: *15 minutes*

Yield: *36 servings*

6 cups cold water

2 12-ounce cans (24 ounces) frozen raspberry lemonade concentrate

2 teaspoons lime juice

6 cups lemon-lime-flavored soft drink, chilled

2 cups crushed ice

2 cups fresh raspberries

1 In a large punch bowl or extra-large drink pitcher, mix the cold water, frozen raspberry lemonade concentrate, and lime juice. Stir until the concentrate and water have thoroughly blended.

2 Add the lemon-lime soft drink, ice, and raspberries and stir. Serve immediately.

Tip: *When you serve drinks, keep in mind that recipes calling for soft drinks will have carbonation. Carbonation adds a lot to any drink, but it must not sit out for an extended period of time, or the drink will go flat.*

Per serving: *Calories 54 (From Fat 1); Fat 0g (Saturated 0g); Cholesterol 0mg; Sodium 5mg; Carbohydrate 14g (Dietary Fiber 1g); Protein 0g.*

Warming Up: Hot Drinks

Nothing warms you up like a steamy, hot cup of your favorite winter beverage. We love to serve hot beverages at winter get-togethers and holidays, and you'll find that hot drinks are always in style.

If you're looking for a hot drink to serve at a Thanksgiving or Christmas crowd event, be sure to check out Chapter 11 for some additional recipes.

Peppermint Hot Cocoa

Hot chocolate is one of those heartwarming drinks, but this one gives you an extra kick with the flavor of peppermint.

Preparation time: *35 minutes*

Yield: *20 servings*

20 cups milk	20 peppermint candies, crushed
15 ounces semisweet chocolate squares, chopped	5 cups whipped cream
	20 small candy canes to garnish (optional)

1 In a stockpot, heat the milk over low heat until it's hot, but not boiling. Stir the milk occasionally so it doesn't scald.

2 Whisk in the chocolate and crushed peppermint candies until both have melted and the mixture is smooth.

3 Pour the hot chocolate into mugs, top it with whipped cream, and garnish with a small candy cane hanging on the side of the mug (if desired).

Per serving: *Calories 374 (From Fat 249); Fat 28g (Saturated 17g); Cholesterol 74mg; Sodium 134mg; Carbohydrate 27g (Dietary Fiber 1g); Protein 10g.*

Café Mocha

Café Mocha means coffee, milk, and chocolate. Coffee is great plain, but thanks to the creation of the coveted coffeehouse, flavored coffees have taken the world by storm, one cup at a time.

This recipe is very easy to make, but the flavor is so good that you and your guests will be surprised.

Preparation time: *15 minutes*

Cooking time: *15 minutes*

Yield: *20 servings*

20 cups hot brewed coffee	*2½ cups milk*
1¼ cups sugar	*whipped cream for garnish (optional)*
1¼ cups unsweetened cocoa powder	

1 Pour the hot coffee into a large stockpot and add the sugar and cocoa powder. Stir the mixture until the cocoa and sugar are completely melted and incorporated into the coffee.

2 Microwave the milk until it's hot, but not boiling.

3 Mix the milk in with the coffee.

4 Pour the mixture into mugs and top it with whipped cream, if desired.

Tip: *If you want to really wow your guests, try placing a chocolate kiss candy in the bottom of each mug before adding the coffee. Extra chocolate is always a good thing!*

Per serving: *Calories 84 (From Fat 16); Fat 2g (Saturated 1g); Cholesterol 4mg; Sodium 21mg; Carbohydrate 18g (Dietary Fiber 2g); Protein 2g.*

Hot Cranberry Tea

This recipe is a bit more unusual, but the hot cranberry taste will be well received by your crowd.

Preparation time: *20 minutes*

Cooking time: *20 minutes*

Yield: *32 servings*

12 cups water

4 tablespoons instant tea powder

2 teaspoons ground allspice

2 teaspoons ground cinnamon

2 3-ounce packages (6 ounces) cherry-flavored gelatin

1 cup sugar

2 cups orange juice

½ cup lemon juice

2 quarts cranberry juice

cinnamon sticks for garnish (optional)

1 In a stockpot, boil the water and add the instant tea and spices, stirring until thoroughly mixed.

2 Remove the stockpot from heat; cover it and allow the tea to steep for 5 minutes.

3 Stir in the gelatin and sugar and mix until both have dissolved.

4 Add the juices and simmer uncovered for 15 minutes. Serve hot, placing one cinnamon stick in each mug of tea, if desired.

Per serving: Calories 89 (From Fat 1); Fat 0g (Saturated 0g); Cholesterol 0mg; Sodium 19mg; Carbohydrate 22g (Dietary Fiber 0g); Protein 1g.

Buttered Maple Apple Cider

This sweet, buttery apple cider is a comforting, soothing beverage to serve on a cold winter's night.

Preparation time: *10 minutes*

Cooking time: *30 minutes*

Yield: *32 servings*

2 gallons apple cider	*2 teaspoons ground nutmeg*
1 cup maple syrup	*2 teaspoons ground allspice*
1½ cups butter, softened	

1 Pour the apple cider into a large pot and add the maple syrup.

2 Cook the cider and syrup mixture over medium heat for 30 minutes, stirring occasionally.

3 Meanwhile, in a small bowl, combine the softened butter and spices and mix well.

4 Pour the apple cider into mugs, add a teaspoon of spiced butter, and serve.

Tip: *If you serve this drink in a self-serve setting where the guests pour their own mugs, try getting creative with the spiced butter. Instead of putting it out in a bowl, try using a small melon baller and making butter balls.*

Per serving: *Calories 223 (From Fat 77); Fat 9g (Saturated 5g); Cholesterol 23mg; Sodium 27mg; Carbohydrate 37g (Dietary Fiber 0g); Protein 0g.*

Chapter 9

Decadent Desserts

In This Chapter

▷ Eating by the dozen — cookies, that is

▷ Coloring your kitchen with brown(ies)

▷ Having your cake (You know the rest)

▷ Going out on a limb: Different desserts that will melt your heart

Ah, desserts. Nothing is quite like a delicious and satisfying dessert to put the perfect ending to the perfect meal. When you cook for a crowd, you naturally want everything to be perfect, so don't let dessert slip to the back of your mind. In fact, many people consider dessert to be the pinnacle of the meal. Knowing that, you should carefully plan ahead. And don't worry — you've come to the right place!

We love desserts, so we're happy to share our favorites with you. We regularly cook these items at a variety of crowd events, and guests always gobble them up immediately. In this chapter, we include desserts that work well for both informal and formal events. Either way, your guests will love these desserts, even if they do add an inch or two to the waistline!

Vegetarians in the mix? Fear no more — all the desserts in this chapter are in the clear.

If you're a die-hard dessert lover, be sure to check out *Desserts For Dummies* by Bill Yosses and Brian Miller, published by Wiley.

Comforting Cookies

Remember coming home from school and being welcomed by the smell of home-baked cookies wafting out from the kitchen? Amazing how a little sugar, flour, and other assorted ingredients can create such a welcoming little piece of heaven, otherwise known as a cookie.

Whether or not they had that school-day welcome, most everyone loves cookies, and we're no exception. We've tried (and consumed!) all kinds, and we share with you our favorites in this section.

Chocolate Chip Cookie Bars

You can't have cookie recipes without at least one really good chocolate chip recipe in the bunch. Chocolate chip cookies are a requirement of most cookie connoisseurs, and this one fits the bill. These cookie bars are easy to make, and because they're bars, they take less time to prepare and are easy to serve.

Preparation time: *10 minutes*

Cooking time: *40 minutes*

Yield: *42 bars*

3 cups flour

1 cup light brown sugar, packed

1 cup cold butter

4 cups semisweet chocolate chips, divided

2 14-ounce cans (28 ounces) sweetened condensed milk (not evaporated)

2 eggs

2 teaspoons vanilla extract

2 cups chopped pecans

1 Preheat the oven to 350 degrees.

2 In a large bowl, stir together the flour and brown sugar.

3 Cut the cold butter into pieces and blend it into the flour and sugar mixture until the mixture resembles coarse crumbs.

4 Stir in 1 cup of the chocolate chips, and then divide the mixture in half.

5 Grease two 13-x-9-x-2-inch pans and press each half of the mixture into the bottom of each pan.

6 Bake the dough for 15 minutes.

7 Meanwhile, in a large bowl, whisk together the sweetened condensed milk, eggs, and vanilla extract.

8 Add the remaining 3 cups of chocolate chips and the pecans and stir.

9 Divide the mixture in half and spread each half on the baked crust.

10 Bake for 25 minutes or until golden brown.

11 Remove the pans from the oven and cool the giant cookies completely — in the pan — on a wire rack. After they've cooled, cut them into bars.

Per serving: Calories 301 (From Fat 148); Fat 17g (Saturated 8g); Cholesterol 28mg; Sodium 30mg; Carbohydrate 37g (Dietary Fiber 2g); Protein 3g.

Raspberry Thumbprints

These cookies aren't only pretty to look at — the almond and raspberry combination is also very satisfying. They're delightful anytime, but they work especially well at holiday meals.

Preparation time: *30 minutes*

Chill time: *3 hours*

Cooking time: *15 to 17 minutes per batch*

Yield: *4 dozen*

1 cup butter, softened	*2½ cups flour*
1 cup sugar	*1⅓ cups sliced blanched almonds, coarsely chopped*
2 eggs	
2 teaspoons vanilla extract	*4 tablespoons seedless raspberry jam*
½ teaspoon salt	*confectioners' sugar*

1 In a large bowl, beat the butter, using an electric mixer, until creamy.

2 Gradually add the sugar and beat the mixture until well blended.

3 As shown in Figure 9-1, carefully separate the egg yolks and whites, making sure none of the yolks get in with the whites, and place them in two small bowls. Cover the egg whites and place them in the refrigerator.

4 Add the egg yolks, vanilla extract, and salt to the butter and sugar mixture and beat until blended.

5 Stir in the flour and mix until well blended. The dough will be crumbly, but you should be able to press it together easily.

6 Form the dough into a ball. Place it back in the bowl, cover it with plastic wrap, and refrigerate it for 3 hours.

7 After the dough has chilled, remove it from the refrigerator and let it stand at room temperature for 5 minutes.

8 Meanwhile, preheat the oven to 350 degrees, grease two baking sheets, and place the chopped almonds on a plate.

9 Shape the dough into 48 1-inch balls.

10 Remove the egg whites from the refrigerator and lightly beat them until they're well mixed.

11 Dip each ball into the egg whites and then roll it in the almonds, pressing firmly. Place the balls on the greased baking sheets about an inch apart.

12 Using your thumb, make an indentation in the middle of each cookie. Fill each indentation with about ¼ teaspoon of the raspberry jam.

13 Bake each sheet of cookies for 15 to 17 minutes or until lightly browned, then remove the cookies to wire racks and allow them to cool.

14 Meanwhile, cut several small circles out of wax paper, about the size of the raspberry centers.

15 Lay the wax paper circles on top of the raspberry centers and dust the cookies with confectioners' sugar, repeating until you've dusted all the cookies.

16 Remove the wax paper circles and serve.

Per serving: Calories 96 (From Fat 49); Fat 5g (Saturated 3g); Cholesterol 19mg; Sodium 28mg; Carbohydrate 11g (Dietary Fiber 1g); Protein 2g.

How to Separate an Egg

Figure 9-1: Separating egg yolks.

1. Hold the egg in one hand over two small bowls.
2. Crack the shell on the side of one bowl.
3. Let the white fall into one of the bowls.
4. Pass the yolk back & forth, each time releasing more white.
5. When all the white is in the bowl, drop yolk in the other bowl.

Anemic nuts, anyone?

If you check your dictionary, you'll see that *blanched* means "deathly pale or anemic." Well, in terms of blanched nuts, we're not talking about deathly pale or anemic nuts (thank goodness). In the nut world, *blanched* means to immerse in boiling water. The purpose is to deactivate the enzymes in the nut in order to loosen the skin and soak away excess salt. In many recipes, the extra skins need to be removed, so if a recipe calls for blanched nuts of any kind, make sure you don't substitute non-blanched options.

Mint Chocolate Candy Cookies

These cookies are delicious, and eating only one is a big challenge! Each cookie contains a surprise center — a melted chocolate mint. The mint chocolate candy centers are a delightful and surprising addition, so make extras because these cookies go quickly!

Preparation time: 10 minutes

Chill time: 2 hours

Cooking time: 10 to 12 minutes per batch

Yield: 7 dozen

2 cups butter

2 cups sugar

1 cup packed brown sugar

4 eggs

2 teaspoons vanilla extract

6 cups flour

2 teaspoons baking powder

1 teaspoon salt

130 chocolate mint candies, such as Andes Mints

1 In a large bowl, beat the butter, sugar, and brown sugar until well blended.

2 Add the eggs, one at a time, beating well after each egg.

3 Beat in the vanilla extract.

4 In a medium bowl, combine the flour, baking powder, and salt.

5 Gradually add the flour mixture to the butter mixture, stirring until they're thoroughly mixed.

6 Cover the mixture and refrigerate it for 2 hours.

7 After the dough is chilled, preheat the oven to 375 degrees and grease a baking sheet.

8 Flour your hands, and then shape a tablespoon of dough around each of 84 chocolate mint candies; place as many as will fit about 2 inches apart on the greased baking sheet.

9 Bake the cookies for 10 to 12 minutes or until the edges are golden brown; don't overcook.

10 Remove the cookies to wire racks to cool. Regrease the baking sheet and bake another batch, repeating this process until all the cookies are baked.

11 While the cookies are cooling, make the glaze: Put the remaining chocolate mint candies in a microwavable bowl and heat them until just melted. Don't overheat the chocolate! The candies may somewhat hold their shape even though they've melted.

12 Stir the melted candy until it's smooth, then drizzle it over the cookies; let the cookies cool, and serve.

Crowd Saver: You can prepare this mixture the day before and refrigerate it overnight.

Per serving: Calories 196 (From Fat 79); Fat 9g (Saturated 5g); Cholesterol 22mg; Sodium 42mg; Carbohydrate 28g (Dietary Fiber 1g); Protein 2g.

Beyond Your Ordinary Brownies

We love brownies, and we've tried a number of different recipes. They're the perfect dessert for crowd cooking because they're easy to store and easy to serve. So try out our favorites!

Peppermint Fudge Brownies

The peppermint and fudge in these brownies makes a tasty combination that's especially enjoyable around Christmas and Valentine's Day. These brownies are easy to make, rich in flavor, and will be enjoyed by all. What's more, you can make this treat *way* in advance without sacrificing taste.

Preparation time: *20 minutes*

Cooking time: *15 to 18 minutes*

Chill time: *15 minutes*

Yield: *4 dozen*

8 eggs	*2 teaspoons vanilla extract*
4 cups sugar	*1 teaspoon peppermint extract*
2 cups flour	*Mint Cream Frosting (see the following recipe)*
2 cups cocoa powder	
2 cups butter, melted	*Chocolate Glaze (see the following recipe)*

1 Preheat the oven to 350 degrees.

2 In a large bowl, beat the eggs with a wire whisk. Add the sugar and stir until the mixture is well blended.

3 In a medium bowl, combine the flour and cocoa powder.

4 Slowly add the flour and cocoa mixture to the egg and sugar mixture.

5 Stir in the melted butter and vanilla and peppermint extracts.

6 Grease two 15-x-10-x-1-inch jellyroll pans.

7 Divide the batter in half and pour each half into a greased pan.

8 Bake the brownies for 15 to 18 minutes or until a wooden toothpick inserted in the center comes out clean.

9 Remove the brownies from the oven and cool them in the pans on a wire rack.

10 While the brownies are cooling, make the mint cream frosting.

11 Spread the frosting over the brownies, and then place them in the freezer for 15 minutes.

12 About 5 minutes before you need to remove the brownies from the freezer, begin making the chocolate glaze.

13 Using a pastry brush, spread the glaze over the frosted brownies.

14 Return the brownies to the freezer and chill about 10 to 15 minutes, until firm.

15 Remove the brownies from the freezer and cut them into squares; serve.

Mint Cream Frosting

½ cup butter, softened
3¼ cups sifted confectioners' sugar
6 tablespoons milk

1 teaspoon peppermint extract
6 to 8 drops green food coloring

1 Beat the butter with an electric mixer on medium speed until smooth.

2 Gradually add the confectioners' sugar, beating after each addition.

3 Add the milk and beat until the frosting is a good spreading consistency.

4 Stir in the peppermint extract and food coloring until even in color.

Chocolate Glaze

6 ounces semisweet chocolate squares   *3 tablespoons butter*

Melt the chocolate squares and butter in a heavy saucepan over low heat, stirring constantly.

Tip: *You can freeze these wonderful treats for up to 3 months. When you're ready to use them, thaw them in the refrigerator overnight and reheat them at 350 degrees for 5 to 10 minutes. You can reheat them in the microwave, but the oven works best in order to maintain the texture.*

Per serving: Calories 247 (From Fat 117); Fat 13g (Saturated 8g); Cholesterol 63mg; Sodium 14mg; Carbohydrate 33g (Dietary Fiber 1g); Protein 3g.

Heavenly Turtle Brownies

If you love caramel, this is the brownie for you! Turtle brownies are a classic, and most people love them. This recipe ensures that you get moist, rich brownies that everyone will enjoy.

Preparation time: *30 minutes*

Cooking time: *55 minutes*

Yield: *4 dozen*

8 squares unsweetened baking chocolate

1½ cups butter

4 cups sugar

8 eggs

2 cups flour

2 14-ounce packages (28 ounces) caramels, unwrapped

⅔ cup heavy cream

4 cups pecan halves, divided

2 12-ounce packages (24 ounces) semisweet chocolate chips, divided

1 Preheat the oven to 350 degrees.

2 In a microwaveable bowl, combine the baking chocolate and butter. Microwave on high for 2 minutes, or until the butter is melted, and stir until well blended.

3 Stir in the sugar until the mixture is well blended.

4 Mix in the eggs and then stir in the flour, making sure it's thoroughly incorporated into the mixture.

5 Roughly divide the batter into fourths.

6 Line two 13-x-9-x-2-inch pans with parchment paper. Leave enough parchment paper at both ends to help lift the brownies out of the pan, and spread one-fourth of the batter into each parchment-lined pan.

7 Bake for 25 minutes or until the batter is firm to the touch.

8 While the brownies are baking, combine the caramels and heavy cream in a microwave-able bowl. Heat on high for 3 minutes or until the caramels begin to melt.

9 Whisk the caramel mixture until it's smooth, then stir in 2 cups of the pecan halves.

10 Divide the mixture in half, and gently spread it over each pan of brownies; sprinkle the chocolate chips on top.

11 Evenly pour the remaining unbaked brownie mix over the caramel and chocolate chips and sprinkle the remaining pecan halves on top.

12 Bake the brownies for 30 minutes, and then remove them from the oven and allow them to cool in the pan.

13 Run a knife along the edges of the pan to loosen the sides. Grasping the parchment paper, lift out the brownies. Cut each pan of brownies into 24 pieces and serve.

Warning: Everyone loves shortcuts, but in the case of this recipe, don't substitute caramel ice cream topping in place of the caramel squares. You won't get the same texture or taste. We made this substitution mistake ourselves, and you won't be happy with the results!

Per serving: *Calories 368 (From Fat 193); Fat 21g (Saturated 10g); Cholesterol 21mg; Sodium 53mg; Carbohydrate 45g (Dietary Fiber 3g); Protein 4g.*

Peanut Butter Brownies

Peanut butter and chocolate is a match made in heaven — these two flavors were meant to be together. You can serve these brownies cool, or for an extraspecial dessert, serve them warm with a scoop of vanilla ice cream on top, a dash of chocolate syrup, and some chopped peanuts.

Preparation time: *15 minutes*

Cooking time: *35 to 40 minutes*

Yield: *6 dozen*

1 cup butter, softened	2 teaspoons vanilla extract
½ cup creamy peanut butter	4 cups flour
2 cups sugar	4 teaspoons baking powder
2 cups packed light brown sugar	½ teaspoon salt
6 eggs	1 cup chocolate syrup, divided

1 Preheat the oven to 350 degrees.

2 In a large bowl, blend the butter and peanut butter. Add the sugar and brown sugar and beat well.

3 Add the eggs one at a time, beating well after each egg.

4 Blend in the vanilla extract.

5 Add the flour, baking powder, and salt and stir until well blended.

6 Grease two 13-x-9-x-2-inch pans and spread one-fourth of the batter into each pan.

7 Spoon ½ cup of the chocolate syrup over the batter in each pan and spread it evenly.

8 Spread the remaining batter carefully over the chocolate syrup, then gently swirl a spatula over the top of the brownies for a marble effect.

9 Bake the brownies for 35 to 40 minutes or until lightly browned.

10 Remove the brownies from the oven and allow them to cool, then cut them into squares and serve.

Per serving: Calories 120 (From Fat 35); Fat 4g (Saturated 2g); Cholesterol 25mg; Sodium 56mg; Carbohydrate 20g (Dietary Fiber 0g); Protein 2g.

Cake, Anyone?

Cake is a mainstay of desserts, and rightly so. It has been around for centuries, and so many different recipes exist that choosing one can be difficult.

As with cookies and brownies, we love cake (see a pattern here?) and have tried a lot of cake recipes over the years. The following recipes give you our tried-and-true favorites.

TIP

The right way to cut cake

Ever freeze up when getting ready to cut a cake or pie? Do you make your first two cuts and then wonder, "How am I going to get 8 (or 6, or 12, or whatever) slices out of this?" Cutting too few servings is never a good idea, and uneven slices aren't pretty. The following illustrations show you a good way to approach cake slicing.

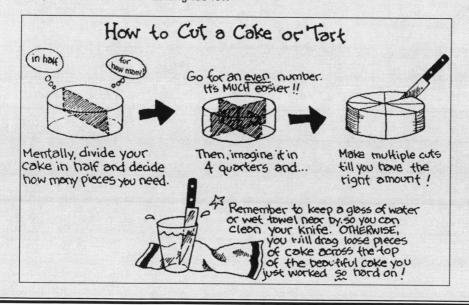

Carrot Cake

Carrot cake is a longstanding favorite, especially when you use cream cheese icing to give it a richer flavor. You can serve carrot cake year-round, but it has a special place at Thanksgiving and Christmas holiday parties.

Preparation time: *35 minutes*

Cooking time: *35 to 40 minutes*

Yield: *24 servings*

Cream Cheese Frosting (see the following recipe)

4 eggs

1½ cups vegetable oil

2 cups sugar

3 cups flour

2 teaspoons baking soda

2 teaspoons baking powder

2 teaspoons ground cinnamon

½ teaspoon salt

3 cups shredded carrots

½ cup crushed pineapple

1⅓ cups chopped pecans, divided

1 Preheat the oven to 350 degrees.

2 In a small bowl, beat the eggs, oil, and sugar until smooth.

3 In a large bowl, combine the flour, baking soda, baking powder, cinnamon, and salt.

4 Add the egg mixture to the flour mixture and stir until well blended.

5 Stir in the carrots, pineapple, and ⅔ cup of chopped pecans.

6 Pour the mixture into a greased 15-x-10-inch baking pan.

7 Bake the cake for 35 minutes, or until a toothpick inserted in the center comes out clean.

8 Remove the cake from the oven and place the pan on a wire rack to cool.

9 After the cake has completely cooled, spread the cream cheese frosting over it and sprinkle it with the remaining ⅔ cup of chopped pecans.

Cream Cheese Frosting

8 ounces cream cheese, softened

½ cup butter, softened

1 teaspoon vanilla extract

4 cups confectioners' sugar

1 Beat the cream cheese, butter, and vanilla extract together until smooth.

2 Add the confectioners' sugar and mix until well blended.

Per serving: *Calories 457 (From Fat 242); Fat 27g (Saturated 6g); Cholesterol 56mg; Sodium 230mg; Carbohydrate 52g (Dietary Fiber 2g); Protein 4g.*

Putting the frosting on the cake

If you've ever tried to frost a cake and decided that brain surgery would probably be easier, you're not alone. After all, getting the frosting to look nice while not tearing the cake apart can be a real chore. However, some helpful tricks of the trade make frosting a cake a real snap. Tuck these tips in your hat:

🖊 Allow the cake to cool for about an hour before you frost it. Also, let the cake stand for an hour after your frost it before slicing.

🖊 Use more frosting than you think you need and work to smooth out the frosting, removing the excess rather than trying to spread the frosting onto the cake. Starting out with more helps prevent tearing.

🖊 To spread the frosting evenly, use a flexible spatula and make light back-and-forth strokes.

🖊 If the frosting seems too thick to work with, stir in a few drops of water.

🖊 To make your frosted cake look smooth and shiny, dip your spatula in hot water for a moment, then wipe off the water. Slide the spatula over the cake in short, decorative strokes. This technique melts the icing slightly to give it that smooth, shiny look.

Rocky Road Cake

If you like Rocky Road ice cream, then you'll love the cake as well. The topping for this cake is made from marshmallows; coconut; pecans, peanuts, or walnuts; and chocolate chips. Sound familiar?

Preparation time: *1 hour*

Cooking time: *20 to 25 minutes*

Yield: *20 to 24 servings*

For the cake:

2 cups flour

2 cups sugar

1 teaspoon baking soda

½ teaspoon salt

1 cup butter

1 cup water

¼ cup cocoa powder

4 eggs

½ cup buttermilk

1 teaspoon vanilla extract

For the topping:

12-ounce can evaporated milk, divided

1¼ cups sugar, divided

20 large marshmallows

14-ounce package coconut flakes

2 cups chopped pecans, peanuts, or walnuts

½ cup butter

1 cup semisweet chocolate chips

1 Preheat the oven to 350 degrees.

2 In a mixing bowl, combine the flour, sugar, baking soda, and salt.

3 In a saucepan, combine the butter, water, and cocoa powder. Heat until the butter is melted, stirring until well blended.

4 Add the butter mixture to the flour mixture and blend thoroughly.

5 Add the eggs, buttermilk, and vanilla extract and mix well.

6 Pour the batter into a greased 15-x-10-x-1-inch pan and bake for 20 to 25 minutes, or until a toothpick inserted in the center comes out clean.

7 After the cake has been in the oven for about 15 minutes, begin making the topping. Combine 1 cup of the evaporated milk, ¾ cup of sugar, and the marshmallows in a saucepan.

8 Heat over medium-low heat, stirring constantly, until the marshmallows have melted.

9 Remove the mixture from heat and stir in the coconut flakes.

10 Sprinkle the cake with 1 cup of the chopped nuts and spread the coconut mixture on top of the nuts. Sprinkle the remaining cup of nuts on top.

11 In a saucepan, combine the butter with the remaining ½ cup of sugar and ½ cup of evaporated milk. Heat until the butter is completely melted, stirring constantly.

12 Remove the butter sauce from heat and immediately stir in the chocolate chips. Stir until the chocolate chips have melted and the mixture is well blended.

13 Drizzle the chocolate sauce over the top of the cake.

14 Allow the cake to cool completely, then serve.

Per serving: Calories 491 (From Fat 256); Fat 29g (Saturated 15g); Cholesterol 71mg; Sodium 178mg; Carbohydrate 71g (Dietary Fiber 3g); Protein 6g.

The birth of Rocky Road

Rocky Road ice cream has been around for a long time, and this cake simply builds on the tradition. In 1929, William Dreyer, an ice-cream maker, and his partner, Joseph Edy, a candy maker by trade, created the world's first batch of Rocky Road ice cream. The original recipe consisted of chocolate ice cream, walnuts, and bits of marshmallow, which Dreyer chopped into bits with his wife's sewing shears. Later, the walnuts were exchanged for almonds. Other than that, this 20th-century ice-cream favorite has remained unchanged.

Surprise Devil's Food Cupcakes

These cupcakes are packed with a sinfully delicious cream cheese center. Not only do they taste great, but they're also very easy to make.

Generally speaking, cupcakes can be really helpful with crowds. After all, they're self-serve by nature and don't require a lot of attention. Also, if you plan to have little ones running around at your event, cupcakes are a good pick because they're always a hit with children.

Preparation time: *40 minutes*

Cooking time: *18 to 20 minutes per batch*

Yield: *5 dozen*

4 3-ounce packages (12 ounces) cream cheese, softened	2 cups milk chocolate morsels
1 cup sugar	2 boxes devil's-food cake mix
2 eggs	4 16-ounce containers (64 ounces) milk chocolate frosting

1 Preheat the oven to 350 degrees.

2 Place the softened cream cheese in a mixing bowl. Using an electric mixer, beat the cream cheese until it's smooth.

3 Add the sugar and beat well.

4 Add one egg at a time, beating until just blended after each egg.

5 Stir in the chocolate morsels and set the mixture to the side.

6 Prepare the cake mix per the box directions.

7 Spoon the cake batter into paper muffin cups placed in muffin pans, filling them about ⅔ full.

8 Spoon a tablespoon of the cream cheese mixture into the center of each cupcake.

9 Bake for 18 to 20 minutes or until you can insert a toothpick in the middle of a cupcake and it comes out clean.

10 Cool the cupcakes in the pan on a wire rack for 5 minutes. Then remove the cupcakes from the pan and allow them to cool completely.

11 Frost the cupcakes and serve.

Vary It! *If these decadent cupcakes aren't rich enough for you, try using cream cheese frosting instead of chocolate frosting.*

Per serving: *Calories 307 (From Fat 138); Fat 15g (Saturated 5g); Cholesterol 36mg; Sodium 211mg; Carbohydrate 40g (Dietary Fiber 1g); Protein 2g.*

Other Stupendous Desserts

Aside from the standards, we couldn't resist sharing with you some additional dessert recipes that we love. These don't fall into any standard category, but your guests will love them!

Punch Bowl Layered Dessert

This dessert is simple to make, goes a long way, and looks great on your table. That combination is hard to find and even more difficult to beat!

Preparation time: *35 minutes*

Chill time: *4 hours*

Yield: *26 1-cup servings*

1 store-bought angel food cake

5.1-ounce box instant vanilla pudding, made per package directions

2 21-ounce cans (42 ounces) cherry pie filling

2 20-ounce cans (40 ounces) crushed pineapple, drained

2 15¼-ounce cans (30½ ounces) fruit cocktail, drained

2 11-ounce cans (22 ounces) mandarin oranges, drained

16 ounces frozen whipped topping, thawed

7 ounces coconut flakes, toasted

1 Cut the angel food cake in half and tear each half into bite-size pieces.

2 Place the pieces from one of the halves into a 6-quart punch bowl.

3 Top the cake pieces with half of the pudding, pie filling, pineapple, fruit cocktail, mandarin oranges, whipped topping, and coconut, in that order.

4 Add the remaining angel food cake and repeat the layering in Step 3 with the remaining ingredients.

5 Cover the bowl and refrigerate it for 4 hours.

Per serving: Calories 254 (From Fat 62); Fat 7g (Saturated 6g); Cholesterol 5mg; Sodium 227mg; Carbohydrate 45g (Dietary Fiber 1g); Protein 3g.

Strawberry Pretzel Delight

Strawberries and pretzels? You bet! Sweet desserts combined with salty snacks are wonderful, and this cold dessert is delicious. Although appropriate for any time of the year, this dessert works particularly well at summer parties. The treat is informal, and the strawberries bring out the feeling of summertime.

Preparation time: *30 minutes*

Cooking time: *10 minutes*

Chill time: *2 hours*

Yield: *24 1-cup servings*

5 cups pretzels, crushed

1 cup, 6 tablespoons sugar

1 cup butter, melted

8 ounces cream cheese, softened

16 ounces frozen whipped topping, thawed

4 6-ounce boxes (24 ounces) strawberry gelatin powder

4 cups boiling water

4 cups sliced strawberries

1 Preheat the oven to 350 degrees.

2 In a small bowl, combine the pretzels, 6 tablespoons of sugar, and melted butter and mix well.

3 Divide the pretzel mixture in half, and press each half into the bottom of two 13-x-9-x-2-inch baking dishes to form the crusts.

4 Bake the crusts for 5 minutes each, then allow them to cool.

5 In a large bowl, mix the cream cheese, 1 cup of sugar, and the whipped topping.

6 Pour half of the cream cheese mixture over each of the crusts, and then cover them with plastic wrap and refrigerate.

7 In a medium bowl, combine the boiling water and strawberry gelatin powder and stir until the powder has dissolved.

8 Chill the gelatin for 40 minutes or until partially set.

9 Add the sliced strawberries to the gelatin and mix well. Then divide the strawberry mixture in half and pour it over each of the cream cheese layers.

10 Cover and refrigerate for 1 hour and 20 minutes, or until very firm. Serve cold.

> **Tip:** *You can use either frozen or fresh strawberries. If you use frozen strawberries, make sure you thaw them and drain any excess liquid.*

Per serving: *Calories 331 (From Fat 129); Fat 14g (Saturated 10g); Cholesterol 31mg; Sodium 195mg; Carbohydrate 47g (Dietary Fiber 1g); Protein 4g.*

Vanilla Pudding Layered Dessert

This dessert is another quick and easy one that works great for crowds. It's delicious, especially if you're a pudding lover. The good news is that one batch goes a long way, so put this dessert on your time- and money-saving list.

Preparation time: *30 minutes*

Chill time: *3 hours*

Yield: *24 1-cup servings*

40 whole graham crackers, divided

2 packages (6 serving size each) vanilla instant pudding and pie filling

4 cups cold milk

2½ cups frozen whipped topping, thawed

4 21-ounce cans (84 ounces) cherry pie filling

1 Line the bottoms of two 13-x-9-x-2-inch pans with graham crackers; if necessary, break the crackers to fit.

2 Prepare the pudding with the cold milk per the package directions, and then let it stand for 5 minutes.

3 In a large bowl, gently stir together the whipped topping and the pudding.

4 Divide the pudding mixture in half and set one half aside; spread the other half over the graham crackers in both pans.

5 Place another layer of graham crackers over the pudding mixture.

6 Add the remaining pudding mixture on top of the graham crackers.

7 Add a third layer of graham crackers on top of the pudding mixture.

8 Top the crackers with the cherry pie filling, cover the dessert, and refrigerate it for 3 hours. Serve cold.

Per serving: *Calories 382 (From Fat 68); Fat 8g (Saturated 3g); Cholesterol 6mg; Sodium 409mg; Carbohydrate 73g (Dietary Fiber 2g); Protein 5g.*

Tempting Tiramisu

Tiramisu (meaning "pick me up") is a tempting Italian dessert that looks complicated to make but is really just different layers of ingredients — usually ladyfingers, a custard and cheese layer, and often a chocolate. In fact, you can put together a fabulous tiramisu in about 30 minutes, so don't let this recipe pass you by.

Preparation time: *30 minutes*

Chill time: *2 hours*

Yield: *24 1-cup servings*

12 egg yolks

1 cup sugar

⅔ cup water

4 cups ricotta cheese

2 cups frozen whipped topping, thawed

64 ladyfingers, split in half

2 tablespoons instant expresso, dissolved in 1½ cups boiling water

2 tablespoons cocoa powder

1 In a double boiler, whisk together the egg yolks, sugar, and water. (See Figure 9-1, earlier in this chapter, to find out how to separate eggs.) Check out Figure 9-2 if you don't know what a double boiler is.

2 Cook for 3 to 5 minutes until the mixture is thickened, whisking constantly. Then remove the mixture from heat and allow it to cool.

3 In a large bowl, beat the cooled egg mixture with the ricotta cheese on medium speed until blended.

4 Fold in the whipped topping.

5 Cover the bottoms of two 13-x-9-x-2-inch pans with the ladyfingers, the cut side facing up.

6 Brush ¾ cup of the instant expresso onto the ladyfingers.

7 Spread the ricotta cheese mixture over the ladyfingers.

8 Put another layer of ladyfingers on top of the ricotta cheese mixture, the cut side facing down; brush the ladyfingers with the remaining instant coffee.

9 Spread another layer of the ricotta cheese mixture on top of the ladyfingers.

10 Sprinkle the cocoa powder on top.

11 Cover the dessert and refrigerate it for 2 hours. Serve cold.

> **Per serving:** *Calories 259 (From Fat 105); Fat 12g (Saturated 6g); Cholesterol 235mg; Sodium 82mg; Carbohydrate 29g (Dietary Fiber 0g); Protein 9g.*

Figure 9-2:
With water simmering in the bottom pan, a double boiler is perfect for slow and gentle cooking.

double boiler

Frozen Treats

Frozen treats are enjoyed by all, young, old, and in between. Although frozen desserts are fine to serve year-round, they especially work well in the summer months (unless you live in Antarctica, in which case, it doesn't matter when you serve them).

Peanut Butter and Chocolate Sundae

This dessert is easy to make, yet the taste is so good — great news when you're cooking for others. You can easily make this dessert ahead of time and keep it in the freezer for up to a month.

Preparation time: *35 minutes*

Chill time: *1 hour*

Yield: *24 1-cup servings*

2 16-ounce cans (32 ounces) chocolate syrup

1½ cups creamy peanut butter

34 ice-cream sandwiches

2 12-ounce containers (24 ounces) frozen whipped topping, thawed

2 cups chopped peanuts

1 Pour the chocolate syrup into a medium microwaveable bowl and microwave on high for about 2 minutes. Don't let the chocolate boil.

2 Stir the peanut butter into the chocolate syrup until the mixture is smooth, then allow the mixture to cool to room temperature.

3 Line the bottoms of two 13-x-9-x-2-inch pans with the ice-cream sandwiches, about 8½ sandwiches per pan.

4 Spoon one-fourth of the whipped topping onto the ice-cream sandwiches in each pan.

5 Spread a thin layer of the peanut-butter-and-chocolate mixture over the whipped topping.

6 Top the chocolate mixture with ½ cup of chopped peanuts per pan.

7 Add another layer of ice-cream sandwiches to each pan and repeat Steps 4 through 6 with the rest of the ingredients.

8 Place the pans in the freezer for 1 hour, or until the dessert is firm. Serve cold.

Vary It! *For a different flavor, try Neapolitan, strawberry, or chocolate-flavored ice-cream sandwiches.*

Per serving: Calories 607 (From Fat 277); Fat 31g (Saturated 13g); Cholesterol 31mg; Sodium 278mg; Carbohydrate 71g (Dietary Fiber 4g); Protein 14g.

Orange Dreamsicle

This refreshing frozen dessert is sure to be a hit. It's great any time of year, especially as the weather outdoors starts warming up. The good news is that you can make it several weeks in advance and store it in the freezer. Before serving, put it in the refrigerator for about 30 minutes to help soften it.

Preparation time: *35 minutes*

Chill time: *4 hours, 5 minutes*

Yield: *24 servings*

2 cups butter	*2 cups coconut flakes*
4 cups flour	*½ gallon orange sherbet, softened*
1 cup sugar	*½ gallon vanilla ice cream, softened*

1 In a large frying pan, melt the butter over medium-high heat.

2 Add the flour, sugar, and coconut to the pan and mix well.

3 Cook for 5 to 6 minutes or until the mixture is golden brown and crumbly, stirring constantly.

4 Remove the mixture from heat, set ½ cup of it aside, and divide the remaining mixture in half.

5 Place each half in an ungreased 13-x-9-x-2-inch baking dish. Using the back of a wooden spoon, press the mixture into the bottoms of the pans, making a crust.

6 Place the crusts in the freezer for 5 minutes.

7 In a large bowl, mix the sherbet and ice cream together. Divide the mixture in half and gently spread each half onto the crust.

8 Sprinkle the ½ cup of reserved crust on top of each dessert.

Tip: *For added visual appeal, swirl the sherbet and ice cream together instead of mixing it thoroughly. This technique gives a marbled appearance to the dessert. Also, add some mandarin orange slices on top for a garnish.*

Per serving: Calories 428 (From Fat 208); Fat 23g (Saturated 15g); Cholesterol 63mg; Sodium 76mg; Carbohydrate 53g (Dietary Fiber 1g); Protein 5g.

Easy Frozen Chocolate Pie

If you need an old standby, here's the recipe for a quick and easy frozen chocolate pie. You can even make it the night before your event and store it in the freezer.

Preparation time: *30 minutes*

Chill time: *8 hours or overnight*

Yield: *24 servings*

18 ounces semisweet chocolate

3 8-ounce packages (24 ounces) cream cheese, softened

3 14-ounce cans (42 ounces) sweetened condensed milk (not evaporated)

4½ cups frozen whipped topping, thawed

3 6-ounce store-bought chocolate cookie pie crusts

1 Melt the chocolate per the package directions.

2 In a large bowl, beat the cream cheese until it's smooth.

3 Add the condensed milk and melted chocolate and beat until the mixture is creamy.

4 Fold in the whipped topping.

5 Pour the mixture evenly into all three pie crusts.

6 Cover and freeze the pies for 8 hours, or until firm.

7 To serve, place the pies in the refrigerator for 30 minutes to soften them.

Per serving: *Calories 505 (From Fat 284); Fat 32g (Saturated 17g); Cholesterol 48mg; Sodium 290mg; Carbohydrate 52g (Dietary Fiber 1g); Protein 9g.*

Part III
Special Events and Holidays

The 5th Wave   By Rich Tennant

©RICHTENNANT

"The Normans are coming and I can't decide on whether to pour a simple consommé on them or a more complex bisque."

In this part . . .

Crowd events lend themselves to special occasions, and depending on the occasion, you'll need to make some decisions about food items. In fact, in our experience, crowds typically gather for special summer get-togethers, holiday meals, and weddings. If you're the designated cook for one of these events, you'll need some special recipes that work well with the event and feed a crowd. In this part, we give you our favorite crowd recipes for summertime shindigs, holidays, and weddings.

Chapter 10

Special Dishes for Summer Get-Togethers

In This Chapter

▶ Breaking out the grill: Summer meats

▶ When raw doesn't cut it: Heating up tasty vegetables

▶ Escaping the traditional salad mentality

▶ Cooling off your taste buds (And making them happy) with treats

▶ Stepping outside the lunchbox: Sandwiches for young and old

Summer is the perfect season for great big get-togethers. After all, nothing is more relaxing than a backyard barbecue or a day at the pool. As such, the crowd cook is in high demand when temperatures and spirits are high, and you'll want to serve some wonderful items to your guests.

We put together some of our tried-and-true summertime dishes in this chapter. You'll find these dishes creative and delicious — perfect for your summertime crowd.

Fire It Up: Grilling Meat

For most people, firing up the grill means the start of something great — summer. There's something wonderful about walking outside and smelling your neighbor's grill, hoping you'll be invited to the party. Now you can be the one cooking all those wonderful-tasting meats. In this section, we show you some of our favorite grilling recipes that are sure to be a hit with your summertime crowd.

Honey-Lime Grilled Chicken

Don't let the short ingredients list fool you. These grilled chicken breasts are anything but bland.

Preparation time: *20 minutes*

Marinating time: *1 hour*

Cooking time: *12 to 16 minutes*

Yield: *20 servings*

2½ cups honey

1⅓ cups soy sauce

1¼ cups lime juice

20 boneless, skinless chicken breast halves

5 limes, each cut into 4 wedges for garnish (optional)

1 In a large bowl, combine the honey, soy sauce, and lime juice and mix well.

2 Place the chicken breasts in extra-large, heavy-duty resealable plastic bags, about 10 breasts per bag, to marinate them. If you prefer, you can place them in shallow glass dishes instead, about 10 breasts per 13-x-9-x-2-inch dish.

3 Pour half of the honey marinade over the chicken in each plastic bag and seal the bags. If you're using glass dishes, cover them with plastic wrap. Refrigerate the chicken for 1 hour.

4 Preheat the grill to medium heat.

5 Remove the chicken from the marinade and shake off the excess.

6 Grill the chicken for 6 to 8 minutes on each side or until the juice runs clear. Arrange the chicken breasts on a platter and garnish with the lime wedges (if desired).

Tip: When chefs prepare meat under normal conditions, they usually add some kind of salt. This marinade has a good amount of soy sauce, though, so it should be plenty salty. If you want, you can use reduced-sodium soy sauce; however, for the best full-bodied flavor, we recommend using regular soy sauce.

Per serving: *Calories 179 (From Fat 28); Fat 3g (Saturated 1g); Cholesterol 73mg; Sodium 371mg; Carbohydrate 9g (Dietary Fiber 0g); Protein 27g.*

Hawaiian Shish Kebabs

Whether you're having a luau or just want something other than barbecue, try these sweet and tasty shish kebabs. They're quick and easy to make and fun to eat.

Preparation time: *20 minutes*

Marinating time: *2 hours*

Cooking time: *20 to 25 minutes*

Yield: *20 servings*

¾ cup, 2 tablespoons soy sauce

¾ cup cider vinegar

⅓ cup honey

⅓ cup, 2 tablespoons vegetable oil

8 green onions, minced

40 small to medium mushrooms

10 boneless, skinless chicken breasts, cut into chunks

2 pounds thickly sliced bacon, cut in half

2 large onions, quartered

4 8-ounce cans (32 ounces) pineapple chunks, drained

20 metal skewers

1 Combine the soy sauce, vinegar, honey, vegetable oil, and green onions in an extra-large plastic or glass bowl and mix well.

2 Add the mushrooms and chicken to the bowl and stir until all the pieces are completely coated.

3 Cover the bowl with plastic wrap and refrigerate it for 2 hours.

4 Preheat the grill to high heat.

5 Remove the chicken and mushrooms from the marinade and set the marinade to the side.

6 Wrap the chunks of chicken with bacon and thread a piece onto each skewer.

7 Add a couple of pieces of onion to each skewer followed by another piece of chicken wrapped in bacon.

8 Add a pineapple chunk and then a mushroom.

9 Repeat Steps 6, 7, and 8 until the skewers are almost full.

10 Lightly oil the grilling rack. Place the skewers on the rack and cook for 20 to 25 minutes, or until the juices run clear and the bacon is crisp, brushing them occasionally with the marinade.

Tip: *You can place the foods on a kebab skewer in any order your heart desires; just remember to make the skewers look attractive.*

Per serving: *Calories 273 (From Fat 128); Fat 14g (Saturated 3g); Cholesterol 49mg; Sodium 922mg; Carbohydrate 16g (Dietary Fiber 1g); Protein 21g.*

Tips for grilling meat

So you love the idea of being a grill master, but every time you grill, you end up disappointed. Don't worry; we have a few helpful tips that will make your grilled meat much better. Keep these ideas in mind the next time you fire up the grill:

✔ **Completely thaw meat or poultry before grilling so it cooks more evenly.** It's best to let frozen meat thaw slowly in the refrigerator.

✔ **Buy quality charcoal, briquettes, or aromatic wood chips.** Make sure your grill is set in a well-ventilated area away from your house, other buildings, trees, and shrubs. Grilling is never much fun if the fire department has to get involved.

✔ **Use a meat thermometer.** Meat and poultry cooked on a grill often brown quickly on the outside, so it's a good idea to make sure the meat has reached a safe temperature. Generally the internal heat of meat should reach a temperature of 160 to 180 degrees. Whole poultry especially should reach 180 degrees.

✔ **Don't smash it.** When you're cooking cuts of meat, don't press on the meat with tongs or other cooking instruments. Most people dry out meat when they're grilling it by pressing out the natural juices and texture of the meat. Pressing on the meat won't make it cook more thoroughly, so avoid this common grilling error.

✔ **Don't get distracted.** Grilling requires your attention, and it's easy to put the meat on the grill and get busy doing other things. Stay focused!

Gourmet Blue Cheese Burgers

Hamburgers are the most commonly grilled item for a backyard get-together. Why not put a little twist on them this time? These gourmet burgers are easy to fix and are packed with flavor.

Preparation time: *25 minutes*

Chill time: *2 hours*

Yield: *24 servings*

6 pounds lean ground beef

½ pound blue cheese, crumbled

1 cup fresh chives, minced

2 teaspoons Worcestershire sauce

2 teaspoons coarse black pepper

1 tablespoon salt

2 teaspoons dry mustard

24 hamburger buns

1 In a large bowl, mix together all the ingredients except the hamburger buns; cover the bowl and refrigerate it for 2 hours.

2 Preheat the grill to high heat and form 24 hamburger patties out of the mixture.

3 Lightly oil the grilling rack and cook the burgers for 4 minutes per side, or until done.

Tip: *When you grill burgers, flip them only once during the cooking process. The number-one reason why grilled burgers sometimes turn out dry is that they were flipped too many times or smashed dry by an overzealous cook.*

Per serving: *Calories 384 (From Fat 167); Fat 19g (Saturated 8g); Cholesterol 91mg; Sodium 738mg; Carbohydrate 22g (Dietary Fiber 1g); Protein 30g.*

Making Vegetables Fun

Vegetables are those foods that most people think of as b-o-r-i-n-g. Perhaps you're one of those people who gives in with a sigh: "Okay, I'll eat them, but only because they're good for me." Although they're certainly healthy, the good news is that you can serve vegetables that go from bland to beautiful by adding just a few ingredients. In this section, we show you some of our favorite summertime recipes.

⌒ Zesty Corn on the Cob

Corn is one of those vegetables that even the pickiest of eaters will enjoy. The Dijon mustard in this recipe gives the corn a tangy twist, so it's full of flavor — and easy to make, of course.

Preparation time: *20 minutes*

Cooking time: *35 to 40 minutes*

Yield: *20 servings*

2 cups butter, melted	*1½ tablespoons salt*
¼ cup Dijon mustard	*1 tablespoon pepper*
3 tablespoons minced fresh parsley	*20 medium ears sweet corn, husks removed*

1 In a bowl, combine the butter, Dijon mustard, parsley, salt, and pepper.

2 Cut two pieces of heavy-duty aluminum foil twice the length of a baking sheet. Place each piece of foil on a baking sheet, with the excess foil hanging off each end. (The excess is to wrap the corn in.)

3 Place 10 ears of corn on each baking sheet and brush the butter mixture on each ear.

4 Fold the foil around the corn and seal it tightly.

5 Preheat the grill to medium heat.

6 Grill the foil-wrapped corn uncovered for 35 to 40 minutes, or until the corn is tender.

Tip: You can use margarine rather than butter if you so desire. We suggest using butter, though, because it gives a richer flavor that enhances the sweet taste of the corn.

Per serving: Calories 249 (From Fat 175); Fat 19g (Saturated 12g); Cholesterol 49mg; Sodium 615mg; Carbohydrate 20g (Dietary Fiber 2g); Protein 3g.

Country-Style Green Beans

If you know anything about real country cooking, you know that lard or bacon grease is usually involved. This recipe uses bacon grease for extra flavor. We realize that people are trying to cut back on fat these days, but the fat in this recipe is what makes it taste so good. Besides, green beans are so low in calories that you don't have to count them.

Preparation time: *60 minutes*

Cooking time: *15 minutes*

Yield: *20 servings*

2 pounds bacon

5 cups chopped onions

¾ cup distilled white vinegar

5 15-ounce cans (75 ounces) cut green beans, drained

1 tablespoon salt

1 In an extra-large skillet, cook the bacon over medium heat until it's crispy.

2 Remove the bacon from the grease, drain it, crumble it, and set it aside.

3 Sauté the onions in the bacon grease for 5 minutes, and then add the vinegar.

4 Cook over low-medium heat until the onions are tender and translucent.

5 Stir in the green beans and salt; heat over low for 15 minutes.

6 Top with the crumbled bacon and serve.

Tip: For a spicier flavor, use thickly cut peppered bacon.

Per serving: *Calories 288 (From Fat 202); Fat 22g (Saturated 8g); Cholesterol 39mg; Sodium 1,302mg; Carbohydrate 6g (Dietary Fiber 2g); Protein 15g.*

☞ *Yellow Squash Casserole*

Yellow squash is a popular vegetable during the summer. It's very versatile; you can fry it, sauté it, eat it raw, or make it into a casserole. This recipe is an old family favorite — enjoy.

Preparation time: *30 minutes*

Cooking time: *30 to 35 minutes*

Yield: *20 servings*

8 cups sliced fresh yellow squash

1 cup chopped onion

¼ cup water

2 cups (8 ounces) shredded cheddar cheese

70 buttery round crackers, crushed

4 eggs, beaten

1½ cups milk

½ cup butter, melted

2 teaspoons salt

2 teaspoons pepper

2 tablespoons butter

1 Preheat the oven to 400 degrees.

2 Place the squash, onions, and water in an extra-large skillet, cover, and cook over medium heat until the squash is tender. Drain the squash and onions well and place them in an extra-large bowl.

3 In a medium bowl, mix together the cheese and crushed crackers.

4 Stir half of the cheese-and-cracker mixture into the squash and onions.

5 In a small bowl, mix together the beaten eggs and milk, and then add them to the squash mixture.

6 Stir in the melted butter, salt, and pepper and mix thoroughly.

7 Divide the mixture between two 13-x-9-x-2-inch baking dishes. Sprinkle the remaining cheese-and-cracker mixture on top of each baking dish. Dot with butter.

8 Bake for 30 to 35 minutes, or until lightly browned. Allow the casseroles to sit for 10 minutes before serving.

Per serving: Calories 196 (From Fat 124); Fat 14g (Saturated 8g); Cholesterol 81mg; Sodium 409mg; Carbohydrate 13g (Dietary Fiber 1g); Protein 6g.

Putting Romaine and Iceberg on Hold: Summer Salads

Salads are a great addition to just about any summer crowd event. After all, salad produce grows during the summer, and a cool salad on a warm day can be really inviting — especially one that strays from the typical lettuce salad. In this section, we show you our favorites.

Summer Broccoli Salad

Although the combination of ingredients may seem a bit odd, this colorful salad is addictive. The first time we tried it, we couldn't get enough — we're sure your guests won't be able to, either.

Preparation time: *25 minutes*

Chill time: *1 hour*

Yield: *20 servings*

2½ cups mayonnaise

1¼ cups sugar

¼ cup, 1 tablespoon white vinegar

4½ heads fresh broccoli, washed and dried

2 medium red onions, diced

1⅔ cups raisins

1 pound bacon, cooked crisp and drained of excess grease

1⅔ cups coarsely chopped pecans

1 In a medium bowl, combine the mayonnaise, sugar, and vinegar and stir until the mixture is smooth. Cover the bowl with plastic wrap and refrigerate it for 1 hour.

2 Cut the broccoli into bite-size pieces, using only the florets, not the stalks.

3 Place the broccoli, onions, and raisins in a large serving bowl.

4 Remove the mayonnaise mixture from the refrigerator and stir. Pour the mixture over the broccoli and mix well.

5 Crumble the bacon over the broccoli mixture, add the pecans, and stir until everything is well coated.

Vary It! *If pecans aren't your nut of choice, try substituting almond slivers or sunflower seeds.*

Per serving: *Calories 440 (From Fat 300); Fat 33g (Saturated 5g); Cholesterol 23mg; Sodium 317mg; Carbohydrate 33g (Dietary Fiber 6g); Protein 8g.*

○ Sage Pea Salad

Pea salads are common fare in the summertime, but why not try something a bit different? You'll love the zing of the sage and Dijon mustard in this recipe.

Preparation time: *20 minutes*

Chill time: *Overnight*

Yield: *24 servings*

1 cup heavy whipping cream

1 cup sour cream

2 teaspoons Dijon mustard

2 tablespoons finely chopped fresh sage

1 teaspoon grated lemon peel

1 teaspoon salt

1 teaspoon pepper

12 cups frozen sweet peas, cooked per package directions, drained, and cooled

4 cups (16 ounces) shredded cheddar cheese

1 In a large bowl, combine all the ingredients except the peas and cheese; blend well.

2 Add the peas and cheese; mix well. Refrigerate overnight.

3 Before serving, stir the salad. If the salad is slightly dry, add 1 tablespoon of milk and stir.

Tip: If necessary, you can use 1 tablespoon of dry sage leaves in place of the fresh sage.

Per serving: Calories 194 (From Fat 110); Fat 12g (Saturated 8g); Cholesterol 38mg; Sodium 303mg; Carbohydrate 13g (Dietary Fiber 4g); Protein 9g.

What's Dijon?

You hear about Dijon mustard all the time, and most people eat it on a regular basis; after all, it tastes great. So what, exactly, is Dijon? *Dijon* is the general term for a style of mustard produced in Dijon, France. Dijon mustard is made from husked and ground mustard seeds, white wine, vinegar, and spices. The condiment is usually highly seasoned, which gives it such a great taste. Grey Poupon is a good American brand of Dijon.

☺ *Creamy Red Potato Salad*

Potato salad is standard fare for any summertime get-together, but people serve it so often that it can be rather boring. Instead, why not put a twist on an old favorite and try this red potato variety? You'll love it.

Preparation time: *20 minutes*

Chill time: *1 hour*

Yield: *24 servings*

16 to 24 small red potatoes, boiled, drained, and cooled	*4 teaspoons horseradish sauce*
6 tablespoons cider vinegar	*2 teaspoons mustard*
½ teaspoon salt	*1 teaspoon coarse black pepper*
½ teaspoon celery salt	*1 cup sliced green onions*
1½ cups mayonnaise	*1 cup sliced celery*
½ cup sour cream	*2 small red bell peppers, coarsely chopped*
2 teaspoons sugar	*4 hard-boiled eggs, cooled, peeled, and chopped*

1 Cut the potatoes into bite-size cubes.

2 Place the potatoes in an extra-large plastic or glass bowl; sprinkle them with the vinegar and salts and toss until coated. Let the mixture stand for 30 minutes.

3 In a small bowl, combine the mayonnaise, sour cream, sugar, horseradish sauce, mustard, and pepper; mix well.

4 Add the green onions, celery, and red bell peppers to the potatoes, and then toss them together until well mixed.

5 Gently stir the eggs into the potato mixture; pour the mayonnaise mixture on top and blend gently.

6 Cover the bowl with plastic wrap and refrigerate it for 1 hour.

Crowd Saver: *Need to save time? Make this salad a day ahead. Just before serving, moisten it by stirring in 2 to 4 tablespoons of milk.*

Per serving: *Calories 211 (From Fat 117); Fat 13g (Saturated 3g); Cholesterol 46mg; Sodium 191mg; Carbohydrate 20g (Dietary Fiber 2g); Protein 4g.*

Chilling Out with Refreshing Summer Treats

We love all kinds of cool summertime treats, and we're sure you do as well. Nothing is better on a sunny day than a cool and creamy dessert, so we've gathered up our favorites in this section. These treats are perfect for any casual summertime get-together, they're easy to make, and they're perfect for crowd cooking.

⌓ Cream Cheese Fruit Dream

Any dessert that contains cream cheese and fruit is hard to beat, and this recipe brings the two together in a perfect way. It's also quick and easy to prepare, making it perfect for a crowd event.

Preparation time: *20 minutes*

Chill time: *4 hours or overnight*

Thaw time: *2 hours*

Yield: *28 servings*

3 8-ounce packages (24 ounces) cream cheese, softened

3 cups, 2 tablespoons sugar

3 15-ounce cans (45 ounces) crushed pineapple, drained

3 16-ounce containers (48 ounces) frozen whipped topping, thawed

3 10-ounce packages (30 ounces) frozen strawberries, thawed

9 bananas, diced

2⅓ cups chopped pecans

1 In an extra-large bowl, cream together the cream cheese and sugar.

2 Fold in the pineapple, whipped topping, and strawberries.

3 Stir in the bananas and pecans.

4 Cover the bowl tightly and freeze it for 4 hours or overnight.

5 Remove the bowl from the freezer 2 hours before serving; stir gently before serving.

Crowd Saver: You can prepare this recipe several days in advance. Just remember to allow thaw time before serving it. Also, keep in mind that some freezers may freeze items harder than others, so you may need to allow additional thawing time.

Per serving: Calories 430 (From Fat 214); Fat 24g (Saturated 14g); Cholesterol 27mg; Sodium 73mg; Carbohydrate 50g (Dietary Fiber 3g); Protein 3g.

Pucker-Up Lemon Ice

This sweet and tart flavored ice is the perfect ending to a summertime meal. Both kids and adults will enjoy its taste, puckering their mouths in satisfaction.

Preparation time: *20 minutes*

Chill time: *8 hours or overnight*

Yield: *40 servings*

½ cup lemon zest

3½ cups lemon juice

8 cups sugar

1 gallon milk

1 In an extra-large bowl, stir together the lemon zest, lemon juice, and sugar until smooth.

2 Stir in the milk until completely blended.

3 Pour the mixture into the canister of an ice-cream maker and freeze it according to the manufacturer's directions. If you don't have an ice-cream maker, you can simply pour the mixture into a couple of large casserole pans, cover them, and place them in your freezer until frozen, about 8 hours or overnight.

4 Allow the dessert to set at room temperature for 5 minutes before serving. This refreshing dessert can be served the same way you serve ice cream.

Tip: *We realize that 8 cups of sugar is a lot, but reducing the amount changes the consistency of the dessert. Instead of having a slightly creamy texture, it'll be more like ice. This dessert is supposed to be rather sweet to offset the tartness of the lemons, so we don't recommend altering the recipe.*

Per serving: *Calories 218 (From Fat 30); Fat 3g (Saturated 2g); Cholesterol 13mg; Sodium 48mg; Carbohydrate 46g (Dietary Fiber 0g); Protein 3g.*

☙ Summertime Fruit Salad

Fruit salad is a common dish at summertime events, and we think this recipe is the best one for a crowd. It's quick, easy, and perfect for a sunny day.

Preparation time: *40 minutes*

Chill time: *Overnight plus 1 hour*

Yield: *24 servings*

2 cups water

4 cups sugar

2 cups packed, fresh basil leaves

6 sprigs fresh mint

2 cinnamon sticks

2 cups fresh blackberries

2 cups fresh raspberries

2 cups fresh strawberries, sliced

2 cups cubed cantaloupe

2 cups fresh blueberries

2 medium apples, sliced

1 In a large saucepan, heat the water and sugar to a boil; remove the pan from heat and add the basil, mint, and cinnamon sticks.

2 Put the mixture in a bowl, cover it, and refrigerate it overnight.

3 The next day, remove the sugar mixture from the refrigerator and remove the herbs and cinnamon sticks.

4 In an extra-large bowl, combine all the fruit. Drizzle the sugar mixture over the top, tossing to coat.

5 Cover the bowl, refrigerate it for 1 hour, and serve.

Vary It! This recipe is rather forgiving, so if you want to try some different fruits, feel free to mix them in.

Per serving: Calories 164 (From Fat 3); Fat 0g (Saturated 0g); Cholesterol 0mg; Sodium 2mg; Carbohydrate 42g (Dietary Fiber 3g); Protein 1g.

More than PB&J: Satisfying Sandwiches

You may not think of sandwiches as crowd fare, but in the summertime, they're often the perfect solution for a big event. Of course, if you make sandwiches, you'll want to serve something better than the normal lunchbox variety, so we give you our favorites in this section.

Chunky Chicken Salad Sandwiches

This filling chicken salad is very satisfying and so easy to make. The good news is that chicken salad goes well with any number of sides and desserts, which is perfect if you need some menu flexibility.

Preparation time: *20 minutes*

Chill time: *3 hours or overnight*

Yield: *24 servings*

6 cups diced cooked chicken	2 cups mayonnaise
2 cups diced apples	2 teaspoons salt
1 cup halved seedless red grapes	1½ cups coarsely chopped pecans
¾ cup thinly sliced green onions	24 croissant rolls
½ cup dill relish	1 head leaf lettuce, washed and dried

1 In an extra-large bowl, combine all the ingredients except the pecans, croissants, and leaf lettuce.

2 Cover the bowl and refrigerate for at least 3 hours or overnight.

3 Remove the bowl from the refrigerator and mix in the pecans.

4 Open each croissant horizontally, place a piece of lettuce on the bottom half, add a scoop of chicken salad, put the top back on, and serve.

Crowd Saver: *If you don't have time to cook the chicken yourself, check out your grocery's freezer section. Many different meat companies now offer precooked diced chicken that tastes great and is a big timesaver.*

Per serving: Calories 494 (From Fat 310); Fat 34g (Saturated 10g); Cholesterol 75mg; Sodium 806mg; Carbohydrate 33g (Dietary Fiber 3g); Protein 15g.

Toasted Muffulettas

This hearty sandwich is a great choice for a summertime gathering. Serve it with some fruit salad and a side of your favorite chips, and you have a complete meal.

Preparation time: *50 minutes*

Cooking time: *25 to 30 minutes*

Yield: *20 to 30 servings, depending on the size of bread slices*

5 7-ounce jars (35 ounces) whole black olives, coarsely chopped

5 6-ounce jars (30 ounces) sliced pimento-stuffed Spanish olives

1¼ cups chopped red onion

5 garlic cloves, minced

1 cup flat-leaf parsley, chopped

1½ cups Italian salad dressing, divided

5 12-inch whole focaccia bread loaves

5 pounds hard salami

2 pounds smoked provolone cheese, thinly sliced

5 13-ounce jars (65 ounces) roasted red bell peppers, drained and patted dry

5 small green bell peppers, thinly sliced into rings

1 Preheat the oven to 350 degrees.

2 In a large bowl, combine the olives, onions, garlic, parsley, and 1 cup of the Italian dressing.

3 Slice the focaccia loaves in half horizontally. Drizzle each piece with the remaining Italian dressing.

4 Place the salami, cheese, red bell peppers, green bell peppers, and the olive mixture on the bottom half of each piece of bread.

5 Replace the tops of the loaves and wrap each loaf in foil.

6 Put the wrapped loaves on baking sheets; bake for 25 to 30 minutes, or until hot.

7 Remove the loaves from the oven and allow them to stand for 5 minutes before slicing and serving.

Crowd Saver: *For extra flavor and to save time, make the olive mixture the day before. Just be sure to cover it tightly and refrigerate it.*

Tip: *Whenever you buy cheese, especially thinly sliced cheese, have the deli place paper between each slice to keep the cheese from sticking together. (Trust us; this will make your life a little easier.)*

Per serving: *Calories 711 (From Fat 451); Fat 50g (Saturated 18g); Cholesterol 81mg; Sodium 2,974mg; Carbohydrate 38g (Dietary Fiber 3g); Protein 29g*

Melt-in-Your-Mouth Barbecue Sandwiches

This recipe tastes so good and is so very easy to make. Just pop everything in your slow cooker and go about your business.

Preparation time: *30 minutes*

Cooking time: *9 to 11 hours*

Yield: *24 servings*

3 cups ketchup

½ cup packed brown sugar

½ cup red wine vinegar

¼ cup Dijon mustard

¼ cup Worcestershire sauce

2 teaspoons liquid smoke flavoring

1 teaspoon salt

½ teaspoon pepper

½ teaspoon garlic powder

1 can cola-flavored drink

2 4-pound boneless chuck roasts

24 sandwich buns

1 In a large bowl, combine all the ingredients except for the roasts and buns.

2 Place each roast in a slow cooker.

3 Divide the mixture between both slow cookers.

4 Cover and cook on low for 8 to 10 hours.

5 Carefully remove each roast from the slow cookers; using a fork, shred the meat and return it to the slow cookers. Stir the meat back into the sauce and cook it on low for an additional hour, then spoon the meat onto the sandwich buns.

Tip: If you don't have two slow cookers (and most people don't), borrow one. Remember, borrowing items from friends and family members when you cook for a crowd is okay, so don't hesitate to ask.

Per serving: Calories 353 (From Fat 81); Fat 9g (Saturated 3g); Cholesterol 79mg; Sodium 840mg; Carbohydrate 37g (Dietary Fiber 2g); Protein 30g.

Keeping chicken salad safe

As you're aware, many foods spoil easily, especially if you're serving them outdoors. Chicken salad is one of those foods that quickly go bad. In fact, anything that has mayonnaise spoils quickly. So how can you keep it safe? The solution is to keep it at the right temperature. You need to keep dishes with mayonnaise cold (40 degrees or under) until they're eaten. If you're eating outside, use a well-packed ice chest or simply keep the sandwiches in the refrigerator until you serve them. Also, be sure to throw away any leftovers. You can find out more about keeping food safe in Chapter 13.

Chapter 11

Special Dishes for Holidays

In This Chapter

▶ Toasting the festivities with holiday-style drinks

▶ Starting off on a good foot: Holiday appetizers

▶ Saving room for the time-tested stars: Holiday main dishes and sides

▶ Satisfying your sweet tooth: Holiday desserts

*N*ovember and December are always prime crowd-cooking times. In fact, our guess is that if you're cooking for a crowd, odds are good that the event has something to do with Thanksgiving or Christmas. Without a doubt, these holidays and the weeks surrounding them are the busiest for crowd cooks.

With that in mind, we know you need some delightful and impressive recipes for your holiday meals. You've come to the right chapter. Here, we explore a number of different recipes, all organized by different courses. We include only those recipes that work great for crowd cooking, but we also include a number of atypical holiday meal items. The drinks and desserts, of course, are vegetarian friendly. In this chapter, you can find what you need to serve something new, interesting, holiday-ish, and completely crowd friendly!

If after you read this chapter you still hunger for more Christmas recipes, check out *Christmas Cooking For Dummies* by Dede Wilson (Wiley).

Welcoming the Holidays: Drinks

Cinnamon and ginger are standard holiday ingredients, and the smell of those spices brings back such warm holiday memories. We love cider during the holidays, and the heartwarming cider in this section is just the ticket to kick off your holiday party and help your guests lose the chill of the winter air. We also love thick and filling eggnog. Without further ado, take a look at some recipes.

Spiced Hot Cider

You can serve standard cider, but why not go the extra mile (actually, a fraction of a mile, because this recipe is so easy). This delicious cider gives you that cinnamon, apple, and ginger taste that can only mean the holidays are nearby.

Preparation time: 10 minutes

Cooking time: 15 minutes

Yield: 40 1-cup servings

10 cinnamon sticks	½ cup brown sugar
2½ tablespoons whole cloves	½ teaspoon ground mace
2½ tablespoons allspice berries	1 teaspoon ground ginger
2½ gallons apple cider	

1 In a clean, white piece of cloth or a piece of cheesecloth, place the cinnamon sticks, cloves, and allspice. Tie the cloth loosely to make a spice bag.

2 In a Dutch oven, combine the apple cider, spice bag, brown sugar, mace, and ginger.

3 Over medium heat, bring the cider to a boil.

4 Reduce the heat to low and simmer for 15 minutes.

5 Remove the pan from heat, remove the spice bag, and let the cider stand for 5 minutes before serving.

Tip: Remember, drinks deserve garnishes, too. Try adding a cinnamon stick to each cup.

Per serving: *Calories 131 (From Fat 0); Fat 0g (Saturated 0g); Cholesterol 0mg; Sodium 26mg; Carbohydrate 33g (Dietary Fiber 0g); Protein 0g.*

Coconut Eggnog

If you want to serve nonalcoholic eggnog, this twist on the old standard will do the trick. It has the traditional eggnog taste, but the coconut gives it an extra flair.

Preparation time: *10 minutes*

Chill time: *4 hours*

Yield: *20 1-cup servings*

12 egg yolks	*1 tablespoon, 1 teaspoon vanilla extract*	*4 cups heavy whipping cream*
6 13.5-ounce cans (81 ounces) coconut milk	*1 tablespoon, 1 teaspoon almond extract*	*ground nutmeg, for garnish*
1½ cups sugar		

1 In a heavy saucepan, mix together the egg yolks, coconut milk, and sugar.

2 Cook over medium heat for 6 to 8 minutes, or until the mixture reaches 160 degrees, stirring often.

3 Remove the saucepan from heat and add the vanilla and almond extracts; stir until well blended.

4 Transfer the mixture from the pan into a pitcher or punch bowl and cover tightly.

5 Place the mixture in the refrigerator and chill it for at least 4 hours.

6 In a medium bowl, beat the whipping cream with an electric mixer on medium speed until soft peaks have formed.

7 Fold the whipping cream into the egg-and-coconut-milk mixture.

8 Garnish the eggnog with a dash of nutmeg and serve.

Per serving: *Calories 491 (From Fat 417); Fat 45g (Saturated 34g); Cholesterol 193mg; Sodium 38mg; Carbohydrate 20g (Dietary Fiber 1g); Protein 5g.*

Eggnog . . . and a trip to the emergency room?

Eggnog is a delicious drink that contains, at its base, eggs. In fact, *eggnog* originally meant "eggs inside a small cup." However, as you look around for eggnog recipes, you may find several that don't require cooking the eggs. The problem with this approach? Salmonella. *Salmonella* is bacteria that causes food poisoning and is commonly found in eggs. So avoid eggnog recipes that use raw eggs. After all, if your crowd has to go to the emergency room, your day will probably be ruined.

Hot Fruit Punch

If you need punch for your crowd gathering, try this delicious hot fruit punch. It's an excellent way to welcome friends and family out of the winter snow and into your home.

Preparation time: *10 minutes*

Cooking time: *45 minutes*

Yield: *32 1-cup servings*

1 gallon cranberry juice

1 gallon pineapple juice

½ cup crushed red hot candies

pineapple wedge, for garnish (optional)

1 In a Dutch oven, combine all the ingredients.

2 Heat to boiling over medium heat, stirring often to thoroughly mix the crushed candies into the juices.

3 Reduce the heat and simmer for 45 minutes. Serve hot. Garnish the punch bowl with a pineapple wedge, if desired.

Per serving: Calories 151 (From Fat 0); Fat 0g (Saturated 0g); Cholesterol 0mg; Sodium 4mg; Carbohydrate 38g (Dietary Fiber 0g); Protein 0g.

Festive Beginnings: Appetizers

Appetizers are the beginning of any meal, so we can't understate their importance. This idea is particularly true with holiday meals. In this section, we show you some of our favorite holiday appetizers. Of course, you should also check out Chapter 4 for more appetizer recipes.

Bacon and Blue Cheese Bites

For a formal finger food, these bacon and blue cheese bites are wonderfully delicious and work well as an appetizer for more elegant meals. If you're skipping the formalities, however, they still function well as a filling appetizer.

Preparation time: *20 minutes*

Cooking time: *20 to 25 minutes*

Yield: *6 dozen*

1½ cups water	6 eggs
½ cup butter	8 ounces crumbled blue cheese
1½ cups flour	10 slices bacon, cooked and crumbled
1 teaspoon salt	4 green onions, finely chopped
1 teaspoon pepper	

1 Preheat the oven to 400 degrees.

2 In a heavy saucepan, bring the water and butter to a boil over medium heat.

3 Add the flour, salt, and pepper. Beat the mixture with a wooden spoon until it pulls away from the sides of the pan and forms a smooth ball of dough.

4 Remove the pan from heat and allow the dough to cool for 5 minutes.

5 Add the eggs one at a time, beating well with a wooden spoon after each egg.

6 Beat in the cheese, bacon, and green onions.

7 Drop the dough by rounded teaspoons onto baking sheets, spacing the balls 2 inches apart.

8 Bake for 20 to 25 minutes, or until golden. The appetizers will be moist in the center.

Crowd Saver: *You can freeze these wonderful treats for up to 3 months. When you're ready for them, thaw them in the refrigerator overnight and reheat them at 350 degrees for 5 to 10 minutes.*

Per serving: *Calories 43 (From Fat 27); Fat 3g (Saturated 2g); Cholesterol 24mg; Sodium 96mg; Carbohydrate 2g (Dietary Fiber 0g); Protein 2g.*

Mini Sausage Quiches

These delightful mini sausage quiches look great and taste wonderful. They're perfect for breakfast appetizers, brunches, or evening meals.

Preparation time: *30 minutes*

Chill time: *1 hour*

Cooking time: *20 to 30 minutes*

Yield: *48 appetizers*

1 cup butter, softened

6 ounces cream cheese, softened

2 cups flour

1 pound bulk Italian-flavored sausage

2 cups (8 ounces) shredded Swiss cheese

2 tablespoons snipped fresh chives

4 eggs

2 cups half-and-half

½ teaspoon salt

½ teaspoon cayenne pepper

1 Preheat the oven to 375 degrees.

2 Beat the butter and cream cheese in a bowl until creamy.

3 Slowly blend in the flour. Refrigerate the dough for 1 hour.

4 Remove the dough from the refrigerator and roll it into 48 1-inch balls.

5 Press each ball into a greased minimuffin cup and set the pan aside.

6 In a large frying pan, crumble the sausage and cook until it's done, stirring occasionally. Drain off the excess grease.

7 Sprinkle the sausage into each dough-lined muffin cup.

8 Sprinkle the cheese and chives on top of the sausage.

9 In a small bowl, whisk the eggs, half-and-half, salt, and pepper until well blended.

10 Pour the egg mixture over each cup, making sure that you don't overfill the cups.

11 Bake for 20 to 30 minutes or until set. Carefully remove the miniquiches and serve them hot.

> **Tip:** *No matter whether you're cooking a full-size quiche or these delightful bite-size versions, it is very important to not overcook the quiche, because doing so causes it to be very dry.*

Per serving: *Calories 117 (From Fat 83); Fat 9g (Saturated 5g); Cholesterol 44mg; Sodium 101mg; Carbohydrate 5g (Dietary Fiber 0g); Protein 4g.*

Quiche 101

If you're new to the idea of quiche or didn't grow up eating it, don't worry. Quiche is, by definition, a rich, unsweetened custard pie. Although the French commonly get the credit for this dish, it actually originated in Germany. In fact, the German name for quiche, *Kuchen,* actually means "cake."

Traditionally, quiches were made of eggs, cream custard, and bacon. Cheese stepped in later, and now all kinds of wonderful variations exist, including vegetable quiches and seafood quiches. If you've never made a quiche, try the mini sausage quiche recipe in this chapter. Your crowd will love the quiche bites, and you'll love the creative look they bring to your table.

☺ *Festive Pumpkin Pie Dip*

This recipe is one that usually causes people to say, "I never thought of serving pumpkin pie this way!" This dip tastes just like Mom's pumpkin pie. Serve it with ginger snaps or sliced apples. Or, for those of you who want to go that extra step, roll out a pie crust and cut it into shapes with a small cookie cutter, then bake the cookies and serve them with the dip. A leaf cookie cutter is always a nice choice.

Preparation time: *15 minutes*

Chill time: *8 to 24 hours*

Yield: *24 ¼-cup servings*

2 8-ounce packages (16 ounces) cream cheese, softened	4 cups confectioners' sugar	2 teaspoons ground cinnamon
	2 15-ounce cans (30 ounces) pumpkin pie filling	1 teaspoon ground ginger

1 Beat the cream cheese and sugar with an electric mixer on medium speed until smooth.

2 Add the pie filling, cinnamon, and ginger and beat well.

3 Cover the mixture and refrigerate it for 8 to 24 hours.

4 Serve the dip in a decorative bowl with apples, cookies, or pie-crust pieces.

Tip: *To garnish, add cinnamon sticks and sprinkle the top of the dip with ground cinnamon. If you want to have some extra fun, purchase a small pumpkin and cut off the top. Hollow out the inside to create a bowl and fill the pumpkin with the dip. You'll be the creative talk of the town!*

Per serving: *Calories 181 (From Fat 61); Fat 7g (Saturated 4g); Cholesterol 21mg; Sodium 130mg; Carbohydrate 30g (Dietary Fiber 3g); Protein 2g.*

Dinner Is Served

When people think of holiday meals, the standard fare comes to mind. Of course, Thanksgiving and Christmas are two holidays when most people tend to lean toward the traditional side, which, by all means, is fine. After all, traditional Thanksgiving and Christmas dinners are wonderful. The following recipes show you some of our favorite holiday meals. Also, check out Chapter 5 for more main course recipes.

Welcome Home Baked Ham

Baked ham always reminds us of the holidays, and we never get through Thanksgiving and Christmas without at least one meal of this staple. Because holiday hams are so popular, you may be tempted to have someone else prepare it for you. All is good and well, but bear in mind that you can cook your own delicious holiday ham without much fuss.

Preparation time: 25 minutes

Cooking time: 2 hours, 50 minutes

Yield: 20 to 24 servings

10-to-12-pound fully cooked ham	*2 teaspoons dried parsley*
1 tablespoon whole cloves	*3 cups pineapple juice*
1½ cups brown sugar, divided	*1 cup honey*
2 teaspoons pork seasoning	*16 ounces canned, sliced pineapple, drained*

1 Preheat the oven to 350 degrees.

2 Remove the skin from the ham. Using a sharp knife, score the surface of the ham, making diamond shapes, about ½-inch deep.

3 Insert a clove into every other diamond.

4 Place the ham on a rack in a shallow roasting pan.

5 In a small bowl, mix ¾ cup of brown sugar with the seasonings.

6 Pat the mixture on top of the ham and some on the sides.

7 Pour the pineapple juice around the ham. Bake the ham uncovered for 2 hours, basting often.

8 Remove the ham from the pan and set it aside. Increase the oven temperature to 400 degrees.

9 Drain the pan of juices, reserving ¼ cup.

10 In a small bowl, combine the honey, remaining brown sugar, and reserved pan juices. Mix until well blended.

11 Return the ham to the pan and spoon half of the honey glaze over the ham.

12 Bake the ham uncovered for an additional 20 minutes.

13 Remove the pan from the oven and place the pineapple slices on it. Drizzle the remaining glaze on top.

14 Bake the ham uncovered for an additional 30 minutes, or until a meat thermometer reads 140 degrees.

15 Remove the pan from the oven and let the ham stand for 15 minutes before carving.

Per serving: Calories 341 (From Fat 71); Fat 8g (Saturated 3g); Cholesterol 78mg; Sodium 1,887mg; Carbohydrate 31g (Dietary Fiber 0g); Protein 36g.

Timesaver Holiday Pork Loin

Time is always a problem around the holidays. After all, the phrase "hustle and bustle" didn't come out of thin air. We're busy, and we know you're busy as well, but you can still cook a great meal for a crowd without ruining your entire schedule. This timesaver holiday pork loin is just one example.

Preparation time: *20 minutes*

Cooking time: *8 hours*

Yield: *18 to 24 servings*

¼ cup vegetable oil, divided

2 3-to-4-pound boneless rolled pork loin roasts, halved

2 16-ounce cans (32 ounces) whole berry cranberry sauce

1 cup cranberry juice

½ cup pineapple juice

1 cup sugar

½ cup brown sugar

2 teaspoons ground mustard

½ teaspoon ground cloves

½ cup cornstarch

½ cup cold water

1 teaspoon salt

1 In two Dutch ovens, heat the oil, 2 tablespoons per pot.

2 Add each pork loin to a Dutch oven and brown the meat on all sides.

3 Place each browned pork loin in a 5-quart slow cooker.

4 In a medium bowl, combine the cranberry sauce, cranberry juice, pineapple juice, sugar, brown sugar, mustard, and cloves and mix well.

5 Divide the mixture in half and pour half into each slow cooker.

6 Cover the slow cookers and cook on low for 8 hours or until a meat thermometer reads 160 degrees.

7 Remove the meat from the slow cookers, wrap it in foil, and put it in the oven on a very low heat setting (just enough to keep it warm).

8 In a saucepan, combine the cornstarch, water, and salt; stir until smooth.

9 Add the liquid from the slow cooker to the saucepan and stir the mixture for 2 minutes or until thickened. Serve the sauce with the meat.

Per serving: Calories 413 (From Fat 121); Fat 13g (Saturated 4g); Cholesterol 85mg; Sodium 205mg; Carbohydrate 42g (Dietary Fiber 1g); Protein 30g.

Peppercorn Beef Tenderloin

Beef tenderloin is another standard holiday meal, and this version will have your guests asking for seconds. You'll find this peppercorn beef tenderloin full of flavor and rather easy to prepare.

Preparation time: *20 minutes*

Cooking time: *50 to 55 minutes*

Yield: *20 to 24 servings*

2 5-to-6-pound beef tenderloins, trimmed

¼ cup Dijon mustard

2 tablespoons dried sage, divided

3 tablespoons whole green peppercorns, ground and divided

3 tablespoons whole black peppercorns, ground and divided

3 tablespoons whole white peppercorns, ground and divided

¼ cup butter, softened and divided

1 tablespoon beef seasoning salt, divided

1 Preheat the oven to 425 degrees.

2 Cut each tenderloin lengthwise to within ½ inch of one side, leaving the edge intact. Open the tenderloins out flat.

3 Place heavy-duty plastic wrap on top of each tenderloin and pound the meat until it's slightly flattened.

4 Remove the plastic wrap and spread the mustard on both tenderloins.

5 Sprinkle 1 tablespoon of the dried sage, 1½ tablespoons of the green peppercorns, and 1 tablespoon each of the black and white ground peppercorns over the mustard on each tenderloin.

6 Fold the tenderloins back over and tie them securely with kitchen string at 3-inch intervals.

7 Spread 2 tablespoons of the butter on the outside of each tenderloin.

8 Sprinkle each tenderloin with half of the remaining ground peppercorns and 1½ teaspoons of the beef seasoning salt.

9 Place each tenderloin on its own rack in a roasting pan.

10 Bake for 50 to 55 minutes or until a meat thermometer reads 160 degrees in the thickest part of the tenderloin. Let the tenderloins stand for 10 minutes before slicing them.

Tip: *A temperature of 160 degrees gives you a medium-cooked piece of beef. This recipe tastes best at medium or medium rare. If medium rare is what you have in mind, the temperature at the thickest part of the meat should be 145 degrees.*

Per serving: *Calories 289 (From Fat 162); Fat 18g (Saturated 7g); Cholesterol 94mg; Sodium 366mg; Carbohydrate 2g (Dietary Fiber 1g); Protein 29g.*

The Perfect Side Dish

Side dishes should always compliment the main course. You'll probably want to have a few of them, such as potatoes, rice, and a green vegetable dish or two. However, the main course should guide your decision making.

Of course, you should check out these holiday side dishes, but also be sure to peruse Chapter 6 for more side dish recipes.

Heavenly Hash-Brown Casserole

Hash-brown casserole is a great side dish because is goes with so many other dishes. It works well for a holiday dinner as well as a brunch, and it's rather filling, which is a big bonus. Try this one out — your crowd will thank you.

Preparation time: *20 minutes*

Cooking time: *1 hour, 10 minutes*

Yield: *24 servings*

4 pounds frozen hash-brown potatoes, thawed

5 cups (20 ounces) shredded cheddar cheese

2 10¾-ounce cans (21.5 ounces) condensed cream of chicken soup

4 cups (32 ounces) sour cream

2 small green bell peppers, chopped

2 small sweet red peppers, chopped

1 large onion, chopped

1 tablespoon pepper

2 teaspoons salt

4 cups crushed cornflakes, divided

1 cup butter, melted

1 Preheat the oven to 350 degrees.

2 In a large bowl, combine all the ingredients, except the cornflakes and butter. Mix well.

3 Divide the mixture between two greased 13-x-9-x-2-inch baking pans. Cover the pans and bake for 45 minutes.

4 Uncover each pan and top the mixtures with 2 cups of the cornflakes.

5 Drizzle ½ cup of the melted butter over the cornflakes in each pan.

6 Bake for 25 to 30 minutes.

7 Remove the pans from the oven and let the casseroles set for 10 minutes before serving.

Per serving: Calories 439 (From Fat 279); Fat 31g (Saturated 17g); Cholesterol 64mg; Sodium 686mg; Carbohydrate 32g (Dietary Fiber 2g); Protein 11g.

☙ Creamy Green Bean and Mushroom Casserole

Traditionally, green bean casseroles have been popular around the holidays. This version keeps the tradition but shakes things up a bit with the addition of mushrooms and soy sauce. Try it!

Preparation time: *20 minutes*

Cooking time: *45 to 50 minutes*

Yield: *24 servings*

5 10¾-ounce cans (50 ounces) condensed cream of mushroom soup	*12 cups canned, cut or French-style green beans*
¾ cup milk	*2 teaspoons pepper*
3 cups canned, sliced mushrooms, drained	*2 teaspoons salt*
2 tablespoons soy sauce	*4 3½-ounce cans (14 ounces) French-fried onions, divided*

1 Preheat the oven to 350 degrees.

2 In a large bowl, combine all the ingredients, except add only 7 ounces of the French-fried onions.

3 Divide the mixture between two greased 13-x-9-x-2-inch pans; cover the pans and bake for 40 minutes, or until bubbly.

4 Remove the pans from the oven and top each pan with half of the remaining French-fried onions.

5 Bake uncovered for an additional 5 to 10 minutes, or until the French-fried onions are golden brown.

6 Remove the casserole from the oven and allow it to set for 10 minutes before serving.

Vary It! *For some people, this holiday classic is perfect just as it is; however, if you want it extra creamy, add an additional can of cream of mushroom soup and an additional ½ cup of milk.*

Per serving: *Calories 191 (From Fat 112); Fat 12g (Saturated 3g); Cholesterol 2mg; Sodium 1,256mg; Carbohydrate 16g (Dietary Fiber 3g); Protein 4g.*

Classic Dressing

We couldn't give you a chapter on holiday recipes without throwing in a classic dressing recipe. Naturally, you may have a family recipe that would cause your banishment to Antarctica if you failed to cook it. If such is the case, by all means, don't rebel — but if you need a really good dressing recipe, this one's for you.

Preparation time: *25 minutes*

Cooking time: *1 hour*

Yield: *24 servings*

3 10½-ounce cans (31.5 ounces) chicken broth	*1½ teaspoons ground sage*
5 cups chopped apple	*1 teaspoon ground nutmeg*
2½ cups chopped onion	*1 teaspoon ground cinnamon*
1½ cups chopped celery	*2 teaspoons salt*
¾ cup sugar	*2 teaspoons pepper*
½ cup butter, melted	*36 cups breadcrumbs*

1 Preheat the oven to 350 degrees.

2 Combine all the ingredients, except the breadcrumbs, in a large pot. Cook the mixture over medium heat until it's almost boiling.

3 Reduce the heat and simmer for 10 minutes.

4 Place the breadcrumbs in a large roasting pan or two large casserole pans.

5 Carefully pour the hot mixture over the breadcrumbs a little at a time, mixing well after each addition.

6 Bake for 50 minutes or until done.

7 Remove the dressing from the oven and let it set for 10 minutes before serving.

Tip: When you cook dressing, texture is subjective. Some people prefer their dressing drier (and crumblier), but others prefer it to be more moist. You can cook it according to your own taste, as long you cook it thoroughly. If you're a Southerner by location or at heart, you can substitute cornbread in place of the breadcrumbs.

Per serving: Calories 728 (From Fat 120); Fat 13g (Saturated 5g); Cholesterol 11mg; Sodium 1,751mg; Carbohydrate 130g (Dietary Fiber 5g); Protein 21g.

You say "stuffing"; I say "dressing" . . .

In truth, stuffing and dressing are two names for the same thing, but how you use them defines what you call them. *Stuffing,* by definition, is stuffed inside of a bird. *Dressing,* on the other hand, is prepared in a pan and is cooked separate from the bird. That's it!

Wrapping It Up: Desserts

You love putting on a little weight over the holidays, don't you? Oh, come on, sure you do! Although no one likes to see the scale after the holidays, everyone loves the wonderful desserts that show up during the holiday season, and you want to give your guests what they love.

In this section, we include a few of our favorite holiday dessert recipes; make sure you read Chapter 9 for additional dessert ideas!

Peanut Butter and Chocolate Cheesecake Bites

This very rich — and very creamy — dessert is perfect for a crowd event. These cheesecake bites scream holiday fun, but they break the traditional springform mold. Also, they're bite size, so they're easy to serve — a big plus!

Preparation time: *40 minutes*

Cooking time: *25 to 30 minutes*

Chill time: *1 to 24 hours*

Yield: *24 servings*

1½ cups finely crushed chocolate wafer cookies

¼ cup butter, melted

⅔ cup, 2 tablespoons sugar, divided

24 chocolate kisses

4 8-ounce packages (32 ounces) cream cheese, softened

4 eggs

1 teaspoon vanilla

1 cup chunky peanut butter

⅔ cup semisweet chocolate chips

2 teaspoons shortening

1 Preheat the oven to 325 degrees. Line 24 2½-inch muffin cups (in pans) with foil liners.

2 In a small bowl, combine the crushed wafers, butter, and 2 tablespoons of the sugar.

3 Divide the mixture evenly among the 24 lined cups. Press it into the bottom of the cups, creating the crusts.

4 In each cup, place a chocolate kiss with the point facing up.

5 In a medium bowl, beat the cream cheese and remaining ⅔ cup of sugar until smooth.

6 Beat in the eggs and vanilla, just until blended.

7 Beat in the peanut butter.

8 Gently spoon about ¼ cup of the cream cheese mixture over the kiss in each cup. The cup should be full.

9 Bake for 25 minutes or until the filling is set. Remove the pans from the oven and cool them on a wire rack for 30 minutes.

10 Melt the chocolate chips and shortening in a microwave on high power until smooth.

11 Remove the cheesecakes from the foil liners and place them on a cookie sheet. Drizzle the melted chocolate over the cheesecakes.

12 Cover the cookie sheet tightly with foil or plastic wrap and refrigerate it for 1 to 24 hours.

Tip: Whenever you cook any kind of cheesecake, always use a water bath. A water bath is simply a pan of water that you place on the rack underneath your cheesecake. (The cheesecake doesn't actually sit in this water bath, of course.) The water bath creates humidity in the oven and helps prevent the cheesecake from cracking on top. When you're cooking with a water bath, you may need to slightly extend the cooking time due to the added moisture.

Per serving: *Calories 330 (From Fat 229); Fat 25g (Saturated 13g); Cholesterol 83mg; Sodium 220mg; Carbohydrate 21g (Dietary Fiber 1g); Protein 8g.*

Peppermint Mousse

We love this festive twist on the standard mousse dessert. Best of all, it's unique, easy to prepare, and perfect for a crowd.

Preparation time: *35 minutes*

Chill time: *1 hour*

Yield: *24 1-cup servings*

1¼ cups sugar	*7 cups cold milk*
½ cup, 3 tablespoons cornstarch	*80 peppermint candies, crushed*
4 eggs	*9 cups frozen whipped topping, thawed*

1 In a saucepan, whisk together the sugar, cornstarch, and eggs.

2 Slowly whisk in the milk, and then whisk in the crushed peppermints.

3 Bring the mixture to a over boil over medium heat, gently stirring at the bottom of the pan.

4 Boil for 2 minutes, then remove the pan from the heat.

5 Pour the mixture into a large bowl, cover the bowl, and refrigerate it for 1 hour.

6 Gently fold in the whipped topping and serve.

Tip: *If you want to make this dessert more festive looking, add a few drops of red food coloring before adding the whipped topping. You can serve this dessert buffet-style in a large pretty bowl or in individual dessert dishes. Why not jazz it up a little bit by hanging a small candy cane on each individual serving dish or several of them around the rim of the large bowl?*

Per serving: *Calories 251 (From Fat 69); Fat 8g (Saturated 6g); Cholesterol 45mg; Sodium 53mg; Carbohydrate 40g (Dietary Fiber 0g); Protein 3g.*

Chocolate Chip Cream Cheese Ball

This dessert gives you a spin on the standard cheese ball and is perfect for a holiday crowd. We love this one because of its unique appeal — it just seems perfect for a holiday crowd.

Preparation time: *30 minutes*

Chill time: *3 hours*

Yield: *24 ¼-cup servings*

3 8-ounce packages (24 ounces) cream cheese, softened

1½ cups butter, softened

2¼ cups confectioners' sugar

⅓ cup, 1 tablespoon brown sugar

1½ teaspoons vanilla extract

2 teaspoons ground cinnamon

2¼ cups miniature semisweet chocolate chips

2¼ cups finely chopped pecans or walnuts

1 In a large bowl, beat the cream cheese and butter until smooth.

2 Mix in the confectioners' sugar, brown sugar, vanilla extract, and cinnamon.

3 Stir in the chocolate chips.

4 Cover the bowl and chill the mixture in the refrigerator for 2 hours.

5 Shape the chilled mixture into two balls. Wrap the balls in plastic and refrigerate them for 1 hour.

6 Place the nuts on a baking sheet.

7 Remove the cream cheese balls from the refrigerator, unwrap them, and roll them in the nuts.

8 Place one or both cheese balls on a large platter; serve them with graham crackers or chocolate wafer cookies neatly arranged around the balls.

Vary It! *If you want to change the taste a little, try rolling the cheese balls in crushed cookies or your favorite chocolate candy bar, crushed.*

Per serving: Calories 413 (From Fat 308); Fat 34g (Saturated 17g); Cholesterol 62mg; Sodium 89mg; Carbohydrate 27g (Dietary Fiber 2g); Protein 4g.

Chapter 12

Special Dishes for Weddings

Ah, weddings. Those blissful days when the birds are singing, a cool breeze is floating through the air, and everyone is completely calm and collected. Yeah, right! Cooking for a wedding can be rather stressful and frustrating; after all, everyone is depending on you to pull the reception together.

Regardless of whether you volunteered to cook for a wedding or the responsibility mysteriously fell in your lap, this chapter is here to help you. Here, you find ten of our favorite wedding recipes.

Don't let the stress of cooking for a wedding crowd overwhelm you. In the end, a wedding is just like any other crowd event. Sure, you'll see more flowers and dressy clothes, but the cooking is really the same. Keep a level head and put to work the skills you gain from this book!

Beautiful Beginnings: Appetizers

Whether you're facing a simple menu of light appetizers or an elegant plated dinner, appetizers are an important part of the wedding meal. As you think about what to serve, be careful. Try to choose recipes that look and taste great but are relatively easy to manage and eat.

The following appetizers are easy to make and are tasty accompaniments to any meal — they can even stand on their own.

Ham and Asparagus Wraps

These delicious wraps give you an elegant appetizer that is easy to make and even easier to serve. This appetizer works great with most other dishes and is sure to be a hit with your wedding crowd.

Preparation time: *30 minutes*

Cooking time: *15 to 20 minutes*

Yield: *60 servings*

2 pounds smoked ham, thinly sliced (not shaved)	*2 8-ounce packages (16 ounces) cream cheese, softened*	*60 fresh asparagus spears, trimmed*

1 Preheat the oven to 350 degrees.

2 In a small bowl, beat the cream cheese with an electric mixer until it's spreadable. If necessary, add about ½ teaspoon of cold water to help it mix easier.

3 Gently spread about 2 teaspoons of the cream cheese on each slice of ham, from one end to the other.

4 Place an asparagus spear along one of the long sides of each piece of ham and roll the ham around it.

5 Place a single layer of appetizers on a baking sheet and cover the sheet with foil.

6 Bake for 15 to 20 minutes, or until heated through. Serve warm.

Tip: *Frozen asparagus that has been thawed is an option, as well as canned asparagus. However, both the canned and the frozen varieties tend to be too soft and limp. Fresh asparagus holds its shape better and has a nice crunch to it.*

Per serving: *Calories 45 (From Fat 30); Fat 3g (Saturated 2g); Cholesterol 16mg; Sodium 204mg; Carbohydrate 1g (Dietary Fiber 0g); Protein 4g.*

Shrimp with Mustard Sauce

Shrimp is a delicious, versatile food. It's great in dip or served with a savory sauce. This recipe is sure to delight even your pickiest guest.

Preparation time: *30 minutes*

Chill time: *6 to 24 hours*

Yield: *72 shrimp*

Mustard Dipping Sauce (see the following recipe)

3 pounds uncooked medium shrimp (21–24 per pound), peeled, tails left on, and deveined

2 bay leaves

2 teaspoons salt

1 Fill a Dutch oven or stockpot halfway to three-quarters full with water and bring it to a boil.

2 Add the shrimp, bay leaves, and salt. Boil until the shrimp are opaque.

3 Drain the shrimp, let them cool, and then cover them and refrigerate until you're ready to serve.

Mustard Dipping Sauce

¼ cup butter

2 tablespoons, 2 teaspoons flour

1 cup half-and-half

1 cup sour cream

½ cup white wine vinegar

¼ cup Dijon mustard

1 teaspoon pepper

1 tablespoon capers, drained (optional)

1 In a large saucepan, melt the butter.

2 Add the flour and stir until smooth.

3 Add the half-and-half and stir.

4 Cook the mixture over medium heat until thickened and bubbly.

5 Reduce the heat to low and cook for an additional minute, stirring constantly.

6 Stir in the sour cream, vinegar, mustard, and pepper.

7 Pour the sauce into a bowl, cover it, and refrigerate for 6 to 24 hours.

8 To serve, place the sauce bowl in the center of a large platter and arrange the shrimp around it. Sprinkle the capers on top of the sauce for a garnish, if desired.

Vary It! *Boiled shrimp have a tendency to be bland, which is why it is important to cook the shrimp with the bay leaves. However, if you want extra flavor, try adding some shrimp boil (also called "crab boil") while the shrimp are cooking.*

Tip: *To really make this appetizer look great, line the tray with some washed (and thoroughly dried) leaf lettuce. The green lettuce with the pink shrimp is visually appealing.*

Per serving: *Calories 33 (From Fat 17); Fat 2g (Saturated 1g); Cholesterol 32mg; Sodium 63mg; Carbohydrate 1g (Dietary Fiber 0g); Protein 3g.*

How to devein shrimp

So you didn't go to medical school, and the idea of deveining something doesn't sound too interesting. Don't worry; deveining shrimp is easy, and in fact, the black vein running down the back of the shrimp is the digestive tract, not really a vein. It's harmless, but not particularly attractive. You can buy deveined shrimp and avoid this icky task. However, if you didn't think about that in advance, you can easily do it yourself (see the following figure); here's how:

1. Hold the tail in one hand and gently remove the shell.

2. Pull off the tail, if desired.

3. At the tail end, pinch the vein and pull it out with your fingers. If you have trouble, try Step 4.

4. Make a shallow slit along the shrimp's back with a sharp paring knife, and then lift the vein out with the knife or wash it away under the tap. This method also gives you an added bonus — the shrimp will cook more quickly and evenly.

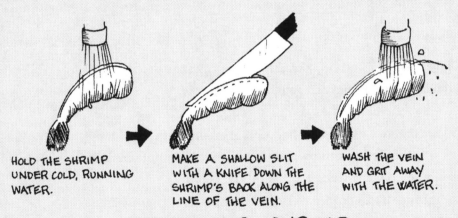

HOLD THE SHRIMP UNDER COLD, RUNNING WATER.

MAKE A SHALLOW SLIT WITH A KNIFE DOWN THE SHRIMP'S BACK ALONG THE LINE OF THE VEIN.

WASH THE VEIN AND GRIT AWAY WITH THE WATER.

DEVEINING SHRIMP

My Big Fat Greek Drummettes

These wonderful, tasty drummettes are a cleaner departure from their counterpart, the buffalo wing. Don't get us wrong — buffalo wings have their place, but not at a formal affair such as a wedding. Served warm with a distinctive, addictive dipping sauce, these appetizers are sure to be a hit.

Preparation time: 30 minutes

Chill time: 8 hours to overnight

Cooking time: 35 to 45 minutes per batch

Yield: 48 drummettes

Cucumber Dill Dipping Sauce (see the following recipe)

½ cup lemon juice

¼ cup olive oil

¼ cup honey

2 teaspoons dried oregano

½ teaspoon salt

2 garlic cloves, minced

48 chicken drummettes

1 In a small bowl, mix all the ingredients for the drummettes, except for the chicken, and stir until well blended.

2 Place the chicken in a large flat dish and pour the mixture over it, making sure all the drummettes are covered.

3 Cover the dish and refrigerate it for 8 hours or overnight. While the chicken is marinating, make the dipping sauce.

4 After the chicken has marinated, preheat the oven to 400 degrees and spray a broiler pan with nonstick cooking spray.

5 Remove the drummettes from the marinade and place them on the broiler pan in a single layer.

6 Bake for 35 to 45 minutes, or until golden brown, turning once about halfway through baking time. Serve hot with the cucumber dill dipping sauce.

Cucumber Dill Dipping Sauce

1 cup peeled, chopped, and seeded cucumber

1 cup plain yogurt

1 cup (4 ounces) crumbled feta cheese

2 tablespoons chopped fresh dill

¼ teaspoon salt

2 garlic cloves, chopped

In a blender, combine all the ingredients and blend until well mixed. Put the dip in a bowl, cover it, and refrigerate until serving time.

Crowd Saver: *To save time, make the dip a day ahead of schedule; the flavors will blend better the longer they sit. You can also make the drummettes ahead of time. To reheat, place them in a microwaveable dish, add a tablespoon of water, and cover the dish in plastic wrap. Heat on medium power until warm.*

Per serving: *Calories 70 (From Fat 44); Fat 5g (Saturated 2g); Cholesterol 21mg; Sodium 75mg; Carbohydrate 1g (Dietary Fiber 0g); Protein 5g.*

◯ Olive Bites

These rich olive bites are sure to be a hit — the cheesy dough and cayenne pepper will delight your guests. This recipe gives you 110 bites, but don't worry, they'll go quickly!

Preparation time: *30 minutes*

Cooking time: *15 minutes*

Yield: *110 bites*

4½ cups (18 ounces) shredded cheddar cheese	*2¼ cups flour*
½ cup, 1 tablespoon butter, softened	*½ teaspoon cayenne pepper*
	110 pimento-stuffed Spanish olives

1 Preheat the oven to 400 degrees.

2 In a medium bowl, combine the cheese and butter.

3 Stir in the flour and pepper; blend well.

4 Wrap a tablespoon of dough around each olive and arrange the wrapped olives on a baking sheet.

5 Bake for 15 minutes, or until golden brown.

Crowd Saver: *You can save some time with this recipe! Make the dough-wrapped olives, and then put them in the refrigerator on a baking sheet until they're cold. After they're cold, put them in a plastic freezer bag and store them in the freezer. You can bake them right out of the freezer — you just need to extend the baking time by a few minutes.*

Per serving: *Calories 40 (From Fat 26); Fat 3g (Saturated 2g); Cholesterol 7mg; Sodium 112mg; Carbohydrate 2g (Dietary Fiber 0g); Protein 2g.*

Creating Sweet Memories: Sweet Treats

Of course, wedding cake will take its place, but face it — those sweet little treats are often what people crave. A wedding is a day of bliss, not a day to worry about calories. So indulge your guests with a sinful assortment of sweets; in this section, you'll find some of our favorite wedding treats. (All, of course, are in the clear for vegetarians.)

Sweet Bruschetta

When you think of bruschetta, you probably think about an Italian appetizer made with tomatoes, basil, and fresh cheese on a piece of garlic bread. This recipe is a dessert version of that Italian favorite. You already know that cream cheese and fruit are wonderful together, but try adding a piece of sweet bread.

Preparation time: *15 minutes*

Cooking time: *10 minutes*

Yield: *48 pieces*

2 8-ounce loaves baguette-style French bread	*2 8-ounce tubs cream cheese*
1 cup butter, melted	*1 teaspoon vanilla extract*
½ cup sugar	*4 cups strawberries, sliced*
1 cup strawberry jelly	

1 Preheat the oven to 375 degrees.

2 Cut each loaf into 24 ¼-inch slices for a total of 48 slices. Place the bread slices in a single layer on an ungreased baking sheet.

3 Lightly brush the melted butter onto each piece, then dust each piece with sugar.

4 Bake the bread for 10 minutes, or until lightly browned.

5 Place the strawberry jelly in a microwaveable bowl and heat it on high for 30 seconds, or until melted.

6 In a medium bowl, combine the cream cheese, vanilla extract, and half of the melted strawberry jelly. Stir until thoroughly blended, then spread the mixture on the toast.

7 Arrange two strawberry slices on each piece of toast.

8 Take the remaining melted jelly and brush it over the strawberries; serve.

Tip: If strawberries aren't your fruit of choice, try substituting raspberries or peaches instead. Just remember to also change the flavor of the jelly.

Per serving: Calories 136 (From Fat 72); Fat 8g (Saturated 5g); Cholesterol 20mg; Sodium 91mg; Carbohydrate 15g (Dietary Fiber 1g); Protein 2g.

Chocolate Peanut Butter Tassies

Peanut butter and chocolate — need we say more? These rich, creamy dessert bites are just the ticket to satisfy your sweet tooth.

Preparation time: *30 minutes*

Cooking time: *20 to 25 minutes*

Chill time: *1 hour*

Yield: *72 tassies*

6 ounces cream cheese, softened

1½ cups butter, softened

3 cups flour

1½ cups sugar, divided

2 eggs, slightly beaten

4 tablespoons butter, melted

½ teaspoon lemon juice

½ teaspoon vanilla extract

1¾ cups peanut butter chips

1¾ cups milk chocolate chips

1 tablespoon, 1 teaspoon shortening

1 Preheat the oven to 350 degrees.

2 In a medium bowl, beat the cream cheese and softened butter until smooth and thoroughly blended.

3 Slowly mix in the flour and ½ cup of the sugar, beating until well blended.

4 Cover the bowl and place it in the refrigerator for 1 hour.

5 Remove the dough from the refrigerator and shape it into 1-inch balls.

6 Press each ball into the bottom and up the sides of the cups in a nonstick minimuffin pan.

7 In a medium bowl, combine the eggs, remaining sugar, melted butter, lemon juice, and vanilla extract and stir until well blended.

8 Set aside ⅔ cup of both the peanut butter chips and the milk chocolate chips and stir the rest of the chips into the egg-and-sugar mixture.

9 Evenly fill each minimuffin cup with the mixture.

10 Bake for 20 to 25 minutes or until the filling is set and lightly browned.

11 In a microwavable bowl, combine the reserved chips with the shortening and melt them on high for approximately 30 seconds. If necessary, melt them for an additional 15 seconds, stirring until the mixture is smooth.

12 Drizzle the chocolate–peanut butter mixture over the tops of the tassies and serve.

Tip: *You can make life a lot easier with recipes like this one by investing in a little device called a tart press, as you can see in Figure 12-1. This little press gives you a quick and easy way to press the tart shell perfectly every time. You can find tart presses at any cooking store.*

Per serving: *Calories 132 (From Fat 74); Fat 8g (Saturated 5g); Cholesterol 22mg; Sodium 22mg; Carbohydrate 13g (Dietary Fiber 1g); Protein 2g.*

Figure 12-1:
A tart press
gives
perfectly
shaped tart
shells each
and every
time.

TART PRESS

Chocolate Chip Cookie Dough Truffles

When was the last time you made chocolate chip cookies? Did you eat any of the dough? Sure you did — everyone does. There's something about the taste and the texture of cookie dough that keeps people coming back for more. The bad news is that raw dough really isn't safe because of the eggs you use to make it.

However, these truffles don't have raw eggs, but you won't be able to tell! This dessert is probably the one that gets the most requests. These easy-to-make truffles are all-around winners, satisfying both the young and the young at heart.

Preparation time: *40 minutes*

Chill time: *35 to 40 minutes*

Yield: *52 truffles*

½ cup butter, softened

¼ cup sugar

½ cup brown sugar, firmly packed

¼ cup egg substitute

1 teaspoon vanilla

1 cup miniature semisweet chocolate morsels

¾ cup pecans or walnuts, chopped

12 ounces semisweet chocolate morsels

1½ tablespoons shortening

1 Place the butter in a medium mixing bowl and, using an electric mixer, beat until creamy.

2 Gradually add the sugar and brown sugar; beat well.

3 Add the egg substitute and vanilla and beat well.

4 Stir in the miniature chocolate chips and the nuts.

5 Cover the bowl and chill the mixture for about 30 minutes.

6 Remove the dough from the refrigerator and shape it into 1-inch balls.

7 Line a baking sheet with wax paper. Place the dough balls on the baking sheet and place it in the freezer until the dough is firm.

8 In a microwavable bowl, combine the chocolate morsels and shortening.

9 Melt the chocolate in the microwave according to the package directions.

10 Remove the truffles from the freezer. Using two forks, dip each ball of dough in the melted chocolate. Make sure you dip the balls quickly and completely.

11 Place the dipped truffles back on the baking sheet and return them to the freezer for 5 to 10 minutes, or until the chocolate coating has hardened.

12 Remove the truffles from the freezer and serve.

Tip: *The trick to dipping these tasty treats is to work quickly and make sure that you let the excess chocolate drip back into the bowl.*

Per serving: *Calories 96 (From Fat 0); Fat 59g (Saturated 3g); Cholesterol 5mg; Sodium 4mg; Carbohydrate 10g (Dietary Fiber 1g); Protein 1g.*

Blissful Entrees

Whether you're having a formal plated dinner reception or a buffet dinner, the following recipes are good choices for wedding crowds.

If you're serving an entree, be sure to check out Chapter 6 for some wonderful side dish recipes as well.

Rosemary Pork Roast

This rosemary pork roast is rather savory and is a perfect choice for a wedding reception. Additionally, this dish isn't fussy — you can serve it with any number of side dishes.

Preparation time: *30 minutes*

Cooking time: *1 hour, 25 minutes*

Yield: *20 to 24 servings*

2 5-to-6-pound boneless pork loin roasts	*3 tablespoons dried rosemary*
4 large garlic cloves, cut into quarters	*2 teaspoons salt*
2 tablespoons olive oil	*2 teaspoons pepper*

1 Preheat the oven to 325 degrees.

2 Place each pork roast, fat side up, in a shallow roasting pan. Cut eight small slits in the top, fat side of each roast.

3 Place a piece of garlic in each slit.

4 Brush a tablespoon of olive oil on each roast, covering them evenly.

5 In a small bowl, combine the rosemary, salt, and pepper and mix well.

6 Rub half of the mixture onto each roast.

7 Cook the roasts uncovered for 1 hour and 25 minutes, or until a meat thermometer reads 160 degrees at the thickest part of the roast.

8 Remove the roasts from the oven and let them stand for 10 to 15 minutes before slicing.

Per serving: Calories 288 (From Fat 125); Fat 14g (Saturated 5g); Cholesterol 107mg; Sodium 271mg; Carbohydrate 1g (Dietary Fiber 0g); Protein 38g.

Beef Stroganoff

This hearty favorite is a great choice for a buffet-style reception. Served with rice or pasta, this filling entree is sure to please.

Preparation time: *50 minutes*

Yield: *20 servings*

3 cups flour	1 large onion, chopped
1 tablespoon salt	4 garlic cloves, minced
2 tablespoons dried parsley	6 cups beef broth
1½ tablespoons pepper	¼ cup tomato paste
1 tablespoon garlic powder	5 cups sour cream
5 pounds sirloin steak, cut into 1-inch slices	15 cups wide egg noodles or white rice, cooked per package directions
3 cups butter, melted	parsley, for garnish (optional)
3 cups sliced, canned or jarred mushrooms	

1 In a large bowl or extra-large zip-top plastic bag, combine the flour, salt, dried parsley, pepper, and garlic powder.

2 Add the meat to the flour mixture; toss until all the pieces of meat are coated.

3 In a large skillet, melt the butter; add the meat and cook, stirring occasionally, until the meat is brown.

4 Remove the meat from the skillet; cover it and keep it warm.

5 Place the mushrooms, onions, and garlic in the skillet, cooking them in the drippings from the meat and stirring constantly. Cook until the onions are translucent, not browned. After they're cooked, remove the items from the pan, drain off the excess grease, and keep them warm.

6 Deglaze the skillet with a couple of tablespoons or so of water, cooking over high heat.

7 Add the beef broth and tomato paste to the skillet. Cook over medium heat, stirring until smooth; the mixture will thicken.

8 After the mixture has thickened, add the meat and the mushroom-and-onion mixture to the pan; continue cooking for 5 minutes.

9 Reduce the heat to low and add the sour cream, stirring constantly until heated through.

10 Remove the mixture from heat and serve it over a bed of pasta or rice; garnish with a sprig of fresh parsley (if desired).

Per serving: Calories 738 (From Fat 418); Fat 46g (Saturated 27g); Cholesterol 148mg; Sodium 731mg; Carbohydrate 52g (Dietary Fiber 1g); Protein 27g.

Regal Beef Tenderloin

This succulent beef tenderloin is the perfect entree for a wedding. You can serve it in a buffet line or in a more formal, plated dinner reception. The marinade is the key to preparing this mouth-watering delight.

Preparation time: *20 minutes*

Chill time: *8 hours*

Cooking time: *55 minutes to 1 hour, 10 minutes*

Yield: *20 to 24 servings*

2 cups soy sauce	2 tablespoons white vinegar
1⅓ cups vegetable oil	2 teaspoons garlic powder
6 tablespoons brown sugar	2 green onions, chopped
4 tablespoons Dijon mustard	2 6-to-7-pound beef tenderloins

1 In a large bowl, combine all the ingredients, except for the tenderloins, and stir well.

2 Place each tenderloin in a large zip-top, heavy-duty plastic bag.

3 Pour half of the marinade over each tenderloin, seal the bags, and refrigerate them for 8 hours, turning occasionally to make sure all the sides are well marinated.

4 Preheat the oven to 400 degrees.

5 Remove the tenderloins from the bags and place each on a rack in a shallow roasting pan.

6 Transfer the marinade from the bags into a saucepan and bring it to a boil; remove the mixture from heat and set it aside.

7 Bake the tenderloins for 55 minutes to 1 hour and 10 minutes, or until a meat thermometer inserted into the thickest part registers 145 to 160 degrees. Baste the meat occasionally with the boiled marinade.

8 Let the tenderloins stand for 10 minutes before slicing.

Tip: This beautiful cut of meat is meant to be tender and juicy, so make sure you pay close attention as it gets closer to the end of its cooking time; you don't want to overcook it. Also, make sure you don't skip the basting part of the recipe; again, this helps the meat taste its very best.

Per serving: Calories 400 (From Fat 209); Fat 23g (Saturated 6g); Cholesterol 114mg; Sodium 1,377mg; Carbohydrate 4g (Dietary Fiber 0g); Protein 41g.

Part IV
Bringing It All Together

The 5th Wave — By Rich Tennant

"I'm having my ornithology club over for brunch."

In this part . . .

So you've made your plans and selected the recipes you'll prepare, and now you need to bring everything together for your crowd. No problem! In this part, you explore some fundamental and important aspects of crowd cooking that will help you be successful. You find out about scheduling, cooking, and managing the big day. We show you our tricks and timesaving tactics, which will help you keep your sanity as guests come knocking at your door.

Chapter 13

Getting Ready for the Event

In This Chapter

▶ Maximizing your kitchen's space

▶ Planning the days (and foods) to come

▶ Developing a workflow so the big day runs smoothly

*O*rganization is a fun part of life. After all, we're sure you enjoy nothing more than cleaning out your closet, systematically putting all your photos in albums, and keeping the clutter from accumulating under the seats of your car. Yeah, right! If you're like us, those tasks are the type you think about doing but never actually accomplish. Yet, organization is vitally important as you get ready to cook for a crowd.

In this chapter, we tackle the issue of getting ready for the event. You find out how to get your kitchen organized, create a calendar, prepare advance items, and create a workflow. By the time you finish this chapter, you'll already be ahead in the cooking-for-crowds game.

Getting Organized

Have you ever stood in your kitchen, aimlessly staring inside your cabinets and thinking, "I really need to get this place under control"? That sentiment is common. From food to forks, your kitchen probably holds a lot of items, and getting everything in the right place so you can quickly access the things you need can be a bit overwhelming. Don't worry. In this section, you find out what you need and how to organize your kitchen.

Making a list and checking it twice

As you get ready to cook for a crowd, you're going to need to create some lists. We know; you're probably not a lists person. We're not either, but lists are very important when cooking for a crowd and trying to keep your sanity.

So what lists do you need? We always find a few standards helpful. Consider spending a little time whipping up these lists:

- ✔ **Ingredients to buy:** Naturally, you need to make a list of ingredients for the food you'll be preparing. Check your recipes carefully.

- ✔ **Supplies to buy:** You need a list of nonfood items, such as napkins, cups, plastic wrap, trash bags, and so on.

- ✔ **Cookware and serving pieces you need:** You should have a solid list of all the cookware and serving pieces you'll need. You can find out more about these items in Chapter 3.

- ✔ **Guests who will attend:** This list helps you keep track of who's coming, which impacts your food preparation. We suggest that you split this master list into two groups: adults and children. Of course, adults eat more than children, which impacts your food preparation, but also keep in mind that children may steer clear of some dishes (spinach dip, for example). Also, you may want to prepare a dish or two especially for the children if you have a number of them attending. As you can see, the guest list will drive your food preparation, so make your list and check it twice (and don't forget to update it as necessary).

- ✔ **SOS:** Have a short list of people who will help you with small inconveniences if necessary. Maybe you have family and friends who will let you borrow items or other people who will help with certain needs. Whatever the need may be, have a short list on hand of dependable people that you can call on.

- ✔ **People you can *really* lean on:** Murphy's Law says that something will always go wrong at the most importune time. Suppose you're cooking for a family get-together of 50 and you break your arm the day before. What do you do? You have a list of three to four good friends or family members whom you trust and depend on and can call to help. This group is different from the SOS list — these people are those you can call at midnight and ask to come help if the chips are down. If something is slowing you down or keeping you from finalizing the meal, you can consult your list and quickly get some help (which is much better than running away from home).

Organizing your kitchen

The kitchen is probably the most diverse room in your house. In it, you probably store such items as food, pots and pans, dishes, silverware, cleaning supplies, storage supplies, and many other items. In fact, if you stop and think about it, you may have everything (including the kitchen sink!) stored in your kitchen. For this reason, organizing your kitchen can be a bit troublesome. The need to get organized when you prepare to cook for a crowd becomes even more important, because you'll need more items than you normally store.

There's no correct way to organize your kitchen for crowd cooking. How you choose to organize will be based on the layout of your kitchen, your available space, and how you like to work. From our point of view, if it works for you, then it works; don't fix it if it isn't broken. However, as you get ready to cook for a crowd, thinking beyond the norm concerning your kitchen is important. More than likely, you don't cook for a crowd on a daily or even weekly basis, so even if your kitchen is somewhat organized, it probably isn't organized in a way that's conducive to crowd cooking.

Don't worry, though. We have some important methods to share with you as you try to get things in order for your crowd.

Zone out

If you have nightmares about kitchen organization, you probably have a good reason: You're thinking about your kitchen as a whole instead of breaking it down into parts. We like to think of our kitchen as a room that has many different parts, which we call zones. A *zone* is an area where certain similar items are organized and stored. You probably already use zones in your kitchen but just don't know it. For example, you probably keep all your canned foods in one place, your silverware in another, cleaning supplies in another, and so on.

This zoning approach will help you get organized and stay organized and will also make inventory much easier to manage. After all, when you cook for a crowd, managing inventory and keeping up with everything is vitally important. Seeing your kitchen as different zones helps you focus on different parts of the whole instead of letting the whole overwhelm you.

First of all, take a close look at each kitchen zone. Try to keep similar items together. In other words, avoid storing your pots and pans on the same kitchen shelf as canned food items. Zones that have specific and logically grouped items are much easier to manage. This idea especially rings true as you purchase items for crowd cooking.

Strive to use subzones. We're not going to lead you into Zone Never-Never Land, but you really should take a close look at subdividing your zones. For example, keep all your plates together, keep glasses together, keep canned vegetables organized by type, and so on. This suborganizational method will help you stay on track as you get ready to cook for a crowd.

Seeing is believing

You should be able to see everything in a zone. When you open a cabinet or drawer, can you see what you have? For example, if you have canned food items stacked in front of each other, you can't see them all, you can't reach them all, and you're more likely to waste money buying duplicate items (which explains why you have ten cans of green beans). When you cook for a crowd, being able to store and see what you have is vitally important, because you'll probably buy more food items than you normally would otherwise. For tips on arranging all those items, see the sidebar "Making kitchen items easy to see."

Rotate it

Keep refrigerator items rotated. For example, when you buy sliced cheese, put the already opened package to the front and put the new package behind it. Because you'll tend to buy many perishable items when cooking for crowds, the rotation method will help you keep track of what's new and what's old and will help you save money. It will also help you stop growing penicillin in your refrigerator.

Making kitchen items easy to see

We know what you're thinking: "Sure, I know I need to organize my pantry so I can see everything, but I have too much stuff!" We understand. We live in a 104-year-old home and know a thing or two about a lack of kitchen cabinets and storage space. The good news is that you can organize pantries and drawers creatively and inexpensively. Consider putting these helpful tips to work:

✔ **Purchase a Lazy Susan.** A *Lazy Susan* is a device that stores items and can fit in a cabinet or on a countertop. It spins around so you can easily see and reach everything stored on it.

✔ **Use drawer organizers.** Drawer organizers essentially divide a drawer into compartments so you can easily store different items. You can find a variety of drawer organizers at any supercenter, kitchen store, or online at www.stacksandstacks.com.

✔ **Use a slide-out organizer.** A slide-out organizer basically provides you with an inexpensive way to create pullout drawers. These easy-to-install items eliminate the need to dig around under the kitchen sink. You can see some examples at www.stacksandstacks.com.

Clean out the clutter. Try to get rid of stuff you don't need so you can make room for the things you do. In other words, that bottle of dishwashing liquid that has been in your cabinet since 1942 needs to go!

Creating a Calendar

A calendar is a key component of successful crowd cooking. By this time, you've accepted, maybe even embraced, the fact that you're going to be cooking for the crowd. Now you need to get out your calendar and start planning.

We know, you're probably thinking, "I'll just get organized mentally," but take our word for it, the process will be much more enjoyable if you have a clear, written-out game plan of what each day's accomplishments need to be.

Mapping out the upcoming event

If you write out everything that you need to do, you'll start realizing what you can do ahead of time. When mapping out the event on your calendar, remember to think ahead. Many tasks can be done several days prior to the event.

For example, if you know that you're going to need 10 dozen cookies, start baking a few batches every day. Or if you're making a recipe that freezes and reheats well, make it a week or so in advance.

By writing out what you need to do, you'll start seeing areas where you can save yourself a great deal of time.

Setting deadlines

Deadlines are never any fun — just as the name implies. Yet, with any cooking event, you have a final deadline at mealtime. However, you'll feel much less stress if you set some incremental deadlines along the way. These incremental deadlines, which we like to call *checkpoints,* help you establish a process for cooking for your crowd.

We usually have a Christmas party in our home for 80 to 100 people. As you can imagine, staring at the final deadline can be a bit overwhelming. So we remove the stress factor by creating checkpoints. We simply mark up a calendar with everything we need to do.

You can do the same. Take a good look at your to-do lists and apply those lists to a calendar. Make realistic but firm checkpoints that will enable you to complete your tasks. These realistic checkpoints will help you get the job done and will make the process more enjoyable.

Working ahead of Schedule

Having a realistic schedule can mean the difference between being able to enjoy the process of cooking for a crowd or wanting to pull out your hair trying to get things done on time. We've found that getting as many things as possible done early is extremely helpful when cooking for a crowd. When you work ahead, the event runs more smoothly, and you can usually catch those last-minute details that you may otherwise overlook.

Preparing foods in advance

At this point in the process, you already know what foods you'll prepare. Take a moment to thoroughly go over your lists of foods and determine which ones you can make ahead of time. Also figure out *how far* ahead of time you can prepare each item.

As you may imagine, preparing food in advance is important for two reasons: saving time and enhancing flavor. This section gives you the details.

Saving time

One of the great reasons to work ahead of schedule is to save time. After all, cooking for a crowd is much more time-consuming than a typical meal, so considering your time is really important. As you're thinking ahead, take a close look at your recipes and all the tasks you must accomplish and keep the following points in mind:

- ✔ Wash, dry, and cut up all the vegetables ahead of schedule. You can store them in individual plastic bags in the refrigerator.
- ✔ Make dips, spreads, and sauces ahead of time and store them in the refrigerator.
- ✔ If the recipe allows it, make desserts ahead of schedule.
- ✔ If refrigerator space allows, make anything that can keep overnight the day before the event.

✔ Clean up the kitchen as you go. This tip may sound silly, but keep everything clean and put away. You don't want to face two hours of kitchen cleaning on the day of the event.

✔ Box up all nonperishable items that you don't need until the day of the event. Doing so will help you transport them more easily. Also, see Chapter 15 for more information about transporting food items.

✔ If possible, set up the tables and chairs and take nonperishable items to the event location the day before the event. If refrigerator space is available at the event location, take what perishable items you can, too.

✔ If other people are assisting you, contact them for a follow-up. Now is the time to delegate tasks, so don't be afraid to tell them what to do.

✔ If you're storing items at other people's homes, follow up with them to make sure they'll be available when you need to come by.

Planning ahead to enhance flavor

Some foods actually taste much better if they're prepared ahead and all the flavors are allowed enough time to thoroughly blend together.

Here's an example from our own experience. We've always tried to prepare ahead of time, but at a recent Christmas party that we hosted for 100 people, we accidentally overbooked ourselves with too many obligations, which meant we had to be even more prepared than usual.

We knew that we were going to be making 10 dozen sausage balls for this party. So to save time, we chopped up the onion and the celery and went ahead and mixed them together with the sausage and the cheese. We put the mixture in a couple of large plastic bags (for easier storage, we've found that plastic bags work better than bowls). The mixture sat in the refrigerator for about 36 hours before we rolled it into balls. We've used this recipe many times before, but this time our guests said these were the absolute best sausage balls they'd ever had.

The difference? The ingredients sat together long enough to give the best flavor possible. Truthfully, we were just trying to save time, but we ended up with a dish that was much better!

Of course, some foods must be prepared just moments before serving. But in case you're wondering, a number of popular food items lend themselves to being prepared well ahead of time. Here are a few examples to get your mind moving in the right direction. You can also check out the recipe chapters in this book; we point out timesaving preparation tips in those chapters as well.

- Vegetable platters
- Salad dressings
- Dips
- Most soups
- Punch bases
- Beans and some other side dishes
- Minicasseroles
- Some cold desserts
- Cookies
- Cheesecake

Keeping prepared items fresh

Now that you've decided what you can prepare ahead of time, take a look at how to keep foods fresh. Of course, the amount of time you save won't matter if the foods don't taste fresh. Don't worry, though. You can put some simple tactics to work.

Preventing odors in your refrigerator and freezer

Much of what you'll prepare ahead of time will probably need to stay cold or frozen. Because foods absorb odors, it's a good idea to make sure your refrigerator, freezer, or ice chest is clean of any food that has turned into a science project. If that piece of tomato you've been saving for a month has long since turned white and fuzzy, get rid of it ASAP.

One of the easiest solutions to help foods stay fresh is to use a box of baking soda. Baking soda helps absorb odors that may be lurking around in your refrigerator, freezer, or ice chest. After all, nothing is worse than chocolate cake that tastes like an onion. Just open the box, pull back the lid slightly, and let it do its job.

Keeping your cold items cold

Another tip that will help you keep your food fresher is to avoid overloading your refrigerator. We realize that when cooking for a crowd, you may have no choice but to stack things in every nook and cranny you can find. However, be careful not to block the air vent in your refrigerator. The more the air can circulate around the food, the more even the temperature will be, and the fresher the food will stay.

Sealing in freshness

Good quality plastic bags are very versatile and are rather inexpensive. Plastic bags come in a variety of sizes, which can help you save room. We find it helpful to always keep a variety of storage bags on hand. We store anything from hamburger meat to cookies to cut vegetables in plastic bags.

Reusable plastic storage containers are also very versatile and affordable. These storage containers come in a variety of shapes and sizes and can be reused for a period of time and then discarded. Many of them are microwavable, which is also a big help.

Of course, another option is permanent plastic containers, such as Tupperware. You probably already have these in your kitchen cabinets, and they work great to seal in freshness.

If you use plastic bags or plastic containers, make sure you always press out the air before sealing the bag or container. The less air you have in the bag or container, the longer the food will stay fresh.

Wrapping your dishes

For most people, foil is as essential to the kitchen as the sink. It's great for cooking and for wrapping up foods you need to store. Just keep in mind that heavy-duty foil is always better than a less expensive, lighter weight foil. The lighter weight foil tends to tear easier, which lets freshness out.

Another standard kitchen wrap is plastic wrap. Everyone knows the slogan: "Sometimes it clings; sometimes it doesn't." Plastic wrap definitely has its place, but too many times we've found that slogan to be true.

Therefore, if you want to keep your New York–style cheesecake from tasting like garlic bread, use a storage item that will give you consistently good results. Again, plastic wrap is a great product, but make sure that it clings where it should if you decide to use it. Also, consider using several layers of plastic wrap for extra protection.

Wax paper and parchment paper are two other kitchen standards that make preparing and cooking food easier. However, these two items aren't meant for food storage. Wax paper is great for keeping foods from sticking together in a storage unit, but used alone, it won't keep foods fresh.

Preserving nonperishables

When you think about freshness, don't forget about nonperishable food items. When you cook for a crowd, money is usually a concern; therefore, looking for sales on the items you need is always wise. As you're shopping, make sure you pay close attention to the expiration date or the sell-by date on the package.

Pay extra attention when you purchase bread. The expiration date may say it's good for another week, but upon closer inspection, you may see telltale signs of mold. In short, many people consider bread a nonperishable item, but they're wrong. Check the expiration date!

You may have never really thought about canned goods in relation to freshness, but the truth remains: Canned foods that are dented can lose their freshness. When foods are canned or placed in a jar, part of the process of packaging them is making them airtight by creating a vacuum. This process prevents bacteria from getting in the can or jar and growing on the food. However, dents or any small cracks can let air in, so avoid damaged packages.

When you buy snack foods, such as chips, crackers, pretzels, and others, again pay attention to the sell-by date. Also, take notice of the packaging. Does that box of crackers have a dent, or does the bag of chips look like it's been tossed around one too many times? Taking just a few extra moments to examine the foods you're buying can save you money and help all your efforts in preparing a wonderful meal.

Making a Workflow for the Day of the Event

The day of the event is drawing near. Your mind is probably running 90 miles an hour. If your life were a movie, would the *Jaws* soundtrack be playing in the background, or would you hear *The Sound of Music*? If you're like we were the first time we cooked for a crowd, you probably switch back and forth between the two.

Planning for the day of the event can greatly reduce the stress that naturally comes when cooking for a crowd. Again, the more prepared you are, the smoother your day will go.

Planning for timeliness

As you make a workflow schedule for the day of the event, being realistic about what needs to be done is very important. Be aware of what time the event will take place.

That reminder sounds simple, but you've probably attended an event where dinner was an hour late. No one likes that scenario, and you don't want it to happen on your watch. You can do some simple things to avoid lateness (and frustrated guests). As for most events, you have to plan to be timely.

You may easily forget to take into consideration a lot of little things when planning your big day. So make sure you take time to really think about all the things that need to get done before, during, and after the event.

Here are some helpful questions to ask yourself that will help you plan:

- ✔ What time of day is the event?
- ✔ Will you be able to take items to the event location ahead of time?
- ✔ Will you be the one responsible for setting up tables and chairs?
- ✔ If the event is somewhere other than your home, do you have the keys to the facility?
- ✔ Will you be able to have someone take care of your children while you're getting everything ready?
- ✔ How many people will be helping you? Do you need more?
- ✔ Are you in charge of absolutely everything?
- ✔ If you aren't in charge of everything, what are the helpers supposed to do or bring, and are they informed? Are you really, really, really sure they're on top of things?
- ✔ Will you need to pick up anyone and take him or her to the event?
- ✔ Is the car full of gas?
- ✔ Is your cellphone battery charged?
- ✔ What is the weather forecast for the day of the event?
- ✔ What is the traffic normally like during the time of day you'll travel?
- ✔ Do you have any foods that you need to take out of the freezer and thaw?
- ✔ Will you need to warm up any foods at the event location? If so, is a microwave or an oven available?
- ✔ How many foods will you need to warm up, and how long will each of them take to heat?

You may read this list and think, "There's no way I can remember all this!" Don't worry. Use the previous questions as a checklist and incorporate them into your master plan. Then, all you have to do is follow your plan and check off the completed items.

"We came early so we could help . . ."

Inevitably, some well-meaning guests will arrive early just so they can "help out," and you may have some guests who are just early people. If you're running around at the last minute trying to get things ready, how can you handle these early birds? Here are a few tactics:

✔ **Plan on having people arrive at least 30 minutes before they're supposed to.** When you're prepared for this likelihood, you can plan ahead and simply be ready 30 minutes early. Of course, doing so may not be entirely practical, but just realize that 1:00 p.m. means 12:30 to some people.

✔ **Give them something to do.** Depending on your culture, some guests feel very uncomfortable coming to a crowd event where they aren't allowed to help or bring food. If you know you have some folks who really need to help, then by all means, have some simple tasks they can do. Again, plan on a few people arriving early and save some noncritical tasks for them to complete. These tasks can be as simple as helping set the table, moving chairs, lighting candles, and so on.

✔ **Have some early appetizers ready.** This way, if some guests are early, they can have something to eat and drink, which helps break the ice and enables the early guests to feel like the party has already started. Always err on the side of making your guests feel warm and welcome, even if they're early.

Creating a preparation workflow and timeline

Creating a realistic game plan for the day of the event should start with a piece of notebook paper. Make a half-hour schedule, starting with whatever time you plan on getting up that day. This workflow will help you stay on schedule and will keep you from forgetting things. Without one, you're much more likely to run behind schedule.

No crowd cook can remember everything that needs to be done, especially when you add the stress and pressure that the event day will surely bring. Hence, the importance of a workflow and timeline.

Here, we provide a pretend schedule so you can see how one should look. Suppose that Cousin Sally is getting married at 2:30 p.m., and a reception of appetizers for 40 people follows the wedding. That job has fallen on your shoulders, and you need to create a workflow. Your workflow and schedule may look something like this:

7:00 a.m.	Rise and shine
7:30	Eat breakfast
	Review lists
	Preheat oven for sausage balls
8:00	Cook first batch of sausage balls
	Make sandwiches, cut into fourths, and put on tray
8:30	Get kids up, dressed, and fed
	Cook second batch of sausage balls
9:00	Make zesty tortilla roll-ups
	Cook third batch of sausage balls
9:30	Coffee break
	Change oven temperature to cook chicken nuggets
10:00	Call Aunt Ann to verify wedding punch
	Cook first batch of chicken nuggets
	Make bread bowl for spinach dip
	Coat bread pieces with garlic butter
10:30	Cook second batch of chicken nuggets
	Clean kitchen
11:00	Cook third batch of chicken nuggets
	Clean kitchen again
11:30	Get showered and dressed
12:00 p.m.	Finish getting ready and eat lunch
12:30	Load items in car; check off all items as they're loaded
1:00	Arrive at event
	Unload car
1:30	Arrange vegetable tray
	Arrange meat and cheese tray
	Arrange fruit tray
2:00	Put spinach dip in bread bowl and tray
	Arrange cracker tray
	Start arranging nonperishable foods on tables

2:30	Pour dipping sauces for chicken in serving bowls
	Wedding starts
	Set out all food items
	Light Sterno cans for chicken and sausage balls
	Breathe — all your hard work is about to pay off
3:00	Reception starts
	Enjoy the compliments on the tasty food!

The more detailed you are as you set your schedule, the less likely you are to get behind or, worse, forget something. A realistic schedule will also help you determine whether you need help and how much. Don't be afraid to make adjustments to the schedule if it seems unrealistic, and, naturally, don't be afraid to find extra help if you need it.

Chapter 14

Getting Ready on the Day of the Event

This is it! Your big day is on the brink and all your planning and hard work will soon pay off. Nothing is quite like the day of the feast. You've worked hard and paid attention to every detail. Naturally, this day is full of excitement (and probably a good dose of butterflies in your stomach).

Yet, the day of the event is much like any other day up to this point. It's helpful to think of the big day as a process — a list of steps and tasks that you must complete on time. If you view the day this way, you'll feel less stressed and more in control. In fact, you'll enjoy the day as much as anyone else. In order to accomplish your tasks, you need to plan ahead and think carefully (and clearly).

We wrote this chapter to help you survive and thrive. Here, you find out how to manage the day of the event and how to serve your crowd, so keep reading!

Getting Your Head in the Game

Naturally, the day of the event will pull your mind in a lot of different directions. *Remember:* Remaining calm and focused as you get ready for your crowd event is important. You can keep your head clear by keeping track of time, reviewing your lists, and rechecking your inventory.

Counting down the hours

The night before the big day is very important. You'll probably be running around trying to make sure you've remembered everything that needs to be done. You've probably had a long day of preparing, but it's nighttime now and time to de-stress. Be sure to allow yourself time the night before the event to have a relaxing evening and a good night's sleep. You've got a busy day tomorrow, and you need to be able to hit the floor running.

On the morning of the event, as you're looking at the busy day ahead of you, remember to stop and take time to care for yourself. Allow time to sit and drink your morning cup of coffee and mentally get ready for your crowd. Hopefully, you got a good night's sleep and are full of energy to start the day.

Now's the time to don your multitasking hat. As you get ready for your day, begin to mentally rehearse the day's events. Sometimes, regardless of how thorough we think we've been, the morning of the event is when we remember details and loose ends that we need to take care of. So think through the events of the day and what will happen at what time. Doing so will help you create a mental workflow for your day.

Consider creating an hour-by-hour workflow for the day of the event in advance. A workflow will help you stay on track and help your day run more smoothly. See Chapter 13 to find out more.

Today will be a busy day, and if your household is anything like ours, especially on the weekends, the phone rings off the hook. Do yourself a favor — let the answering machine get it. You can screen your calls this way. When you're at your busiest moment, Aunt Chatty Cathy never fails to call and tell you play-by-play about her bridge game.

Reviewing your lists

Remember those lists you made? (If you didn't, see Chapter 13 for some guidance.) Get them out and review them. Start with the workflow list for that day. Hopefully, you took our advice and already have your workflow list written up. Review the list to make sure everything is still on track. However, feel free to make changes to it as necessary.

You should also go back over the guest list just to make sure no radical changes have happened. In our experience, no matter how many times you ask people to RSVP by a certain date, some of them invariably wait until the night before or the day of the event to let you know. This late notice usually isn't a problem, unless a lot of people have made the social blunder of not responding on time.

Check your SOS list and the list of people you can really lean on — are they still accurate? Keep in mind as you're reviewing these lists who you'll call for some assistance if necessary.

Reviewing your lists shouldn't take very long at all. Again, the reason for the review is to help you get mentally on track for the day. The most important thing to remember is to note any last-minute changes. Roll with any changes and be sure to ask for help if you feel like things are getting out of control.

Confirming your inventory

It's time to start getting everything together, so get out your food, nonfood items, and your cookware and serving pieces lists. Thoroughly review these lists as you're packing everything up so you avoid the "Oh no — I forgot" scenario. In our busy, multitasking world, it's easy to simply believe that you have everything you need. But believing isn't always seeing; take the little bit of time to check off everything on your inventory lists to make sure you've got it all.

When going over your inventory, if you think of some additional items that you may need but aren't sure, remember this saying: "Better to have it and not need it than to need it and not have it." Keeping that saying in mind has helped us many times.

As you're confirming your inventory, if you find that you've forgotten something major or have inadvertently forgotten an entire dish, don't panic. Remember your lists of people to call on? Use them and calmly call and tell your friends what you need, then go back and finish going over your inventory. Don't start stressing, because if you do, you'll likely be distracted, which can cause more problems to arise.

Although you should certainly check your lists the day of the event, we recommend checking them beforehand as well. Better to be overprepared than underprepared.

Packing Up and Moving Out

Unless you're hosting the event in your home, you'll have to transport all your food items to the event location. For some people, the idea of having to transport everything can seem rather overwhelming. You may worry about glass breaking, cookies and crackers crumbling, and your perfectly round cheese ball becoming a pancake. However, with a little organization and the right tools, transporting your food doesn't have to be stressful.

Think of transporting food items as packing for a move to a new house or apartment. In other words, you need boxes, boxes, and more boxes — and make sure they're heavy-duty boxes. You can usually get boxes for free from your local grocery store. Just make sure they're durable — packing everything up doesn't do much good if the bottom falls out. If you can't get them from the grocery store, go to a moving company to purchase a few so you'll have them on hand.

A friend of ours introduced us to the big tub concept of storage and transportation. You can find large plastic tubs at most supercenters, which are great for transporting everything from food to dishes to decorations. Plastic tubs are rather inexpensive and can be used over and over. If you cook for a crowd more than once a year, they're more than worth the money. And again, when you're not storing food in them, you can store your Christmas decorations, children's toys, and so on.

Another everyday item that can be useful in transporting things is a laundry basket. Our kids refer to it as the breadbasket more often than they call it the laundry basket. You probably have one or two around your house, so put them to work and keep your belongings organized.

Depending on your event, you may have a lot of stuff to transport. You can probably fit everything your car. However, if you have small car and there's no way you can fit everything in it in one trip, either ask someone to drive his or her car loaded with items or borrow someone's vehicle that can hold everything. It's better to ask for help than try to stuff everything in too small of a space.

Organizing supplies

Here's that word again — organization. Organizing items according to type will greatly help in saving time and preventing accidents. We realize that for some of you the following may seem obvious, but let us tell you, we've seen it all.

We've had the unfortunate experience of eating a cheesecake at a large gathering that had the faint smell of lighter fluid. The hostess was rather embarrassed as people started smelling each other's cheesecake and then ultimately throwing it in the trash. The gathering was at an outdoor pavilion, and shish kebabs were served, hence the need for lighter fluid. The moral of the story: Food items belong with food items only. Decorations belong with decorations. Pots and pans belong with pots and pans — and so on.

Packing nonfood items

The nonfood items are usually what we pack first and load into the car first. The following are what we mean by nonfood items: glasses, cups, pots, pans, flatware, trash bags, and so forth. Remember as you're packing your nonfood items to check them off of your lists — just because they aren't food doesn't mean they won't be missed.

When you pack nonfood items, remember to pay attention to the items you're packing together and organize them logically. Place all your trash bags, foil, plastic wrap, leftover containers, and so on together. Pack all your glasses together, pots and pans together, and so on. If you're packing pots and pans, make sure that you use a heavy-duty box or tub to transport them, and remember to label the boxes. We've learned from the school of hard knocks that it's easier to find what you're looking for when it's labeled.

Protecting breakables

Packing breakables, such as plates, platters, cups, and glasses, can be challenging, but with a little extra work up front, you won't have to worry about breaking anything while you're transporting it.

Most people wrap breakable items in newspaper. Newspaper is a really good way to pack if you're moving, but not when you're transporting breakables to a crowd function. The simple reason is that newspaper is unsanitary. If you must wrap your dishes in newspaper for the event, allow enough time to wash and thoroughly dry them when you arrive at the event location.

To avoid having to rewash your dishes and such, pack them in freshly washed and dried towels. A word of caution: Don't use dryer sheets — you know, those things that make your laundry smell sunshine fresh. You don't want your guests thinking of laundry when they pick up a glass to drink. You want them thinking how great all the food is going to taste.

If you have extra money in the budget, go to your local moving company and purchase some of the boxes that are purposely designed to move glasses and plates. Also consider purchasing some tissue paper to wrap the dishes in.

Loading up for the road

When you load the nonfood items, be aware of what boxes contain the fragile items. Clearly label the boxes *FRAGILE;* that way, if other people are helping you out, they'll be aware of what's in the box. The last thing you want to happen is to have a box of plates become a box of shattered pieces. Also, make sure you pack the fragile items on top of the nonbreakable items.

If you're one of those highly organized people, you can pack and load most nonfood items the night before the event. Not all nonfood items should be packed in your car the night before, however. Keep in mind that temperatures can affect these items, such as candles. If it's the middle of summer and you live in a hot climate, then you know that leaving candles in a parked car, even at night, can result a big, waxy mess.

Packing nonperishable food items

Nonperishable food items are such things as chips, crackers, most breads, canned goods, soft drinks, and so on. Basically, anything you can eat that doesn't require refrigeration or freezing is nonperishable. Packing these items requires just a little bit of thought to help prevent the foods from getting broken, munched, squished, and crushed.

Get your food list out again. As you're packing up to transport, go over it and mark through each item as you pack it.

Get organized! You can pack all your nonperishable food items days in advance. Don't wait until the last minute to pack these items.

If you're transporting canned food items, place them in the bottom of your box or container. Try to place all canned foods together, keeping in mind the weight limit of the box or container.

When packing boxes of crackers or cookies, for example, stand them up side by side. Doing so will help prevent them from getting crushed. If room allows in your box or container, place other fragile nonperishable food items on top, such as bags of chips or bread. Make sure there's plenty of room in the box so the lid can close without smashing anything on top.

Common sense is the first thing to go

As you read through this chapter, you may think, "This is all common sense." True enough, but we'll be the first to tell you that common sense is the first thing to go on the day of the event. You'll have a lot of demands on your time and your mind. As you're putting boxes in the car, you'll likely be thinking about 15 other things at the same time. Most crowd cooks make a lot of simple mistakes on the day of the event, and often those mistakes cause a lot of problems. Do yourself a favor and get highly organized. Plan, plan, and plan some more. You want the day of the event to be a system of tasks that you've rehearsed. If you leave things to chance, your eight cans of creamed corn will likely end up on top of the bags of chips.

When you load the boxes of nonperishable food items into your vehicle, be mindful of the contents of each box. It's helpful to use a removable sticky label to place on the outside of each box, briefly listing the contents. Again, pretend that you're moving. You don't want to stack a box of canned goods on top of a box of chips. You won't face this issue if you're using the hard plastic storage containers, but otherwise, common sense goes a long way.

Managing perishable food items

Get your food list out again. When the time comes for you to go to the event location, you'll need to pack the perishable food items and make sure you get everything. With a little common sense and preparation, packing and transporting perishable items doesn't have to be a big problem.

Packing and transporting cold food items

For cold food items, ice chests are a must. Unless you're an avid camper, you probably don't own more than one ice chest. The odds are good that you'll need more than one, so feel free to borrow one from a friend or family member, and make sure you have it in your possession and ready to use before the day of the event arrives.

We recommend the hard, plastic, durable ice chests. If you're in a pinch, a Styrofoam ice chest will work. The reason we don't recommend the Styrofoam version is because it isn't as insulated as the hard shell variety and also has a tendency to crack and break easily.

This thought may sound simplistic, but we feel it's noteworthy to remind you to make sure that the ice chest, regardless of type, has been thoroughly cleaned inside and out. You don't want to show up at cousin Sally's semi-formal wedding with an ice chest that has a fragrant reminder of last month's fishing trip.

Because you're going to be packing things in the ice chests that have either been in your fridge or freezer, the dishes should already be sealed, covered, and/or wrapped sufficiently to prevent *cross-smellation*. If not, err on the side of overwrapping and oversealing the different food items.

Place a thin layer of ice cubes on the bottom of the ice chest, then start placing items on top of the ice. Again, remember to pay attention to how much items weigh. Place heavier items on the bottom and lighter ones on top.

Make sure you pack plenty of ice in the chest to keep everything cold until you arrive at the event. If you're only going a short distance, you won't need as much. With that said, you're better off anticipating that the food will stay in the cooler longer than you may expect. That way, if you get to the event and the refrigerator you planned on using is full, the food still has a place to stay cool as you make alternate plans.

Cold foods need to stay cold — meaning, they need to be stored at 40 degrees or lower to prevent food poisoning.

Packing and transporting hot food items

When transporting hot foods, you need to make sure you keep the foods as hot as possible to help prevent food poisoning. Hopefully you don't have to travel any great distance to the place where the event is going to take place.

If you're traveling farther than an hour away, cook the food at the location if at all possible. This way, you'll avoid any possible food transportation problems.

Over the years, we've learned some pretty interesting tips on transporting hot food items. One of our favorites is using a baking stone, and we keep several of them on hand at all times.

A *baking stone* is a flat piece of crockery that distributes heat evenly. You can find them in the shape of a pizza pan, a cookie sheet, a casserole dish, and a variety of other shapes. Heat these stones in the oven right before you have to load everything. Take a heavy-duty box, place a folded bath towel on the bottom of it, and then place the heated stone on top of the towel. Place your covered casserole dish or whatever hot food item you're taking on the stone. To find out more about baking stones, visit www.cooking.com.

If you don't have a baking stone, don't fret; you probably have another every-day item on hand that can help keep things warm. Take a terry cloth or an extra-thick bath towel and place it in the dryer on high for 15 minutes before using it. Wrap the pot, pan, or casserole dish in the towel and place it in a box for carrying.

You can also transport hot items in a slow cooker or roasting pan. Always use a box and a towel as with the baking stones. If you're using an electric roasting pan or a slow cooker, don't forget the cord. Also, make sure you plug in the item as soon as you arrive in order to maintain the proper heat.

Hot foods need to stay at a temperature of 140 degrees or higher to prevent the chance of food poisoning.

Keeping Everything Safe and Fresh

Keeping foods fresh is of the utmost importance. You can greatly prevent food-borne illness by following a few common-sense tips and some maybe not so commonly known tips.

- **Wash your hands; wash your hands; wash your hands.** We realize that the importance of hand-washing is one of those things that everyone should know. However, most people don't realize how often they need to wash their hands or how to properly do so. To do it right, wet your hands under warm water, put soap on them, rub them together for *at least 20 seconds,* rinse them with warm water, and dry them with a clean towel, preferably a paper towel. Unclean hands carry germs, so keep them clean.

  Everyone knows that you need to wash your hands after handling raw meat, but remember that after unloading all your supplies at the event, your hands need to be washed. When you're working with food, you can't be too careful. You must properly wash and dry your hands after each task you do or after you handle food. We aren't suggesting that you develop an obsessive-compulsive disorder, but it's better to wash too much than too little.

  Have you ever noticed that restaurants often have signs in the restrooms telling employees that they must wash their hands before returning to work? The employers do that for a reason: A specific food-borne illness is caused by using the restroom and not washing your hands. As disgusting as it sounds, fecal material gets on a person's hands, he or she goes to prepare food, and the chain of events starts — contamination and sickness.

- **Use paper towels to dry your hands and keep things clean.** We truly believe in using things that can be recycled, but we also want to do everything we can to ensure that the food we serve is safe. Paper towels are good to use in lieu of cloth towels because you use them once and throw them away. Cloth towels in a kitchen have a tendency to get used for too many things.

  The following is a common scenario of how a simple kitchen towel can cause a food-borne illness: You're busy preparing the hamburgers to go on the grill, some blood from the meat spills on the counter, and you're in a hurry so you grab your hand towel and wipe it up. Later, you're placing the potato salad in the pretty decorative bowl and you spill some on the side. You grab the same towel and clean off the bowl, and you just created a potentially bad food-poisoning scenario.

✔ **When you arrive at the event, wash all the counters with hot soapy water, and then dry them thoroughly.** Those countertops are your work surface and need to be cleaned before, during, and after the event.

✔ **Don't set out perishable foods until right before you serve them.** In an effort to have everything go smoothly and promptly, it's easy to get gung-ho and set up too early.

✔ **When setting out nonperishable foods, leave them properly covered until right before serving.** Even the most sanitary of places can have flies and gnats buzzing around, and you don't want them to be landing on your food.

✔ **Remember, cold foods must stay at 40 degrees or colder, and hot foods must stay at least 140 degrees.** Foods should never sit out more than 2 hours. When food temperatures are between 60 and 125 degrees, they become a breeding ground for bacteria.

Dishing It Out

You've successfully arrived at the event. Everything is in perfect order, the car is unloaded, and all your items are accounted for. You've organized your work area and know where everything is. Now is the time to serve this wonderful meal that you've carefully prepared.

You'll serve the food in one of two ways:

✔ **Buffet style,** where everything is attractively set out on a table and your guests serve themselves

✔ **A plated meal,** where someone else has placed the food on the plates and the plates are served to the guests

Most often when cooking for a crowd event, the serving style will be buffet, because plated affairs are difficult to manage. Please don't misunderstand; plated affairs aren't overly difficult, they just require more people helping you and more time.

Gathering around the bountiful table

Buffet-style meals are great because you can do so many things ahead of time, and the more you can do in advance, the less stressful the event will be for you. When serving buffet-style, try to plan ahead how the buffet will be arranged. We realize that you may not be able to if you're having the event away from your home, but at least try to have a good idea of how the buffet should be organized. Here are some tips to guide you:

✔ Write the name of each item you're serving on its own sheet of paper. You can then lay out the papers on a table to get a visual idea of how the buffet will be arranged.

✔ If you're hosting the event at your home, physically place each serving dish on the table where you think you may want it and place the name of the item on the corresponding dish.

✔ If you're using a centerpiece, keep it in mind, because it'll take up room on the table.

Getting things ready ahead of time

Hopefully, at this point you'll have a pretty good idea where things will go so you can set the following things out on the buffet table(s) a few hours ahead of time:

✔ Set the cups on the drink table, and if you're serving soft drinks, whether bottles or cans, place them on the table in an orderly fashion. In other words, place the same flavors of drinks together.

✔ Remember to include a container with ice and a scoop for the beverage table if necessary. Get the container in place ahead of time.

✔ If you're serving iced tea, go ahead and place slices or wedges of lemon in it, and if desired, place mint sprigs in attractive containers on the table. Cover them and place them in the desired place on the buffet.

✔ Place crackers, chips, cookies, brownies, cakes, and any other nonperishable food items on the table in the appropriate place, making sure they're all properly covered. You don't want the crackers losing their crunch or the brownies drying out.

✔ Set out decorations, such as tablecloths or greenery.

✔ Set out napkins, plates, and silverware.

✔ Set out any nonperishable food items, such as pickles, ketchup, salt, pepper, and sugar.

Arranging the food on the table

As you're thinking about the buffet line, you need to determine the order of the food. Generally speaking, different food groups should stick together. Here's a guide for a logical order:

✔ Plates, bowls, silverware, and napkins.

✔ Appetizers.

✔ Soups and salads. If the salad dressing isn't already on the salad, make sure you place the dressing next to the salads.

If you're serving soup on a buffet, set the baskets of crackers, mini-muffins, and other soup sides next to the soup.

✔ Side dishes — cold dishes first, followed by the hot sides.

✔ Entree, followed by bread. If you're serving butter, place it next to the bread and make sure it's softened so it's easy to serve.

✔ Drinks.

We know that some buffet restaurants have the drinks at the beginning of the line, but we strongly recommend placing them at the end, because juggling a drink is tough when you're trying to fill up your plate.

✔ Desserts (finally!).

Depending on the size of the event and the actual size of the room you're using, you can use a table for the appetizers, salads, soups, and cold sides and another table for the hot side dishes, main entree, and bread and butter. The drinks can be on a smaller table nearby, followed by the dessert table.

Plating the food for your guests

Most people save plated events for very formal occasions. We caution you about doing such an event without a good bit of crowd-cooking experience under your belt. Plated events require a great deal of organization, skill, and extra help for some very good reasons.

When you host a plated event, timing is very crucial, especially if you're serving more than ten people. We realize that many of you probably fix dinner plates at home every night for your family. But there's a very big difference between fixing 4 to 6 plates for your immediate family and fixing 20 plates for a dinner party.

One of the reasons timing is so important is keeping food warm. You don't want the first couple of plates you've made to become cold while you're working on plate number 20. Most people don't have warming carts or those nifty covers you get when you order room service that help keep food warm. For these reasons, plated affairs can be difficult to accomplish, and we strongly encourage you to avoid them.

However, sometimes you just can't avoid plated events. Suppose you're a novice and this is the first time you've ever cooked for more than your immediate family of four. You're cooking for your niece's wedding, and she has her heart set on a plated meal. If you're in this predicament, how can you survive with style? This section can help.

Make an impact with butter balls

A common question concerns serving butter. Sure, you can serve butter on a buffet from a stick or in individual pats. However, with just a tad of work, you can create butter balls. They look great and provide just the right serving portion for people moving through the buffet line. Here's how:

1. Take slightly softened butter or margarine and use a small melon baller to scoop out balls. Place the balls on a wax- or parchment-paper-lined cookie sheet.

2. Place the butter balls in the freezer for about 10 minutes to help firm them back up. Re-chilling also helps them to not stick together.

3. Remove the butter balls from the cookie sheet and place them in a serving container. You can do this ahead of time, but make sure you securely seal the container, as butter or margarine can quickly absorb other odors from your refrigerator.

Setting up

Here are some tips you need to commit to memory when planning a plated event:

- ✔ Make sure you have at least two other people to help you plate the food. The larger your crowd, the more people you'll need. For every 20 people, you need at least two additional people to plate the food.

- ✔ Have your kitchen area well organized and cleaned before plating the food; you'll need all available counter and table space.

- ✔ Put tablecloths out ahead of time (the day before the event, if possible).

- ✔ Place salt and pepper shakers on each table ahead of time.

- ✔ If you're serving salad without dressing already on it, place the salad dressing on the table ahead of time.

- ✔ If you're serving bread, give each table its own breadbasket.

- ✔ Place a set of condiments on each table, such as ketchup, mustard, mayonnaise, steak sauce, and so on.

- ✔ Set up an assembly line in the kitchen, with the first item to be served at the front of the line.

- ✔ Use slotted spoons for items such as vegetables or beans to help remove excess liquid before placing them on the plate.

- ✔ Placed the food on the plates in an attractive, appealing manner, and make sure that all the plates look alike.

- Garnish each plate. A small sprig of washed and thoroughly dried parsley is a universal garnish. Orange slices also make an impressive colorful garnish.

- Have someone else (if at all possible) be in charge of drinks. Pouring the drinks shortly before serving them is best. This way, the ice won't melt and dilute the beverage. You'll also need to have someone moving from table to table for beverage refill service.

Serving the grub

For plated meals, you use the same basic order as a buffet line. Begin with appetizers (if you're serving them), then move to the soup and salad, side dishes, entrees, and bread. Finally, serve the desserts and coffee.

As you can see, having to set each table with a host of items will cause more work and will run up the price of the event due to the duplicate numbers of items needed. And if everything is done in true plated style (meaning you serve everything to the guests at their tables), you're looking at a lot of work to serve each item and then pick it up before moving on to the next item.

A few words of encouragement

Let us just say that we aren't against plated affairs. Our goal with this book, however, is to help you be successful as you cook for a crowd, and plated affairs come with a host of difficulties and potential problems (not to mention a lot of extra work). Cooking for a crowd can be stressful enough without having to play waiter to a sit-down party of 30. It certainly can be done, and beautifully so with the right amount of extra hands and a great deal of organization and timing.

However, we don't want you collapsing at the end from working your fingers to the bone. Our suggestion is that if you know that you have a large plated event coming up, practice ahead of time. Have a dinner party at your home for 12 people. This practice will greatly help you prepare for the bigger event, and again, the more prepared you are, the less stressful things will be.

Relaxing and Enjoying the Event

Whether you had a buffet spread fit for a king or a plated formal affair, the work has been done, the food has been presented, and it's time to sit back and enjoy the event with your guests.

Trust us, we know your adrenaline will be pumping, and you'll be looking over everything to make sure it's going smoothly, but after you serve the food, allow yourself some time to reap the harvest of all your work.

Your guests will want to visit with you, so don't become so engrossed in the process that you forget the reason you cooked for them in the first place — the people! After the food is served, do a once-over and go on. If you aren't careful, and this is the voice of experience talking, you'll work yourself to death for absolutely no reason. Plus, you never want your guests to think things are out of control. And they'll surely think you don't have control if you're running around like a chicken with its head cut off. You know the saying, "Never let 'em see you sweat" — that saying is so important when you're cooking for a crowd.

Please don't misunderstand us; we're not saying the party is over and you're done. You do need to keep an eye on the landscape and attend to any issues that may pop up, such as running out of ice, or occasionally stir the gravy so that an ugly skin won't form on it. Again, use common sense, make sure all your guests have gotten their food, and remember that you need to eat, too. Grab a plate and have a seat. Try to enjoy the time. The event will go quickly, and before you know it, it'll be tomorrow, and you'll be thinking to yourself, "Wow! I can't believe I pulled off that awesome crowd meal!"

Part V
The Part of Tens

In this part . . .

*E*very *Dummies* book has a *part of tens,* a section con-
taining quick and helpful top-ten lists. Ours is no
exception to the rule, so in this part, we give you our top
ten ways to avoid common food preparation problems,
more than ten decorating tips, ten ways to keep from
pulling out your hair, and more than ten bits of info on
food safety.

Chapter 15

Ten Ways to Avoid Common Food Preparation Problems

In This Chapter

▶ Letting planning work for you

▶ Making sure you cook safely, store tightly, and serve neatly

Cooking is a complex process, especially when you're doing it for a crowd. Naturally, during complex processes things have a tendency to go wrong. However, with just a little planning on your part in light of the ten tips you find in this chapter, you can avoid most crowd-cooking problems and mishaps. So read through these tips and tuck them in your hat.

Before You Start, See What You Need

Nothing is worse for a cook than being halfway through a recipe and realizing that you're out of butter. Before you ever start working on a recipe, check all the ingredients, pans, tools, and anything else you may need and be sure you have them all on hand. Yes, we know you bought the ingredients last week, but we're always amazed how quickly and easily different ingredients seem to disappear. So play it safe and double-check that you have everything before you get started.

Follow the Recipe

Sure, this tip seems like a no-brainer, but you'd be surprised at the number of people who give a recipe a cursory look, then proceed on their own. In many ways, cooking and baking are more science than art. You have to have the right combination of ingredients in order for meals to turn out the way you want. The best way to ensure that you'll get the right dish is to carefully follow the recipe exactly as you see it. When you're cooking for a crowd, you don't have time for experimentation, so now isn't the time to exercise your creativity.

Be Careful with Substitutions

Substitutions often work great, but you have to be careful. Just because you commonly substitute one ingredient for another doesn't mean that the substitution will work for every recipe. Many of the recipes in this book, for example, require that you use butter, not margarine. To keep things simple, we suggest in the intro that you don't substitute margarine for any of the recipes you find here.

So err on the side of caution. If you want to make a substitution in a recipe, make a small-portioned size of the recipe and try it out before you make the crowd-sized serving. You don't want any surprises on the day of your event, and substitutions can get you into trouble if you don't test them out first.

Use Parchment Paper

You may be surprised that parchment paper made our top-ten list, but this handy item is a great kitchen invention. Parchment paper is a grease- and moisture-resistant paper used to keep things from sticking. It'll save your cheesecakes, sausage balls, rolls, cookies, and other baked items from sticking to the pan. It also makes cleanup much quicker and easier. Parchment paper is inexpensive and available at most grocery stores, so pick some up and put it to work. Your food will thank you.

Tightly Seal All Containers

Unless you love cheesecake that tastes like onion, refrigerator-stored items can be a real nightmare. When you cook for a crowd, you need to make some foods in advance and store them in the refrigerator. Yet, refrigerators can easily cycle odors, and you may end up with foods that have absorbed tastes and smells that you don't want.

We're fanatical about making sure all the containers and bags are thoroughly sealed when we store food in the refrigerator. We commonly use heavy-duty storage bags, and we often double and triple the bags to make absolutely sure no odors can get in or out.

 If you need to store onion in the refrigerator, here's a quick tip. Get a canning jar with a sealable lid and store the onion in it. Glass doesn't breathe, so no odors will escape into your refrigerator.

Avoid Last-Minute Preparation When Possible

Some food items can be made at the last minute, and some can't. For example, sauces, dips, marinades, and other foods with combined ingredients often need time to chill and set. Otherwise, the foods don't taste good. The important point here is to plan. You can't rush a good sauce or dip, so make sure you adhere to the recipe's directions concerning chill time. Plan, plan, and plan some more. Make sure your last-minute food preparation is reserved for foods that you really can and should make at the last minute.

Wash Your Hands Religiously

Raw meat and eggs commonly contain germs and bacteria, such as salmonella. Mix a little salmonella in your Caesar salad, and you're asking for trouble. Because proper cooking kills germs and bacteria, your meat and eggs will be fine to eat; however, you always run the risk of cross-contamination, which happens when you don't wash your hands, the counter, or utensils with hot water and antibacterial dish soap before you use them on another food item.

Trust us — you should become fanatical about washing everything after working with raw meat and eggs. Cooking for a crowd and having a bunch of people get sick because of cross-contamination is devastating. It only takes a few moments to play it safe!

Avoid Having Too Many Recipes in the Works at Once

Yes, we know you're smart and can multitask in the kitchen. After all, you probably do it all the time. But cooking for a crowd requires a lot of mental attention and focus that you don't need for a typical family meal. As such, avoid trying to do too many things at the same time. You're asking for mistakes and recipe errors if you do. Be sure you note what items you can make ahead of time. Don't wait until the last minute and think you can bring together five different dishes at once.

Be Aware of What You Can't Do Ahead of Time

We stress preparing items ahead of time in this book, which is wise advice for a crowd cook. However, you can't make everything in advance, so plan carefully. That chocolate soufflé will fall if you make it much in advance, and other desserts and dishes will have similar repercussions. In short, prepare what you can ahead of time, but if the dish doesn't allow for it, then don't.

Be Attentive to Personal Hygiene

Would you like some hair with your brisket? How about a fake fingernail in your pudding or a beautiful bracelet charm in your salad? You get the picture. Personal hygiene does matter, because the consequences are very embarrassing. So play it safe. Use a hairnet, or at least put your hair up if it's long. Keep your fingernails short and don't wear any jewelry when you're preparing food.

Chapter 16

More Than Ten Decorating Tips for Crowds

*W*hen you cook for a crowd, getting the food on the table is of paramount importance; after all, serving your wonderful dishes is the whole point of crowd cooking. However, with just a little planning and a few minutes of work, you can also throw in a bit of table decorating, which will really make you look like a hero.

"Decorating?" you may ask, "I'll just be happy to get the food ready in time." If this is your feeling as you think about decorating for your event, don't worry. You won't have to become a professional party planner to make the ideas in this chapter work, and you won't have to spend much money, either.

Let's face it; everyone loves food, but those extra touches will really make your event special. After all, decorating shows that you've put some careful thought and care into the event, and everyone will appreciate that fact. So put your decoration ideas to work and be sure and keep these ten tips in mind.

Getting into the Theme

If you're having a themed event, try to incorporate the theme on your table. For example, work in little American flags or other patriotic decorations at your July 4th party (you can find inexpensive decorations at any party store). For a baby shower, take a close look at the invitation and model your colors and theme items after the invitation — have someone make a cake that looks like the invitation. You don't have to go overboard, but find a central concept and stick with it. The little details make a big difference!

Dressing Up with Table Linens

There's something to be said for a table dressed in a pressed, stain-free tablecloth, because that piece of linen is the backdrop for your food. You can find a variety of tablecloths available for purchase. Like most everything else, they come in a wide range of prices: You can shell out the big bucks on an expensive damask, or you can pinch your pennies and pick up a checked paper tablecloth — of you can go with any of the many variations in between. Tablecloths are usually made of out of cloth, paper, or plastic, and you can usually purchase them at your local supercenter, department store, a large grocery store, and your basic dollar store.

When you're deciding what kind of tablecloth to use (cloth, paper, or plastic), let the overall theme and feel of the event be your guide. If the event is formal or semiformal, cloth is the appropriate choice.

If money is an issue (which it usually is), considering borrowing the table linens. You can also rent them if necessary. When renting table linens, make sure you carefully examine all the pieces to make sure they're stain free.

When the event is more relaxed and casual, you may be able to use paper or plastic tablecloths. At a backyard barbecue or a family get-together, either paper or plastic will work nicely. Remember that when you decide what to use, make sure it goes with the event. If you're hosting a summer cookout, a red and white checked tablecloth may be just what you need to pull the overall look of the event together.

Napkins, like tablecloths, are available in cloth and paper. If you're having a formal event, in which case you should only use cloth, make sure the napkins are cloth as well. If the event is semiformal (again, you should use cloth tablecloths), cloth napkins are best. However, you can use paper napkins for a semiformal event as long as they're upper-class napkins (steer clear of the packs of 250 for a buck for these events). These nice paper napkins are usually smoother in texture and have a clothlike appearance.

Making a Visual Impact with Your Food

You've worked hard on carefully deciding what foods to serve and have chosen the finest ingredients, writing list after list to make sure that all your ducks are in a row — now it's time to serve all that wonderful food. So why not make it a little more special by getting creative and creating some visual impact with the food you're going to serve?

Isn't it nice when you go to a restaurant or attend a catered event and the food is thoughtfully laid out on the table rather than placed without much thought? Your guests will appreciate your extra bit of thought, too. Don't worry if you think you don't have a creative bone in your body; here are some simple ideas to let your food work for you:

- **Make your own dip bowls.** When serving a vegetable tray with dip, rather than using a traditional bowl for the dip, try making a bowl out of a vegetable — red, yellow, or green bell peppers work great. Simply wash the pepper, cut off the top portion (about ¼ to ½ of it from the top), and remove the insides. Wash the pepper thoroughly with water and allow it to dry. Then fill her up!

  Likewise, when you serve a fruit tray with dip or fruit salsa with cinnamon chips (check out the recipe in Chapter 4), try using a piece of fruit for the bowl. A large orange, grapefruit, small cantaloupe, or honeydew melon works great as a bowl. Just cut off the top ¼ of it, hollow out the inside, wash it with water, and *voilà!*

- **Carve holes in your bread.** Breadbaskets or -bowls are a great way to serve dips, soups, sandwiches, and individual servings of bread, such as muffins and sliced bread. To make a breadbasket, take a large loaf of bread, cut a circle in the top, and remove its insides. You can also use smaller round loaves of bread, preparing them as you do the larger loaves and using them to serve soup.

- **One word: Garnish.** Garnishing your food takes only a few moments and is an inexpensive way to add that special touch to the food you've worked so hard to prepare. Fresh mint sprigs, cilantro, and parsley are the most common garnishes. Not sure where to stick these little green additions? Place them in the center of the food item, and you won't go wrong. The addition of the small piece of greenery can have a huge visual impact.

- **Pull an Edward Scissorhands on your food.** For those of you wanting to try something a little more creative, try garnishing with a tomato rose or a strawberry fan. Don't worry; these garnishes are easier to make than you may think. To make a tomato rose, first wash and dry a tomato (the size of the tomato will determine the size of the rose — you can use any tomato except for cherry or grape, because they're too small). Take a sharp paring knife and, starting at the top, gently "peel" the skin off in the same manner you'd peel an apple. Then gently take one end of the peel and start rolling it up to create a rose shape. The end result is a beautiful garnish that will make you look like a pro!

To fashion a strawberry fan, take a washed and dried strawberry (with the green stem still attached) and, using a paring knife, and starting at the bottom, cut thin slices into the strawberry. Slice up to the green stem. Gently fan the pieces of the strawberry out and place it on the food as a garnish.

You can find all kinds of tips and suggestions for decorating with food online at www.diynet.com.

Breaking Out the Baskets

A tisket, a tasket, let us use some baskets. Okay, we know that's not really how the song goes, but you get the point. Baskets can serve a number of different purposes. You can purchase them at just about any store, and like everything else, they range in price from very inexpensive to rather costly. Your best bet is to look around your own house and see what baskets you have or borrow some from your friends, neighbors, and family.

Baskets make great serving pieces. Serving whole pieces of fruit? Try placing them in a basket instead of just a bowl to add some visual interest. Just remember to make sure that you keep the event's theme and feel in mind when deciding whether to go with baskets or to nix the idea.

When serving bread, rolls, or muffins, try placing them in a basket that you've lined with a color-coordinated napkin. Cookies are also a good choice to serve out of a basket, as long as they're of the crunchy variety, not chewy. The chewy kind is best served on a platter so they don't break apart.

Chips and crackers also take well to baskets. Again, line the basket with a cloth or paper napkin, and remember to make sure the size of the basket is in proportion to the item being served.

Don't forget your nonfood items — eating utensils and napkins can also be served in baskets.

Using Decorative Bowls

Bowls are an essential serving dish, as they're perfect for holding everything from salads to sides to desserts. What's great about them is that you likely already have them on hand.

Bowls come in just about every size and can be made out of paper, plastic, ceramic, glass, or metal — and for those of you who are feeling creative, you can make them out of food (see the "Making a Visual Impact with Your Food" section, earlier in this chapter). Remember to keep the theme of the event or the occasion in mind so that your serving bowls go along with the event. Also, consider using festive bowls or even decorated bowls for holiday and fun crowd events.

Putting Platters to Work

Platters, plates, and other flat serving dishes most certainly have a leading role in displaying and serving food. If the only platters you have seem to be left over from your child's birthday party, don't worry. You can easily disguise them and dress them up just by using a little imagination Consider a few ideas on how to use flat serving dishes to display your food and how to make what you have work:

- **Mask your dishes with leafy greens.** If all you have are plastic serving platters, but the event is semiformal (in which case plastic simply won't work) let leaf lettuce come to your rescue. Leaf lettuce and kale cover a multitude of ugly platters, plates, and the like, and they also add texture to both the food being served and the overall appearance of the table. Make sure you thoroughly wash and completely dry each piece of the greens, then line the platter with them and place the food on top.

- **Borrow Grandma's paper doilies.** When you're serving a food such as chips, cookies, or anything else that doesn't belong on a bed of lettuce, line the platter with foil and then place paper doilies on top. You can purchase these doilies at just about any cooking store, supercenter, or arts and crafts store, and they're usually available wherever cake-decorating supplies are sold.

- **Use baking pans as big platters.** Have a large piece of meat to serve and no platter big enough? Use a cookie sheet or a jellyroll pan lined with lettuce.

At our annual Christmas party, we serve food only in glass or silver serving dishes, because the event is more formal. However, for our summer pool parties, we use only plastic dishes, cups, and utensils. Just let the style of the event guide you, and try to have your platters, serving dishes, and decorations match the event.

Of course, remember your humble authors' philosophy: borrow, borrow, and borrow some more.

Varying the Heights of Food

You can greatly boost your table's appeal by using various heights with your dishes. For example, use a cake pedestal to serve cookies or a tiered serving dish to serve snacks. With just a little planning, you can give the food a whole new look. These various levels greatly enhance the visual appeal of your table and make you look like a pro (and they don't cause you any extra work).

Bringing Nature Inside

The power of green — and we're not talking about money — is an important part of any decorating scheme. Greenery is useful for decorating the buffet table and for decorating the tables where everyone will be eating. It also spices up the room itself. Plants, whether real or faux, always seem to help events come to life. They tend to brighten up the room and make people feel more relaxed.

Of course, you can go the real chloroform route, but because insects also love plants, we usually go for the artificial versions. Artificial ivy is our greenery of choice. It compliments just about any type of event, whether formal or very casual, and better yet, it's easy to find and relatively inexpensive. You can usually pick some up at your local supercenter as well as at arts and crafts stores.

The following list gives you some tips to help you arrange the greenery and decide where to place it:

✔ **On your buffet table:** Artificial greenery is available by the bunch or by the string, and both styles work great. After you've set all the food in place on the table, go back and add the ivy around the serving dishes. Remember, when you're using a chaffing dish or any other serving dish that will be warm or hot, keep the greenery at a safe distance from it to prevent a fire.

- **Around tiers and poles:** When using a tiered plate stand to serve food, try wrapping the stand with a string of greenery.

- **In and around baskets:** You know those baskets we talk about earlier in this chapter? If the basket needs a little touch, try wrapping some greenery around it. You'll be surprised at how much the green adds to the overall look of the table.

- **With lighting:** Will trees, real or otherwise, be at your event location? If so, try stringing clear lights in them for a beautiful, natural effect.

Serving Things Up in Unusual Ways

To us, the idea of using objects in unconventional ways is always fun, because our creative juices get to flow. Don't worry if you feel that you don't have a creative bone in your body — in this section, we give you some easy-to-follow ideas.

When using unusual objects to serve food from, you must think outside the box. For example, when you think of stemware, you think of drinks. However, stemware is useful for many other reasons as well. Serving coffee or tea and need something to put the artificial sweetener packets and sugar packets in? Try using a piece of stemware instead of a bowl.

Stemware also works well for serving nuts, small candies, and olives. Just make sure that the mouth of the glass is wide enough for people to easily get whatever is inside.

Here are some other ideas for serving items in unusual ways:

- For a baby shower, use old-fashioned glass baby bottles adorned with color-coordinated ribbon to serve the punch in rather than glasses.

- Having a backyard barbecue? Use an old wash pot or a child's pool, filled with ice, to serve the canned drinks.

- For a springtime tea or brunch, try using clean (preferably never used) flowerpots, lined with a green napkin, to serve various items such as chips or crackers.

- Having a Mexican fiesta? Try using a sombrero lined with wax paper or napkins to serve the tortilla chips.

As you can see, you have all kinds of fun ways to serve food by using unusual serving pieces. As you think about your event, think about the theme or the occasion. Then turn your attention to unusual serving ideas that go along with that theme or occasion. You'll be amazed at the fun serving pieces you can invent!

Creating Beautiful Centerpieces without a Lot of Fuss

Centerpieces can be labor intensive and dramatic or simple and elegant, not to mention easy to make. Usually, when you think of a centerpiece for a table, you probably think of flowers — that old standby is great, but don't think that flowers are the only thing you can use. Just remember to consider the overall theme and feel of the event to help you get ideas on some different kinds of centerpieces.

- **Rely on the old standby.** Flowers, real or otherwise, always add that special touch to any table. The flower arrangement doesn't have to be fancy to have an impact; a simple red rose in a thin glass base with a sprig or two of baby's breath works great for many occasions. Do keep in mind that the size of the table and the size of the arrangement need to complement each other. For example, if you have a large table that sits ten people, the single rose idea may be a little lacking. For a table that size, try a half-dozen roses (or whatever your flower of choice may be) in an appropriate size vase.

- **Leave the vase in the cupboard.** Like the idea of using flowers but don't want to put them in a vase? Try a bouquet tied together with a piece of color-coordinated ribbon and placed in the center of the table. Remember, fresh flowers need water, so if you go this route, don't set out the arrangements until the event is about to begin.

- **Bring the outside in.** Potted plants make wonderful centerpieces, and even better, you or one of your guests can take them home. When you use a potted plant, make sure that the pot is clean and that it hasn't recently been sprayed with any chemicals. Remember, it will be around food, so take some basic precautions.

- **Make your own conglomeration.** Want to get really creative for a wedding reception? Do a combination centerpiece. We've used this concept many times and have gotten overwhelmingly great responses. Place a small-to-medium sized floral arrangement in the middle of each table where guests will sit and add to the arrangements some disposable cameras. Many times you can find disposal cameras that look like they've been wrapped in wedding paper, instead of the bright yellow packaging they normally come in. At the beginning of the reception, announce to the guests that they should feel free to pick up one of the cameras and snap as many pictures as they want. At the end of the reception, have a designated area for the guests to place the cameras. With this interactive centerpiece, guests get to take an active role in helping the newlyweds preserve their magical day with pictures.

Want to make a bridal shower or a baby shower extra special for both the guests of honor and their loved ones? In addition to a floral arrangement, try adding some small journals or shower-themed pads of paper with some coordinated pens and ask each guest to write down some words of encouragement or ideas that may help them with their marriage or child. Again, this adds a personal element to the centerpiece, giving the guests of honor a wonderful keepsake.

You can use fresh cut flowers for a centerpiece, but if you do, make sure the flowers don't have an overpowering smell and are free of any insects. Nobody wants creepy-crawlies around the table.

Setting the Mood with Candles

The flicker of candles and their soft warm glow add a lot to just about any setting, not to mention the obvious benefits that they're inexpensive and are readily available at just about any store.

Candles come in a variety of shapes, sizes, and scents. A word of caution with scented candles — be very particular about the scent you choose. Scented candles are wonderful, but you need to make sure the scent won't compete or overpower the smells of all the wonderful foods you've worked so hard to prepare. For this reason, we strongly suggest that you stick with the unscented variety.

When decorating with candles, keep in mind that you should arrange them in a way that prevents the chance of anything catching on fire. The warning should go without saying, but for good measure we remind you: Never leave candles burning unattended. We realize you know this, but in case you get too busy and forget, we wanted to remind you. Candles are common causes of house fires, so beware.

Candles are incredibly flexible when it comes to decorating, and the following are a few ideas:

- **Use them as a centerpiece.** Candles make a beautiful centerpiece at a more formal event such as wedding receptions or anniversary parties. To create a centerpiece with candles, try placing the candles on a decorative plate or a mirror. Use different heights of the same color candles to add even more appeal.

✔ **Let them float.** Floating candles are one of our favorites for center-pieces. You can use a variety of glass pieces filled with water to float them in. At a recent wedding reception, we used stemware of varying heights, filled them with water about half to three-quarters full, and placed individual floating candles in each glass. The simple elegance of the stemware combined with the romantic feel of the candles was just what the reception needed to make it go from "Oh, this is nice" to "Oh, how beautiful."

✔ **Nail them to the wall (sort of).** Depending on where the event will take place, candle wall sconces may be available for use. Take advantage of them! The additional candlelight will add to the overall look and feel of the gathering. When using candle wall sconces, make sure they're high enough on the wall and out of the way of people walking by so no one catches their hair or clothing on fire. Trust us, this ugly scenario has happened. But with a little common sense and attention to detail, you can easily prevent it from happening. We also suggest that if you can find dripless candles, especially dripless taper candles, use them. They help prevent wax from getting on everything.

✔ **Arrange them on the buffet table.** Candles can really add visual interest to your buffet table. Hopefully you've taken a little time to design the setup of your table and your food is displayed at a number of varying heights; simply add to the arrangement some votive candles or tea lights in small glass candleholders. These small candles will emphasize the varying food heights (mentioned earlier in this chapter), which will add to the overall appeal of the table.

When you use candles, always remember to bring a lighter, preferably the kind specifically made for lighting candles, as opposed to a cigarette lighter. Matches, of course, will work, but they tend to leave the just-lit smell. It's also a good idea to have a candle snuffer and a pitcher of water available just in case a rogue candle decides to burn out of control.

Topping It Off with Background Music

Have you ever noticed that just about every restaurant, from fancy and elegant to your local burger joint and everything in between, always has music playing in the background? From rock-and-roll and country to Mozart, the right music makes all the difference.

Your crowd event should be no exception to the rule. As you plan, think about music. The tunes you choose should naturally match the theme of the event and the occasion. Also, be careful not to play it too loudly. Music should add a nice feel to the room, but it shouldn't take center stage.

If you have an overzealous friend or relative who insists on helping, put that person in charge of the music. In fact, if your friend or relative has a computer, put him or her in charge of making a custom CD for the event, with songs that are special or meaningful to your crowd. Extra touches like this one have a great impact and show your crowd how thoughtful you've been.

Chapter 17

Ten Ways to Keep from Pulling Out Your Hair

In This Chapter

▶ Getting in gear way before the big day

▶ Keeping preparations under control

▶ Taking care of the cook (that is, you)

*L*et's face it: Cooking for a crowd can be rather stressful. After all, you have to plan, prepare, and serve a meal that is much larger than your typical family meal.

If you've read the other chapters in this book, you're armed with plenty of techniques to help reduce stress and make your crowd event a smashing success. However, if you need a little inspiration, here are our ten best tips all conveniently wrapped up in one chapter to make your crowd event less stressful and keep your hair attached to your head.

Plan, Plan, Plan!

A lack of planning is probably the greatest stressor for crowd cooks. You know you have a crowd event coming up, you know it can be a challenge, but you wait until the last minute to try and pull off the event. Unfortunately, a prior lack of planning keeps you from having all your ingredients and tools readily available, from anticipating problems and issues, and from being able to organize effectively. So if you want your crowd event to run smoothly and keep you from aging ten years over the course of a week, you must plan carefully well in advance. You'll thank yourself later. (For the details of all that planning entails, flip back to Chapter 13.)

Organize, Organize, Organize!

Naturally, organization is the sister of planning, and you can't cook well for a crowd without both. Remember, you're cooking for a much larger group than you normally do, and you'll face some fundamental differences. Namely, you have more ingredients, more tools, and more information to juggle than ever before. The only way to control your crowd event is to make sure you've organized everything carefully. Know exactly what you'll need, round up the items, and organize them in a way that makes them accessible. (For tips on organizing your kitchen, see Chapter 13.)

Keep a General Head Count

Crowds tend to be ever-changing animals. At first, Uncle Joe and Aunt Juanita plan to come, then they decide they can't, then they decide they can. . . . Add about ten more people to the "I don't know whether I'm coming" list, and you'll be bald-headed in no time. The reality is that crowds are often shifty, so it's up to you to try and keep an accurate head count as you move forward. However, don't spend all your time trying to keep a solid count. You can expect some adjustments along the way, so always err on the side of too much food than too little. Just try to keep a general head count running at all times so you know what you're up against.

Carefully Determine Your Menu

It's easy to get excited about a crowd event and go overboard with your menu. As you plan it, keep your head out of the clouds and think carefully about everything you must do to create each dish. Plan to have a few items that are more difficult and take more time and a few items that are quick and easy. We try to strike this balance with every crowd event we cook for. As such, be sure to check out the recipes in this book. We include some complicated items as well as a number of items that are quick and easy and still make a great impact.

Prepare Some Items in Advance

A vital trick for crowd cooking is preparing as many items in advance as possible. If you look through the recipe chapters in this book, you'll see that we often say things such as "You can prepare this dish and store it in the refrigerator for a week." Keep these tips in mind! The more items you can prepare in advance, the easier the big day will be on your psyche.

Don't Be Afraid to Borrow

We're quite sure you don't have a kitchen that is readily set up to handle cooking for 50 guests, and if you're serving them at your home, you're probably not set up to handle that many people, either. Many times, the crowd cook thinks he or she must have supernatural powers and be able to handle all these issues, but this approach is unrealistic. When we cook for a crowd, we're often on the phone asking questions such as "Hey, Kim, can we borrow your card table?" or "Hi, Aunt Martha, I need to borrow your cookie sheets." Borrowing is perfectly fine, and most people are more than willing to help. You don't need to buy everything you may need, and you don't need to suffer in silence, either.

Create a Workflow

We mention a few times in this book that a workflow for the day of the crowd event is vitally important, and we want to re-emphasize that idea here. The big day will certainly be stressful, and stress has a way of getting you off-track, causing you to forget things. For this reason, a workflow will help you manage the day and make sure everything gets done, because you prepare it in advance, when you're cool, calm, and thinking clearly. Use a workflow: It makes all the difference!

Eat Well, Exercise, and Sleep Well

Everyone has gone into panic mode at some point. In those times, reality seems to go out the window, and you zone in on one particular task. If you're not careful, cooking for a crowd will do the same. You'll spend days before the event working, fretting, and trying to avoid every possible problem. During that time, you'll likely stop eating well, stop getting any exercise, and stop sleeping well. Combine those situations, and you're asking for trouble.

As you're getting ready for your crowd event, try to keep the same schedule. Eat the same kind of foods you normally do, get some exercise, and go to bed and get up at the same times as usual. If you keep your body in sync, you'll keep a level head on your shoulders.

Take a Breather

This tip is especially helpful on the day of the event, and we often build it into our workflow for the day. Your mind and body work better if they both can take a break, so on the day of the event, build in a 15-minute break in the middle of the preparation. Put your feet up, read an article, and completely stop working for a few minutes. You'll feel refreshed, and those overwhelmed feelings will remain at bay.

Get Help (When You Need It)

The Superman and Superwoman syndrome runs high when you cook for a crowd, but keep in mind that circumstances may get out of control, and you may need a few extra hands. That's fine. After all, if your crowd has grown from 30 to 60, you'll probably need extra help, anyway. The trick is knowing when you need help. As you move toward the day of the event, continue making plans, and be realistic. If you simply have too much to do, make some phone calls and get extra help. Your goal is to have a fun, successful crowd event, and if you need a bit of help to meet that goal, you're not a failure!

Chapter 18

More Than Ten Things You Need to Know about Food Safety

*I*magine a crowd cook's absolute nightmare: You host a pool party for all your friends. The party is a smashing success and you drift to sleep later that night feeling like you deserve a trophy. At 7 a.m., the phone rings and you find out that half of your guests have spent the night at the hospital with food poisoning. Your crowd-cooking days are over.

You can wake up now; the nightmare is over. Food poisoning is a serious matter, and if you've ever had it, you know how serious it can be. Yet you can employ simple tactics to make sure that you never serve spoiled food to anyone. This chapter will help you keep food safe, so read it carefully.

Clean Like There's No Tomorrow

It seems as though this should go without saying, but you must keep things clean. You may be the neatest, cleanest person in the world, but cooking for a crowd is stressful, and food safety slip-ups can easily occur. So keep food safety at the front of your mind — your first line of defense is cleanliness:

✔ **Those beautiful hands:** Cross-contamination of different food items (especially when handling meat) most often occurs from unwashed hands. Make sure you wash your hands with antibacterial soap after you handle a certain kind of food — meat, for example.

> ✔ **Dishes:** Make sure dishes are kept clean. It's easy to reuse a dish when you're preparing different food items. However, dishes need to be washed after each use. If you've used a dish for raw meat, make sure you don't put anything else on that dish until you've washed it with antibacterial soap.

> ✔ **Counters:** Another common area of cross-contamination is counter space. When you work with food, make sure you regularly clean the counters with soap — don't just wipe them off with a dishcloth. You can easily spread bacteria from raw meat or eggs to other foods because of contamination on counter spaces.

Keep Temperatures Where They Need to Be

When you're serving buffet-style foods, you need to make sure that hot items stay hot and cold items stay cold. As a general rule, hot foods should be held at 140 degrees or warmer, and cold foods should stay 40 degrees or colder. Don't allow foods to sit at room temperature for more than two hours. If you're eating picnic-style outside, discard food after one hour. Here are a few more tips to remember:

> ✔ If serving food outside, keep the food cold in an ice chest for as long as possible.

> ✔ Thaw and marinate meats in the refrigerator, not at room temperature.

> ✔ When you cook meat, cook it at one time and thoroughly. In other words, don't start to cook meat, stop, and then return to it later.

> ✔ Eat grilled foods immediately.

Mind Your Eggs

Eggs are used in many dishes and are great served in a variety of ways, but they spoil easily and are probably the greatest source of salmonella poisoning. As such, eggs and dishes that contain them must be handled carefully to avoid spoilage. Here are some important tips to keep in mind:

- ✔ Always keep eggs refrigerated and take them out only when you're going to use them.

- ✔ Discard any eggs that are cracked.

- ✔ After you use raw eggs, wash your hands, utensils, dishes, and the counter with hot water and antibacterial soap.

- ✔ Refrigerate leftovers in small, shallow dishes that enable quick cooling.

Be Careful What You Buy

You also need to keep food safety in mind when you're buying it. Here are a few reminders:

- ✔ Don't buy food past the sell-by date or expiration date. In fact, stay as far away from the expiration date as possible.

- ✔ Never purchase torn, leaking, or damaged packages.

- ✔ Put raw meat and poultry in plastic bags so that nothing leaks to other foods.

- ✔ When you're shopping, don't get the refrigerated items until the very last. This way, you're not letting them warm up or thaw as you continue to shop.

- ✔ During the summer, when you load the car, keep cold or frozen items in the air-conditioned part of the car. Don't put them in the trunk, especially on warm days. In the winter, keep cold items in the trunk since the heat will be on in the car.

- ✔ If you live more than 30 minutes from the store, bring a cooler to hold cold items until you get home.

Store Your Fruits and Vegetables Properly

You just came home from the grocery store with a couple of armloads of veggies. How long will your food keep in the fridge? Table 18-1 answers all your cold storage questions when it comes to vegetables, and Table 18-2 covers fruit.

Don't wash vegetables before refrigerating them, and remember to store odorous veggies in some kind of plastic wrap.

Table 18-1	Cold Storage for Vegetables	
Fresh Vegetables	**Refrigerator Time**	**Freezer Time**
Asparagus	2–3 days	8–12 months
Broccoli and Brussels sprouts	3–5 days	8–12 months
Cabbage	1–2 weeks	8–12 months
Carrots, beets, and turnips	2 weeks	8–12 months
Cauliflower	1 week	8–12 months
Celery	1–2 weeks	Don't freeze
Corn on the cob	1–2 days	8 months
Cucumbers	4–5 days	Don't freeze
Eggplant	3–4 days	6–8 months
Green beans	3–4 days	8 months
Green peas and lima beans	3–5 days	8–12 months
Lettuce	1 week	Don't freeze
Mushrooms	3–5 days	Don't freeze
Okra	2–3 days	8–12 months
Onions	3–5 days	8–12 months
Parsley and cilantro	1 week	1–2 months
Peppers	1 week	8–12 months
Squash	2 weeks	8–12 months
Tomatoes	2–3 days	8–10 months

Table 18-2	Cold Storage for Fruits	
Fresh Fruit	**Refrigerator Time**	**Freezer Time**
Apples	3 weeks	8 months if cooked
Apricots	2–3 days	Don't freeze

Fresh Fruit	Refrigerator Time	Freezer Time
Avocados	3–4 days	Don't freeze
Bananas	2 days	1 month if frozen whole and peeled
Cherries and berries	1–2 days	4 months
Citrus fruit	1–2 weeks	Don't freeze
Grapes	1 week	1 month
Kiwi	3–4 days	Don't freeze
Melons	3–4 days	Don't freeze
Peaches	3–4 days	Don't freeze
Pears and plums	3–4 days	Don't freeze

Keep Your Dairy Items Safe

As you probably know, dairy and other cold foods spoil easily, so you have to make sure that you keep cold foods cold. However, cold foods don't last forever, so it's important that you move stuff out of the refrigerator and freezer after the allotted storage time expires. Check out Table 18-3 for a list of allotted storage times.

Table 18-3	Cold Storage for Dairy Products	
Product	Refrigerator Time	Freezer Time
Butter	1–3 months	6–9 months
Buttermilk	1–2 weeks	3 months
Cheddar and Swiss cheese	3–4 weeks if opened	6 months
Cottage cheese	1 week	Don't freeze
Cream cheese	2 weeks	Don't freeze
Egg substitutes	10 days, 3 days if opened	Don't freeze
Eggs (in shell)	3–5 days	6 months
Half-and-half	3–4 days	4 months

(continued)

Table 18-3 (continued)

Product	Refrigerator Time	Freezer Time
Margarine	6 months	12 months
Milk	1 week	3 months
Parmesan cheese and other shredded cheeses	1 month	3–4 months
Pudding	2 days if opened	Don't freeze
Sour cream	7–21 days	Don't freeze
Sour-cream-based dips	2 weeks	Don't freeze
Whipping cream	1 month	Don't freeze
Yogurt	7–14 days	Don't freeze

Butter can easily pick up odors from other foods in your refrigerator, and the original packaging usually doesn't provide much protection. If your butter is going to be in the fridge for more than a few days, consider wrapping it in plastic wrap or storing in an airtight container.

Be Careful with Your Meat

Meat spoils easily, as everyone knows. You can store it in the refrigerator, and the freezer greatly extends shelf life. Table 18-4 tells you how long to expect your meat to stick it out.

Table 18-4	Cold Storage for Meat	
Product	**Refrigerator Time**	**Freezer Time**
Bacon	7 days	1 month
Beef roasts	3–5 days	6–12 months
Beef steaks	3–5 days	6–12 months
Chicken and turkey (giblets)	1–2 days	3–4 month
Chicken and turkey (pieces)	1–2 days	9 months

Product	Refrigerator Time	Freezer Time
Chicken and turkey (whole)	1–2 days	1 year
Cooked meat and meat dishes	3–4 days	3–4 months
Corned beef	5–7 days	1–2 months
Ground meats	1–2 days	3–4 months
Ham (canned)	6–9 months	Don't freeze
Ham (cooked and whole)	7 days	1–2 months
Ham (cooked slices)	3–5 days	1–2 months
Hot dogs, opened	1 week	Don't freeze
Liver, heart, or kidneys	3–4 days	3–4 months
Lamb chops	3–5 days	6–12 months
Lamb roasts	3–5 days	6–9 months
Pork chops	3–5 days	4–6 months
Pork and veal roasts	3–5 days	4–6 months
Sausage	1–2 days	1–2 months
Stew meats	1–2 days	3–4 months

No, Table 18-4 doesn't have a typo. You really can store a canned ham in the refrigerator for 6 to 9 months.

Appendix A

Metric Conversion Guide

*N**ote:* The recipes in this cookbook were developed and tested using nonmetric measures. You may notice some variation in quality when converting to metric units.

Common Abbreviations

Abbreviation(s)	What It Stands For
C, c	cup
g	gram
kg	kilogram
L, l	liter
lb	pound
mL, ml	milliliter
oz	ounce
pt	pint
t, tsp	teaspoon
T, TB, Tbl, Tbsp	tablespoon

Volume

U.S. Units	Canadian Metric	Australian Metric
¼ teaspoon	1 milliliter	1 milliliter
½ teaspoon	2 milliliters	2 milliliters
1 teaspoon	5 milliliters	5 milliliters
1 tablespoon	15 milliliters	20 milliliters

(continued)

Volume (continued)

U.S. Units	Canadian Metric	Australian Metric
¼ cup	50 milliliters	60 milliliters
⅓ cup	75 milliliters	80 milliliters
½ cup	125 milliliters	125 milliliters
⅔ cup	150 milliliters	170 milliliters
¾ cup	175 milliliters	190 milliliters
1 cup	250 milliliters	250 milliliters
1 quart	1 liter	1 liter
1½ quarts	1.5 liters	1.5 liters
2 quarts	2 liters	2 liters
2½ quarts	2.5 liters	2.5 liters
3 quarts	3 liters	3 liters
4 quarts	4 liters	4 liters

Weight

U.S. Units	Canadian Metric	Australian Metric
1 ounce	30 grams	30 grams
2 ounces	55 grams	60 grams
3 ounces	85 grams	90 grams
4 ounces (¼ pound)	115 grams	125 grams
8 ounces (½ pound)	225 grams	225 grams
16 ounces (1 pound)	455 grams	500 grams (½ kilogram)

Measurements

Inches	Centimeters
½	1.5
1	2.5
2	5

Inches	*Centimeters*
3	7.5
4	10
5	12.5
6	15
7	17.5
8	20.5
9	23
10	25.5
11	28
12	30.5
13	33

Temperature (Degrees)

Fahrenheit	*Celsius*
32	0
212	100
250	120
275	140
300	150
325	160
350	180
375	190
400	200
425	220
450	230
475	240
500	260

Appendix B
Helpful Web Sites

The Web is an ever-so-helpful place, and you can find information galore when it comes to crowd cooking. We've given you a bunch of good crowd recipes in this chapter, but you can find a plethora of them on the Internet, as well as other sites that can help you host a crowd or throw a knock-out party. In this appendix, we share some of our favorite sites.

Recipe Rewards

Recipe Rewards is a nicely designed Web site that has a great database of recipes (see Figure B-1). You can browse through different recipe categories and holiday categories or you can search for the recipe you want. Check out this site at ww2.reciperewards.com.

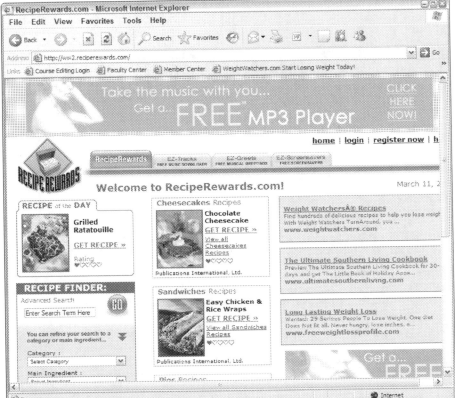

Figure B-1:
Recipe
Rewards.

About.com

If you want to read a quick article about cooking for a crowd, then check out
`http://homecooking.about.com/library/weekly/aa022299.htm`. This
page gives you some helpful reminders and especially some good links to
other content on the Internet.

Recipe Gal

The Recipe Gal site has a lot of recipes that are well organized, so you can quickly find what you want. In fact, you'll find that many of the recipes here are crowd ready with a helpful number of servings. Visit this site at `www.recipegal.com`.

Recipe Goldmine

Recipe Goldmine is exactly what it suggests — a gold mine of recipes. You can search for a specific recipe or look through a very long list of categories. In fact, you'll even find a "quantity" category, which is perfect for crowd cooks. Be sure to look through this site at `www.recipegoldmine.com` — you'll probably find many recipes you like! See Figure B-2 for a screen shot.

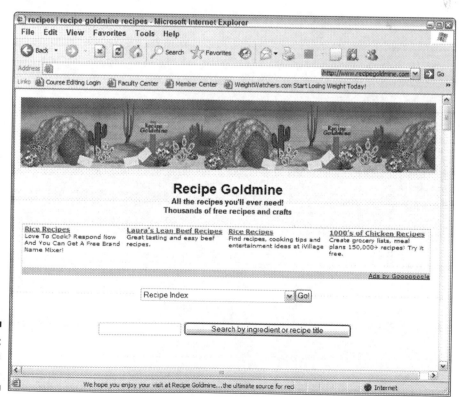

Figure B-2:
Recipe
Goldmine.

Razzle Dazzle Recipes

The Razzle Dazzle Recipes site has many great recipes for crowd cooks, as you can see in Figure B-3. Simple click on a category and you find plenty of recipes that are already adjusted to a larger quantity. You can find the crowd recipes at www.razzledazzlerecipes.com/quantity.

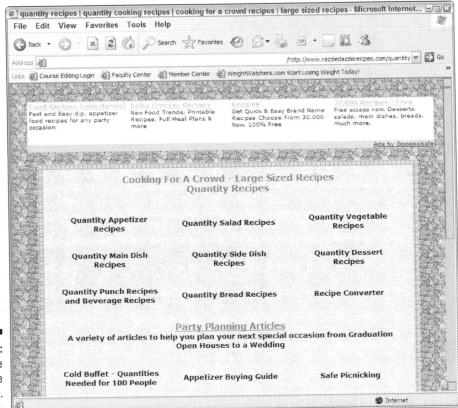

Figure B-3:
Razzle
Dazzle
Recipes.

Joyce's Fine Cooking

Joyce's Fine Cooking presents a nice Web site full of recipes that are crowd-specific (see Figure B-4). Most of these recipes serve between 50 and 100 people. You simply click on a recipe name and go from there. Check out the crowd portion of the site at `www.joycesfinecooking.com/cooking_for_ a_crowd.htm`.

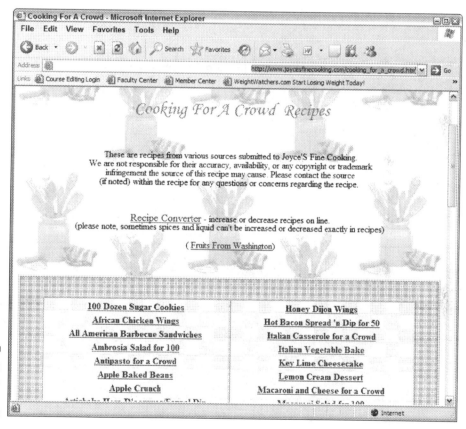

Figure B-4: Joyce's Fine Cooking.

Pioneer Thinking

Pioneer Thinking has a good article about using theme meals during the holidays. You can find some great tips and advice here along with a few recipes you may want to try. Visit the page at www.pioneerthinking. com/ara-holidaycrowd.html.

Food Network

Naturally, Food Network is a great place to explore. At www.foodnetwork.com, you find lots of recipes and general information about cooking. This site is a great place to visit if you need a certain kind of recipe or have some general questions about cooking (see Figure B-5).

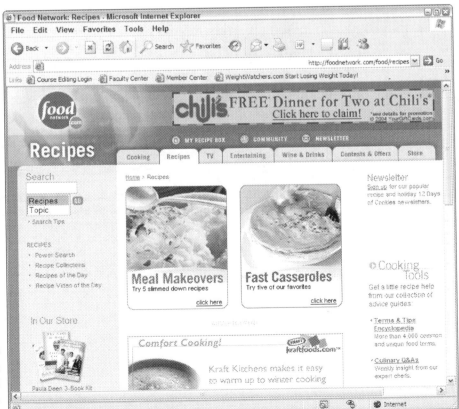

Figure B-5:
Food
Network.

Growlies for Groups

Growlies for Groups has over 500 large-quantity recipes, many of which you can make ahead of time. Check out this site at `http://members.tripod.com/~lotsofinfo` and see Figure B-6 for a screen shot.

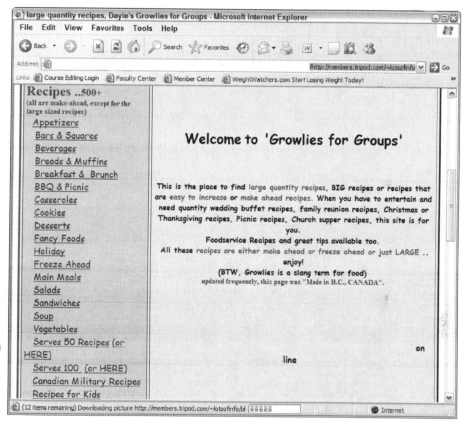

Figure B-6:
Growlies for Groups.

The Recipe Link

The Recipe Link site has several different items that you may find useful, from conversion calculators to cooking tips to several links to other helpful Web sites. Check it out at www.recipelink.com/faqs.html.

Epicurious

Epicurious has more recipes than you can count. If you're trying to find something specific or just want to spend some time browsing through thousands of recipes, this is the site for you (see Figure B-7). Visit it at www.epicurious.com.

Figure B-7: Epicurious.

Recipe Source

Recipe Source is another great source for recipes (hence the name). At www.recipesource.com you find all kinds of recipes organized according to different geographic regions or food type. See Figure B-8 for a screen shot.

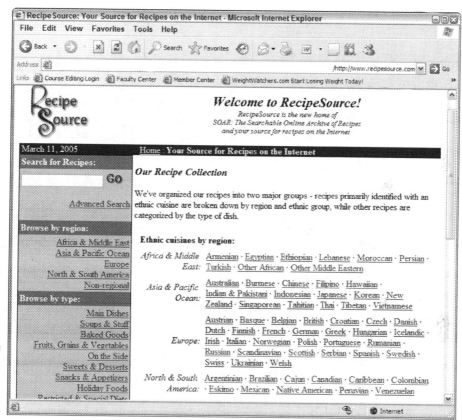

Figure B-8:
Recipe
Source.

All Recipes

We love this recipe site! Here you find many different kinds of recipes that are well organized and quickly searchable. Be sure to check this one out (see Figure B-9). You can visit the site at `www.allrecipes.com`.

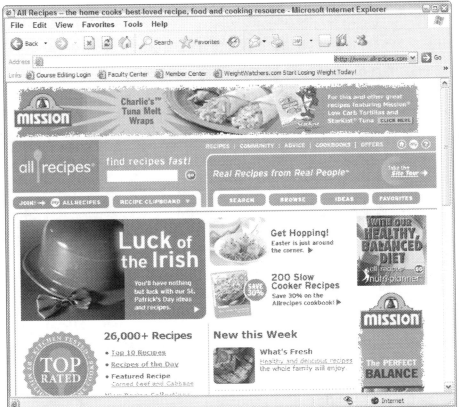

Figure B-9:
All Recipes.

Theme Parties 'n' More

Are you throwing a party and need some quick decorating tips or theme ideas? Then check out this site. Here you find all kinds of fun and practical suggestions. Check out the site at `www.themepartiesnmore.com`.

DIY Network

DIY (Do It Yourself) Network is one of our favorite places to visit because it has so much to offer (see Figure B-10). From cooking to decorating tips, you can search for topics and find a wealth of information. Visit the site at `www.diynet.com`.

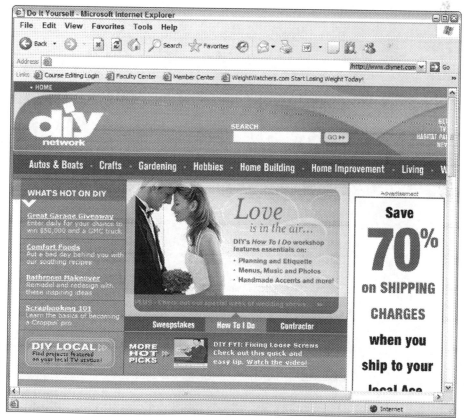

Figure B-10: DIY Network.

Appendix C

Fun and Easy Garnishes

The food is prepared, the table is set, but something seems to be missing. Chances are your naked foods need to accessorize — enter garnishes. With just a little bit of imagination, you can make homely food seem fit for a queen. After all, if you're going to do all the work it takes to prepare your good eats, you may as well spend a few extra minutes making them look enticing, too.

Consider some age-old sayings: Beauty is in the eye of the beholder, you only get one chance to make a first impression, your eyes are bigger than your stomach, and so on. You're probably wondering what in the world those sayings have to do with garnishing food. In fact, aspiring crowd cook, they have everything to do with it.

Dining together is one of the most important social events the modern world shares. Everyone has to eat, although most people eat for enjoyment, not just to sustain themselves. But one of the biggest parts of a meal is the anticipation of delectable foods, encouraged by the allure of the visual presentation — the five human senses work together, and a carefully prepared meal is really a hit when your guests are encouraged to taste with their eyes before tasting with their mouths.

In this appendix, we help you engage the oft-forgotten visual sense, tuning you in to our favorite garnish ideas and the best ways to use them.

Spell It Out — Literally

Although this first garnish isn't appropriate for every occasion, it provides a creative, unusual touch for a family gathering, backyard barbecue, or birthday party — pretty much any informal event. The trick? Create messages with your food, either letting the words stand on their own as part of the table decorations or placing them on a fruit tray. Are you having a summer party with a Hawaiian theme? Try spelling out the word "Aloha" with pineapple. Just have a pineapple and a set of alphabetical cookie cutters handy (if pineapple doesn't suit your mood, get as creative as you like with other foods) and follow these steps:

1. **Slice the pineapple in rings, about ¾ inch thick.**

2. **Using your cookie cutters, place each letter of the word you're spelling on a ring of pineapple, and press down firmly to cut out each letter.**

3. **Slice enough pineapple rings an inch thick to serve as a base for each letter.**

4. **Attach each letter to a pineapple ring base with toothpicks.**

   Remember, these pineapple letters are a garnish, so attach the toothpicks from the backside so as to have a cleaner, prettier presentation.

Keep in mind that if the word you're spelling is long or the pineapple is small, you may need to purchase more than one pineapple.

Alphabetic cookie cutters are usually quite inexpensive, and you can purchase them at your local superstore, cooking store, or at an online cooking store. We strongly suggest that you buy the metal ones instead of plastic, because the metal ones make a cleaner cut.

The following are some other foods you can use to spell out words:

- Cantaloupe
- Cheese
- Chocolate
- Cookies
- Crackers
- Seedless watermelon

Play with Shapes

Making a cheese tray and hankering for a presentation that stands out from that of its peers? Instead of the standard cheese tray that consists of either slices or cubes of cheese, dress it up a bit by cutting the cheese into different shapes.

To make different shapes, simply cut the cheese to the desired thickness and use a small cookie cutter to fashion the shapes. Place the cheese on a serving platter in a cool pattern, cover the platter tightly, and refrigerate until it's time to serve.

Not sure what shape to make? Keep the theme of your event in mind. Here are a few ideas to get you going:

- **July 4th party:** Try using star shapes.
- **Christmas party:** Christmas tree shapes.
- **Super Bowl party:** You guessed it — football shapes.
- **Mexican fiesta:** Pepper shapes.
- **Hawaiian luau:** Pineapple shapes.
- **Graduation:** Graduation cap shapes.
- **Fall fling:** Leaf shapes.
- **Valentine's Day party:** Hearts — what else?
- **A formal celebration:** Try using flower, circle, or triangle shapes.

You're probably thinking that these are some great ideas but simply too much work for a crowd event. If you have a huge platter of food, you can simply cut every fourth piece of cheese into a shape, and your tray will still have some variation and flair. Don't have much time at all? Just cut enough pieces to use as a garnish.

Want some more ideas of foods that lend themselves to shaping? Consider these greats — of course, some of them require that you shape them before cooking:

- Cookies
- Finger sandwiches
- Homemade crackers
- Homemade ice-cream sandwiches
- Homemade tortilla chips
- Melons
- Summer sausage

Create Animal Figures

From whimsical to elegant, animal-shaped garnishes are sure to impress your guests. The good news is that these garnishes are much easier to craft than they look, and they're all cheap, too.

Radish mouse

This cute little mouse made out of two radishes is the perfect creative garnish for a vegetable tray (of course, you may want to forgo this one for a formal event). Or be cute and put it on a cheese tray for added whimsy. To make a radish mouse, you need two radishes with the root still attached and two small cloves.

Follow these instructions, and in no time you'll have a cute little mouse.

1. **Wash and dry the radishes, and then remove the root gently from one of the radishes.**

2. **Hold the radish with the root attached horizontally, so the root extends to the left or right.**

3. **Using a sharp paring knife, cut a thin slice off the bottom thick enough that when the radish lies cut side down, the root lies flat.**

   The root will serve as the tail.

4. **For the eyes, place a small clove on each side of the radish, slightly above the stem.**

5. **For the ears, cut off the end of the other radish, and then cut two thin slices. Make a slit in the other radish above the clove eyes and place the two slices in the openings.**

Apple bird

This garnish — a bird made out of an apple — is sure to impress your guests and works well as an addition to any type of dish. You can use it as the centerpiece of a fruit tray, as part of the decorations around the serving dishes, or anywhere else that needs an extra touch. We realize the project may seem a little difficult, but with a sharp knife, a little confidence, and a little practice, you'll be a pro in no time. Just in case, you may want to practice making this garnish before the big event, and you may want to have a few extra apples on hand as you practice.

To make these impressive flights of fancy you need only three things: An apple (well rounded and free of bruises), toothpicks, and a sharp serrated steak knife.

1. **Cut ⅓ of the apple from the side.**

   Set the piece you cut off to the side; you'll use it later.

2. **Place the apple cut side down with the stem facing you — this part will serve as the body. Using a light sawing motion, cut a slit in the top of the apple.**

3. Cut another slit to the right of the first one, angling the cut toward the bottom of the first one to make a wedge. Continue making wedge-shaped cuts, each a bit larger than the next, until you reach the bottom of the apple.

4. Repeat Step 3 on the left side of the apple, forming three sets of feathers.

   Don't worry if a piece breaks; the sections will fit together so that the break won't show.

5. Starting with the largest wedge first, overlap each smaller piece until feathers are formed. Repeat this step for the other side of the apple. Set the body aside.

   The juice from the apple will help hold the wedges together.

6. To form the head and neck, take the piece that you originally cut out in Step 1, and cut a ¼-inch slice from the center section.

7. Cut a V at the front of the slice, leaving some fruit at the front, and then cut the fruit away following the natural shape of the skin.

8. Insert a toothpick into the body on an angle and attach the head and neck.

9. To prevent the apple from becoming discolored, squeeze lemon juice over the entire bird.

Hard-boiled egg bunnies

These bunnies are a cute garnish that work well with an Easter theme, baby shower, or spring gathering. To make them, you need a hard-boiled egg, two whole cloves, and one cauliflower floret. Simply follow the instructions:

1. Gently remove the shell from the hard-boiled egg.

2. Wash the egg and gently pat it dry.

3. To allow the egg, which will serve as the bunny's body, to sit flat, cut a ¼-inch slice off the side of the egg.

4. To make the ears, cut in half lengthwise the slice that you just cut off.

5. Cut a small slit in the top of the pointed end of the egg to attach the ears. Gently squeeze the cut open and insert the ears.

6. Take the two whole cloves and gently push them to form the eyes.

7. Use a small piece of the cauliflower floret for the tail.

How to boil the perfect hard-boiled egg

Having trouble with your hard-boiled eggs? Are they discolored in some places and is removing the shell difficult? Never fear . . . follow these steps to cook the perfect hard-boiled egg.

1. Lay the desired amount of eggs in the bottom of a saucepan and cover them with an inch of water.

2. Cook over high heat, just to a boil. Remove the pan from heat, cover it, and let it set for 17 minutes.

3. Remove the eggs from the pan and place them in a bowl of ice water. Chill for 2 minutes. (Chilling the eggs helps shrink them from the shell.) While eggs are chilling, return the pan of water to the stove and bring it to a boil. (This second boiling expands the shell, which greatly helps in removing the shell.)

4. After the eggs have chilled, return them to the pan of water and allow the water to come to a boil. Allow the eggs to boil for 10 seconds, and then remove them and place them back in the ice water. Chill for 15 to 20 minutes. (Cooling the eggs between each step prevents those unsightly dark lines.)

5. Remove the shells from the eggs and wash them to make sure no additional pieces of shell are still attached.

6. Gently dry and prepare the eggs as you so desire.

Frost Your Fruit

Frosted fruit, also known as sugared fruit, is so easy to make, and at the same time, it's a beautiful garnish. This attractive colorful garnish holds its own as a centerpiece and also adds a sweet touch as a garnish for a number of desserts as well as cheese trays, fruit trays, and platters of meat. Sugared fruit slices even work great as drink garnishes.

Many different fruits will serve you well:

- Apples
- Blackberries
- Blueberries
- Cherries
- Cranberries
- Kiwi slices
- Lemon and lime slices
- Peaches

- Pears
- Raspberries
- Red or green grapes
- Strawberries

You may have readily available many of the supplies that you need for this garnish:

- Pastry brush
- Cookie sheet
- Fruit
- Granulated sugar
- Light-colored corn syrup
- Wax paper

Various cookbooks boast different sugaring techniques, but we find this technique to work the best:

1. **Wash and dry the fruit.**

   It's important to make sure fruit is completely dried.

2. **Pour the corn syrup into a small bowl, such as a cereal bowl.**

3. **Pour the sugar into another small bowl.**

4. **Line the cookie sheet with wax paper.**

5. **Using the pastry brush, coat a piece of fruit with the corn syrup.**

6. **Roll the coated fruit in sugar.**

7. **Gently shake off the excess sugar and place the fruit on the lined cookie sheet.**

8. **Place the sugared fruit in the refrigerator until ready to use.**

If you like the frosted look, you don't have to limit yourself to fruit. Here are a few more ideas.

- Edible flowers
- Fresh peppermint leaves
- Fresh spearmint leaves
- Nuts

Behold the Power of Chocolate

What is it about chocolate the drives the vast majority of the human population wild? Is it the anticipation of its sweet, velvety taste that lavishes our tongues with sheer delight? Who knows — all we know is that we love our chocolate and like to find ways to use more of it.

Chocolate is one of those food items that can be shaped and formed into a number of different items. With a little creativity you can turn that taste of heaven into a feast for the eyes as well.

Chocolate flowers

Chocolate flowers make for garnishes for a variety of desserts that you and your guests will want to indulge in. To make them, you need 10 ounces of chocolate (chopped in chunks or chocolate chips), almond bark (dark or white, your choice), ⅛ cup of light corn syrup, and wax paper.

Here are the steps for making the chocolate flowers:

1. **Place the chocolate in a microwaveable bowl and microwave on high for 1 minute. Stir the chocolate; if it isn't completely melted, continue microwaving it in 10-second intervals until melted, stirring after each 10 seconds.**

   Be very careful not to overheat chocolate, as the texture will change and so will the taste.

2. **Stir the corn syrup into the melted chocolate. Mix until well blended.**

3. **Place a sheet of wax paper on a flat surface, and then pour the chocolate mixture onto the wax paper.**

4. **Spread the chocolate with a rubber spatula, flat knife, or your clean fingers until it's roughly ½ inch thick.**

5. **Cover the chocolate loosely with another piece of wax paper. Allow the chocolate to stiffen, until it's pliable like clay.**

   The chocolate will need at least a couple of hours to stiffen. If necessary, allow it to set overnight.

6. **Form approximately ten balls out of the chocolate.**

7. **Place a clean sheet of wax paper on the table, and then place the chocolate balls on the paper, about 1 inch apart.**

8. **Place a piece of wax paper on top of the chocolate balls. Using your thumb, press down on each chocolate ball so that it becomes a circle,**

about the size of a quarter. You may need to apply a fair amount of
pressure.

9. Remove one chocolate circle from the wax paper and form a funnel
with it; the opening of the funnel should be rather small.

10. Take another chocolate circle and wrap it around the opening of the
funnel.

11. Take another chocolate circle and make another funnel, and then
place it at the back of the original funnel. This is the rosebud.

12. Continue adding chocolate circles around the rosebud, forming the
petals.

Are you really creative? Because this chocolate is the texture of clay, you can
form just about any item you want.

Chocolate curls and chocolate shavings

Chocolate curls and shavings are easy-to-make garnish that go great with
all kinds of desserts. All you need are two items: Semisweet or bittersweet
chocolate or almond bark and a vegetable peeler.

To make chocolate curls, the chocolate needs to be at room temperature or
warmer. When the chocolate is at the right temperature, peel off slices of
chocolate with a vegetable peeler, adding enough pressure to obtain desired
thickness of the curls.

To make chocolate shavings, which are great garnishes for ice cream, cakes,
pies, and hot beverages, follow the instructions for the curls, only make sure
the chocolate or almond bark is cool to cold.

Chocolate stars

Need a little extra something for that cake, ice cream, or pie? Add some chocolate stars. To make them, you need almond bark or chocolate chips and a
pastry bag. You also need a star tip for the pastry bag and wax paper to put
the stars on. Follow these steps:

1. Place the almond bark or chocolate in a microwaveable bowl and
microwave on high for 1 minute. Stir the chocolate; if it isn't completely melted, continue microwaving it in 10-second intervals until
melted, stirring after each 10 seconds.

Remember to stop every 10 seconds or so and stir. Do not overheat the
chocolate.

2. **Place the star tip on the pastry bag.**

3. **Pour the melted chocolate into the pastry bag.**

4. **Squeeze chocolate stars onto the wax paper and allow them to set for 1 hour.**

You can use any other decorating tips that you would normally use to decorate a cake, such as the rosette tip. For additional visual interest, make some of the stars out of white almond bark and the others out of the dark.

Chocolate-dipped garnishes

When using chocolate as a dip, it's important to work with small amounts of melted chocolate at a time. You also need to remember to work somewhat quickly with chocolate because it quickly becomes tacky. Another important tip is that if you're covering fruit with chocolate, the fruit must be thoroughly washed and dried before dipping — water and chocolate don't mix.

If the chocolate isn't thin enough, add a small amount of shortening to it and stir until the desired consistency is achieved. Never add water, milk, or butter to thin chocolate that you're going to use for coating.

Here's how to make chocolate-dipped foods:

1. **Melt the chocolate in the microwave or in a double boiler on top of the stove.**

   We normally choose the microwave for speed and convenience.

2. **Quickly dip the food of your choice in the chocolate and remove it, gently shaking off any excess chocolate.**

3. **Place the food on wax paper and allow the dipped item to set for about an hour.**

The following are some suggestions of food items that work well dipped in chocolate:

- ✔ Brownie bits
- ✔ Cherries
- ✔ Cookies
- ✔ Minimuffins
- ✔ Nuts

- Petit Fours
- Pretzels
- Strawberries

Want to impress your coffee-loving guests? Try making some homemade chocolate-covered spoons, like the kind the fancy coffeehouses serve.

Remember to be creative. If you're dipping cookies, try dipping half of the cookie in white almond bark and the other half in dark. If you're making chocolate-covered pretzels. Dip them all in white chocolate, and then take a fork and fling some dark chocolate over the top for the marbled look.

Chocolate molds

If the chocolate flower idea sounds great, but you just don't have the time to commit to the idea, or if you need to make a different shape and aren't quite sure how to do it, we have an easy fix for your quandary: candy molds. You can find these molds at just about any cooking store, craft store, or super-center, in the craft area along with the wedding supplies, and you can even snatch them on the Web. These little plastic molds are very inexpensive and very easy to use.

Before you use a candy mold, be sure to wash and thoroughly dry it. Remember, water and chocolate don't mix.

Place the chocolate in a microwavable bowl and microwave until melted, stirring halfway through cook time. There's one point we can't stress enough: *Don't overheat the chocolate.*

1. **After the chocolate has melted and is the consistency of syrup, begin filling the molds.**

   You can fill the molds in one of two ways: by spooning it in or by using a plastic squeeze bottle. Using a spoon certainly works but can be somewhat on the messy side. So for a quicker, cleaner method, use the squeeze bottle.

2. **After the molds are filled, pick them up and gently tap them on the table or countertop.**

   This gentle tapping will help prevent any air bubbles from developing.

3. **Place the molds in the freezer for 10 minutes.**

   If you're using molds larger than a standard-size lollipop, you'll need to leave them in for an additional 10 to 15 minutes. Remember, better to keep them in the freezer too long than not long enough.

4. **Remove the candies from the molds by turning the molds upside down and placing them on a counter or tabletop and then gently tapping them.**

   The candies will usually pop right out. If they don't, however, don't worry — gently push on the mold with your fingers until the candy releases.

You can place the chocolate molds in the refrigerator instead of the freezer, but if you do, the candies will lose some of their shine and will take at least three times as long to harden. In addition, the candies may be harder to remove from the molds.

Looking for something different to use as a centerpiece at your next ladies' get-together or dessert social? Try making a centerpiece out of different chocolate molds. Follow the preceding directions, except this time add some lollipop sticks. Placing the molds on the sticks will allow you to use the sticks to create an arrangement similar to a floral arrangement. This one, however, you can eat. To add visual interest to your arrangement, cut the sticks to different lengths. Not sure what to put the sticks in to make them stand up? A piece of angel food cake in the base of the vase you're using works great in place of floral foam. If you want to take it a step further and add some florist's moss on top, try using green-colored coconut.

Dress Up Your Drinks

Picture this: A hot summer day, a tall cool glass of tea with just the right amount of ice cubes, a bright yellow wedge of lemon, perfectly placed on the lip of the glass, with two velvety pieces of mint floating carelessly on top. You're not enjoying just any glass of tea — you're savoring liquid refreshment. Sounds like a television commercial, doesn't it? Well sit tight because you can easily dress up your own drinks. The following is a list of really easy garnishes.

Garnishes for iced tea:

- Lemon wedges, circles, or half-circles
- Lime wedges, circles, or half-circles
- Orange wedges, circles, or half-circles
- Peach wedges
- Fresh mint sprigs

Garnishes for punches, lemonades, and all other cold drinks:

- ✔ Lemon wedges, circles, or half-circles
- ✔ Lime wedges, circles, or half-circles
- ✔ Orange wedges, circles, or half-circles
- ✔ Kiwi circles
- ✔ Starfruit slices
- ✔ Maraschino cherries
- ✔ Strawberry fans
- ✔ Small fruit kebabs
- ✔ Drink umbrellas

To help prevent cold drinks from getting watered down, make flavored ice cubes. Simply fill your ice-cube trays with your drink of choice, freeze, and serve.

Coffee, hot chocolate, hot cider, and every other hot drink in between can be garnished with a few simple items:

- ✔ A dollop of whipped cream
- ✔ Chocolate shavings
- ✔ Cinnamon sticks
- ✔ Cocoa powder
- ✔ Cookies
- ✔ Ground cinnamon
- ✔ Nutmeg powder
- ✔ Peppermint sticks

Try Edible Flowers

Edible flowers make beautiful natural garnishes and are easy to use. In addition, you have many varieties to pick from. The good news is that edible flowers can be used with all kinds of dishes.

If you want to use edible flowers, you must make certain that you get them from an organic source to ensure that they haven't been sprayed with pesticides.

The following list tells you about our favorites.

- **Alliums:** We have some allium bulbs in our yard, and they always remind us of onions. Rightfully so, because they're commonly known as "flowering onions." All alliums are edible, but keep in mind that they have a mild taste of onion, leek, or garlic, depending on the variety.

- **Angelica:** These flowers range from pale lavender-blue to deep rose. They have a flavor similar to licorice, and you can use it as a garnish for many dishes.

- **Anise hyssop:** Both flowers and leaves have a slight licorice or root-beer taste.

- **Apple blossoms:** Apple blossoms have a light flavor and work well as garnishes for fruit dishes.

- **Arugula:** The flowers are small and white with dark centers and can be used on salads for a simple garnish. They typically have a light, spicy flavor.

- **Basil:** Flowers can be white, pink, or lavender, and the flavor is very mild. Basil flowers work well on salads and even pasta dishes.

- **Borage:** These star-shaped flowers have a cucumber taste, which makes them perfect for salads.

- **Calendula:** Calendula is also known as a marigold and is a perfect edible flower because it's so versatile. It has a strong garnish impact and works well with many foods, such as soups, salads, pasta, and other related dishes.

- **Carnations:** These beautiful and edible flowers work well with all kinds of desserts and decor. The petals are sweet but the base is bitter, so keep that in mind.

- **Chamomile:** These small, daisy-type flowers taste something like apple.

- **Chicory:** This small flower has a bitter taste, but it can work well as a garnish because it's so pretty.

- **Chrysanthemums:** You have many colors of mums to choose from, and they typically have a bitter to pepper taste. They're beautiful flowers and can be used as a garnish in many ways, especially on salads.

- **Cornflower:** Better known as "bachelor's button," these flowers have a sweet to spicy taste and are beautiful as a garnish.

- **Daylilies:** Daylilies are generally too big to work as a simple garnish, but you can use them on your table and with food because they're edible.

  Not all types of lilies are edible.

- **English daisy:** These flowers have a slightly bitter taste, but they're pretty when used as a garnish for salads.

- **Fennel:** These starburst yellow flowers work well as a garnish for entrees.

- **Fuchsia:** These flowers really don't have a taste but are boldly colorful, making them a good garnish choice.

- **Gardenia:** These flowers are edible, but they're often overpoweringly fragrant. They're pretty as a garnish, but the smell may overpower the food.

- **Gladiolas:** These beautiful flowers don't have much of a taste. They're perfect garnishes for salads and other fresh spring dishes.

- **Hollyhock:** Like gladiolas, hollyhock doesn't have much taste but is very pretty when used as a garnish.

- **Impatiens:** These beautiful flowers are commonly used as a garnish. They have little to no taste.

- **Lavender:** These light purple sprigs have a sweet flavor and are very nice as a garnish, especially with cake and ice cream.

- **Nasturtiums:** This beautiful garnish has a peppery taste, but because of its beauty, it's one of the most commonly used edible flowers.

- **Petunia:** Petunias are an excellent garnish choice for spring crowd events. They have a big impact and a mild taste.

- **Roses:** Rose petals are edible and are highly versatile as garnish items. You can use them on everything from salads to desserts, and they work particularly well for romantic or formal gatherings.

Tulips are also edible, but some people have allergic reactions to them. For this reason, you should avoid using them at crowd events.

Appendix D

Special Cooking Tricks

*T*hroughout this book we've given you a multitude of tips and tricks, but we couldn't pass up one more special section that highlights some of our favorites. Frankly, we've learned some of these from painful experience or that of our friends, so we're happy to share them with you because they can certainly save your big crowd event.

Stifling the Stench of Onions

Although onions add a nice kick to a good dish, the problem with them is that these smelly roots are difficult to contain. You can wrap them in layers of plastic wrap and put them in the refrigerator, but the smell always leaks out. Perhaps that doesn't seem like a catastrophe, but if you're also storing foods you've prepared in the fridge, it certainly can be one. After all, no one honestly enjoys Key lime pie with a hint of onion.

You can avoid this stinky problem with a simple trick: Always store cut onions or onion pieces in a glass jar with a sealed lid. Glass doesn't breathe, so the odor will be safely contained inside the jar. Works every time.

Why do onions smell?

Onions are a part of the allium family, which includes leeks, shallots, garlic, chives, and even strains of beautiful ball-shaped flowers you may have planted in your yard. Over 500 types of allium exist, and they all smell. They all contain thioallyl compounds, otherwise called *alliins*. When you cut or crush the alliin, an enzymatic reaction converts it into allicin, which then breaks down into sulphide compounds, commonly called sulphur. Sulphur stinks, and that's why everything in the allium family stinks. Interestingly, the onion doesn't have much nutritional value but is full of flavor and may even have a health benefit: As it turns out, alliins may be able to prevent the growth of malignant cells. In areas where onions and garlic are commonly eaten, the rate of stomach cancer is low.

The Tale of the Towel and Fabric Softener

Okay, here's a true story for you. A dear friend of ours recently bought a café. During the first week, she used a laundered towel to keep a breadbasket warm. No problem, right? You've probably done that as well. Her dilemma was that she'd used fabric softener with the laundry, so when the towel warmed up, the bread absorbed the smell of the fabric softener. April fresh bread, anyone?

This funny story could've been quite embarrassing if she hadn't discovered the problem ahead of time. The moral of the story: Avoid any kind of fabric softener or perfumed dryer sheets if you plan on using towels to keep bread warm. Remember — smells can be your friend, or they can be your worst enemy.

Lettuce and Knives Are Not Friends

Sure, you've probably cut lettuce with a knife many times in your life. If you have, you've been doing it all wrong, friend. Instead, you should tear lettuce to create a salad. Why, you might ask? The metal in the knife reacts with the lettuce and causes it to brown more quickly, so avoid cutting lettuce with a knife. Your guests will be much more interested in green lettuce over brown.

Cutting Greasy Soup

If you're cooking soup, stew, or a sauce for a crowd (or any other time, for that matter), you may find that the mixture is a bit too greasy. No problem — you can solve that scenario with a little trick we've learned. Drop a leaf of lettuce or cabbage in the mixture for the last 30 minutes of cooking time. The leaf will absorb the excess grease and solve your greasy soup problems.

Avoiding Soggy Potatoes with Pot Roast

We love a good pot roast, but we're not a big fan if the potatoes get too soggy. That problem is common with pot roast dishes, but we have the perfect solution — you can have your cake and eat it, too (as well as the pot roast).

Simply peel and cut up the potatoes the night before and put them in cold water. The next day, cook them with the pot roast as usual. With minimal effort, you'll have crisper, tastier taters.

Reviving Fainting Parsley

Parsley is probably the most commonly used garnish. However, it goes limp rather easily, and face it, if the garnish looks tired and worn out, it isn't doing a whole lot to boost your food's confidence.

You can stop this wimpy behavior by putting the parsley in a bowl of ice water for 15 minutes before you use it. The ice water helps the parsley stay perky and keeps your dish looking happy.

Oh, No! The Dish Is Too Salty!

Suppose you're working on a soup, stew, or sauce, but when you taste the dish, it's much too salty. Don't worry — you can fix it with no problem. Simply peel a raw potato and put it in the dish. The potato will absorb the excess salt, and then you can simply throw the potato away. Salty dish problem solved!

The Dry Ham and Coke Trick

There once was a ham that had a dry sense of humor . . . sorry, wrong story. Suppose you cook a ham a bit too long and it comes out dry. You don't want to serve it to your crowd, so is the ham tomorrow's trash? Not at all.

Rather, pour a can of Coke over the ham and cook it again for an hour at 250 degrees. The ham will absorb the moisture from the Coke and the tale of the dry ham will have a happy ending.

To Sift or Not to Sift

Here's a quick tip to remember. No matter what you're baking (cakes, cookies, breads, and so on), always sift the flour to put air in it. This simple action makes the flour lighter and produces a better baked good. The small tricks are the ones that count, so keep this one in mind.

And a Few More . . .

Here are a few more quick tricks to keep in mind:

- ✓ If you overcook cookies and they're a bit hard, put them in a zip-top bag with a piece of bread and let them sit overnight. The cookies will absorb the moisture from the bread and turn soft again.

- ✓ If you're boiling new potatoes or cauliflower, you can keep them from turning brown by simply adding a quarter wedge of lemon to the pot.

- ✓ If you make guacamole, put the avocado seed in it to help keep the dip from turning brown.

- ✓ If you need to peel garlic cloves, microwave them for 10 seconds first, and they'll easily pop out of their skins (which is better than jumping out of their skins).

- ✓ Don't store apples and carrots in the refrigerator in the same place. The apples emit a gas that makes the carrots bitter (we're not even going to attempt a joke here).

Index

• I •

• J •

• K •

• *N* •

• S •

Notes

Notes

BUSINESS, CAREERS & PERSONAL FINANCE

0-7645-5307-0

0-7645-5331-3 *†

Also available:
- ✔ Accounting For Dummies †
  0-7645-5314-3
- ✔ Business Plans Kit For Dummies †
  0-7645-5365-8
- ✔ Cover Letters For Dummies
  0-7645-5224-4
- ✔ Frugal Living For Dummies
  0-7645-5403-4
- ✔ Leadership For Dummies
  0-7645-5176-0
- ✔ Managing For Dummies
  0-7645-1771-6

- ✔ Marketing For Dummies
  0-7645-5600-2
- ✔ Personal Finance For Dummies *
  0-7645-2590-5
- ✔ Project Management For Dummies
  0-7645-5283-X
- ✔ Resumes For Dummies †
  0-7645-5471-9
- ✔ Selling For Dummies
  0-7645-5363-1
- ✔ Small Business Kit For Dummies *†
  0-7645-5093-4

HOME & BUSINESS COMPUTER BASICS

0-7645-4074-2

0-7645-3758-X

Also available:
- ✔ ACT! 6 For Dummies
  0-7645-2645-6
- ✔ iLife '04 All-in-One Desk Reference
  For Dummies
  0-7645-7347-0
- ✔ iPAQ For Dummies
  0-7645-6769-1
- ✔ Mac OS X Panther Timesaving
  Techniques For Dummies
  0-7645-5812-9
- ✔ Macs For Dummies
  0-7645-5656-8

- ✔ Microsoft Money 2004 For Dummies
  0-7645-4195-1
- ✔ Office 2003 All-in-One Desk Reference
  For Dummies
  0-7645-3883-7
- ✔ Outlook 2003 For Dummies
  0-7645-3759-8
- ✔ PCs For Dummies
  0-7645-4074-2
- ✔ TiVo For Dummies
  0-7645-6923-6
- ✔ Upgrading and Fixing PCs For Dummies
  0-7645-1665-5
- ✔ Windows XP Timesaving Techniques
  For Dummies
  0-7645-3748-2

FOOD, HOME, GARDEN, HOBBIES, MUSIC & PETS

0-7645-5295-3

0-7645-5232-5

Also available:
- ✔ Bass Guitar For Dummies
  0-7645-2487-9
- ✔ Diabetes Cookbook For Dummies
  0-7645-5230-9
- ✔ Gardening For Dummies *
  0-7645-5130-2
- ✔ Guitar For Dummies
  0-7645-5106-X
- ✔ Holiday Decorating For Dummies
  0-7645-2570-0
- ✔ Home Improvement All-in-One
  For Dummies
  0-7645-5680-0

- ✔ Knitting For Dummies
  0-7645-5395-X
- ✔ Piano For Dummies
  0-7645-5105-1
- ✔ Puppies For Dummies
  0-7645-5255-4
- ✔ Scrapbooking For Dummies
  0-7645-7208-3
- ✔ Senior Dogs For Dummies
  0-7645-5818-8
- ✔ Singing For Dummies
  0-7645-2475-5
- ✔ 30-Minute Meals For Dummies
  0-7645-2589-1

INTERNET & DIGITAL MEDIA

0-7645-1664-7

0-7645-6924-4

Also available:
- ✔ 2005 Online Shopping Directory
  For Dummies
  0-7645-7495-7
- ✔ CD & DVD Recording For Dummies
  0-7645-5956-7
- ✔ eBay For Dummies
  0-7645-5654-1
- ✔ Fighting Spam For Dummies
  0-7645-5965-6
- ✔ Genealogy Online For Dummies
  0-7645-5964-8
- ✔ Google For Dummies
  0-7645-4420-9

- ✔ Home Recording For Musicians
  For Dummies
  0-7645-1634-5
- ✔ The Internet For Dummies
  0-7645-4173-0
- ✔ iPod & iTunes For Dummies
  0-7645-7772-7
- ✔ Preventing Identity Theft For Dummies
  0-7645-7336-5
- ✔ Pro Tools All-in-One Desk Reference
  For Dummies
  0-7645-5714-9
- ✔ Roxio Easy Media Creator For Dummies
  0-7645-7131-1

* Separate Canadian edition also available
† Separate U.K. edition also available

Available wherever books are sold. For more information or to order direct: U.S. customers visit www.dummies.com or call 1-877-762-2974.
U.K. customers visit www.wileyeurope.com or call 0800 243407. Canadian customers visit www.wiley.ca or call 1-800-567-4797.

SPORTS, FITNESS, PARENTING, RELIGION & SPIRITUALITY

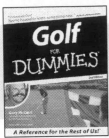

0-7645-5146-9

0-7645-5418-2

Also available:

- Adoption For Dummies
0-7645-5488-3
- Basketball For Dummies
0-7645-5248-1
- The Bible For Dummies
0-7645-5296-1
- Buddhism For Dummies
0-7645-5359-3
- Catholicism For Dummies
0-7645-5391-7
- Hockey For Dummies
0-7645-5228-7

- Judaism For Dummies
0-7645-5299-6
- Martial Arts For Dummies
0-7645-5358-5
- Pilates For Dummies
0-7645-5397-6
- Religion For Dummies
0-7645-5264-3
- Teaching Kids to Read For Dummies
0-7645-4043-2
- Weight Training For Dummies
0-7645-5168-X
- Yoga For Dummies
0-7645-5117-5

TRAVEL

0-7645-5438-7

0-7645-5453-0

Also available:

- Alaska For Dummies
0-7645-1761-9
- Arizona For Dummies
0-7645-6938-4
- Cancún and the Yucatán For Dummies
0-7645-2437-2
- Cruise Vacations For Dummies
0-7645-6941-4
- Europe For Dummies
0-7645-5456-5
- Ireland For Dummies
0-7645-5455-7

- Las Vegas For Dummies
0-7645-5448-4
- London For Dummies
0-7645-4277-X
- New York City For Dummies
0-7645-6945-7
- Paris For Dummies
0-7645-5494-8
- RV Vacations For Dummies
0-7645-5443-3
- Walt Disney World & Orlando For Dummies
0-7645-6943-0

GRAPHICS, DESIGN & WEB DEVELOPMENT

0-7645-4345-8

0-7645-5589-8

Also available:

- Adobe Acrobat 6 PDF For Dummies
0-7645-3760-1
- Building a Web Site For Dummies
0-7645-7144-3
- Dreamweaver MX 2004 For Dummies
0-7645-4342-3
- FrontPage 2003 For Dummies
0-7645-3882-9
- HTML 4 For Dummies
0-7645-1995-6
- Illustrator CS For Dummies
0-7645-4084-X

- Macromedia Flash MX 2004 For Dummies
0-7645-4358-X
- Photoshop 7 All-in-One Desk Reference For Dummies
0-7645-1667-1
- Photoshop CS Timesaving Techniques For Dummies
0-7645-6782-9
- PHP 5 For Dummies
0-7645-4166-8
- PowerPoint 2003 For Dummies
0-7645-3908-6
- QuarkXPress 6 For Dummies
0-7645-2593-X

NETWORKING, SECURITY, PROGRAMMING & DATABASES

0-7645-6852-3

0-7645-5784-X

Also available:

- A+ Certification For Dummies
0-7645-4187-0
- Access 2003 All-in-One Desk Reference For Dummies
0-7645-3988-4
- Beginning Programming For Dummies
0-7645-4997-9
- C For Dummies
0-7645-7068-4
- Firewalls For Dummies
0-7645-4048-3
- Home Networking For Dummies
0-7645-42796

- Network Security For Dummies
0-7645-1679-5
- Networking For Dummies
0-7645-1677-9
- TCP/IP For Dummies
0-7645-1760-0
- VBA For Dummies
0-7645-3989-2
- Wireless All In-One Desk Reference For Dummies
0-7645-7496-5
- Wireless Home Networking For Dummies
0-7645-3910-8

HEALTH & SELF-HELP

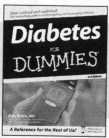

0-7645-6820-5 *†

0-7645-2566-2

Also available:

- Alzheimer's For Dummies
  0-7645-3899-3
- Asthma For Dummies
  0-7645-4233-8
- Controlling Cholesterol For Dummies
  0-7645-5440-9
- Depression For Dummies
  0-7645-3900-0
- Dieting For Dummies
  0-7645-4149-8
- Fertility For Dummies
  0-7645-2549-2
- Fibromyalgia For Dummies
  0-7645-5441-7
- Improving Your Memory For Dummies
  0-7645-5435-2
- Pregnancy For Dummies †
  0-7645-4483-7
- Quitting Smoking For Dummies
  0-7645-2629-4
- Relationships For Dummies
  0-7645-5384-4
- Thyroid For Dummies
  0-7645-5385-2

EDUCATION, HISTORY, REFERENCE & TEST PREPARATION

0-7645-5194-9

0-7645-4186-2

Also available:

- Algebra For Dummies
  0-7645-5325-9
- British History For Dummies
  0-7645-7021-8
- Calculus For Dummies
  0-7645-2498-4
- English Grammar For Dummies
  0-7645-5322-4
- Forensics For Dummies
  0-7645-5580-4
- The GMAT For Dummies
  0-7645-5251-1
- Inglés Para Dummies
  0-7645-5427-1
- Italian For Dummies
  0-7645-5196-5
- Latin For Dummies
  0-7645-5431-X
- Lewis & Clark For Dummies
  0-7645-2545-X
- Research Papers For Dummies
  0-7645-5426-3
- The SAT I For Dummies
  0-7645-7193-1
- Science Fair Projects For Dummies
  0-7645-5460-3
- U.S. History For Dummies
  0-7645-5249-X

Get smart @ dummies.com®

- **Find a full list of Dummies titles**
- **Look into loads of FREE on-site articles**
- **Sign up for FREE eTips e-mailed to you weekly**
- **See what other products carry the Dummies name**
- **Shop directly from the Dummies bookstore**
- **Enter to win new prizes every month!**

Separate Canadian edition also available
Separate U.K. edition also available

Available wherever books are sold. For more information or to order direct: U.S. customers visit www.dummies.com or call 1-877-762-2974.
U.K. customers visit www.wileyeurope.com or call 0800 243407. Canadian customers visit www.wiley.ca or call 1-800-567-4797.